D1605674

What Successful People Say About Darryl Hickman

"WRITTEN BY A CHAMP! What Darryl Hickman has learned from his multi-faceted career as a first-rate film actor, Broadway star, TV executive and teacher all leaps off the pages of this thoughtful, valuable book. It's insightful, informative and a great read for anyone interested in the theatre or just improving their own navigating skills through the minefields in today's world."
  —**Robert Osborne**, host of Turner Classic Movies & columnist/ critic, *The Hollywood Reporter*

"Darryl Hickman stands for truth, and his pupils who soon become working actors give such honest performances that one has a tendency to believe he's watching candid camera."
  —**Burt Reynolds**, actor, director, producer, Academy Award® nominee

"I found that working with Darryl Hickman gave me greater insight into the creative process, both personally and professionally. He knows what he's talking about when it comes to teaching optimal creativity."
  —**Bo Derek**, actor, author—former student

"Read this book. It's fascinating, it's fun, and it works."
  —**Gordon Hunt**, director, teacher, author *(How to Audition)*

"The knowledge Darryl has passed on to me in his passionate, creative, casual and intellectual style has helped me become tops in my field."
—**Edward Scott**, Emmy-winning producer *(Young and the Restless)*—former student

"*The Unconscious Actor* is a must read for actors, directors and anyone involved in the creative process. It is brilliantly innovative."
—**Eric Morris**, actor, teacher, author *(No Acting Please)*

"Bringing Darryl's Stanislavski-based work back to the revered halls of The Moscow Art Theatre was like a spiritual, global homecoming. As a young actress, what I discovered to be a profound way of acting has become a profound way of living, fully embodied in great clarity, humility, and truth."
—**Diane Benedict**, former faculty at The Moscow Art Theatre, Fulbright Scholar, Professor of Theatre Arts at Loyola Marymount University, director, actor—former student

"You don't have to be an acting student to learn from Darryl Hickman's journey of discovery, from his early career in Hollywood to his true calling as a teacher."
—**Leonard Maltin**, film historian, author

"Darryl has such a wealth of knowledge to offer his students — the important fundamentals of acting, learning to get in touch with your true emotions when you need them. I learned to act from Darryl Hickman."

—**Bob Saget**, actor, comedian, writer, producer—former student

"Rudyard Kipling, the British poet, wrote a poem called "If." To paraphrase the last lines: If you can walk among the kings, but never lose the common touch, then you are a man, my son! In his book, *The Unconscious Actor*, Darryl Hickman proves that during his long career he has, indeed, walked among the kings but never lost the common touch!"

—**Jonathan Winters**, actor, comedian, author, artist

"One of the elements of being successful in my profession involves the art of negotiation. And attending Darryl's class helped me improve my skills to an enormous degree. Even though my activities are focused in real estate negotiations and oil deals, I believe his Process has broad applications for many professions other than acting."

—**Leonard Jaffe**, real estate and oil developer—former student

"*The Unconscious Actor* isn't limited to being a manual for the aspiring actor; it's really a manual for the aspiring human who wants to learn how to live—freely, fully and joyfully. And Hickman tells a hell of a lot of good old Hollywood stories along the way. I intend to give it to my therapist, my stock broker and my eighty-four-year-old Aunt Ethel."

—**Gary Dontzig**, triple Emmy Award-winning writer / executive producer—former student

"Darryl's Process had a profound impact on all aspects of my life. It enabled me to tear down the walls of fear and insecurity that I had built around myself allowing me to live in the present moment and to discover myself. I have a heightened sense of awareness. I have learned to trust my instincts and embrace the unknown, which holds infinite possibilities. Life for me is full of joy, wonder, curiosity and creativity. I simply would not be the person I am today if I had not had those wonderful years with Darryl."

—**Laurie Cantwell Rosenthal**, co-owner/Gorilla Travel Agency—former student

"The lessons I learned as an actor and a person about the creative process and how it impacts life development began in Darryl Hickman's workshop. There is not a day that passes that I don't reflect on something that I learned in that classroom and see the application in my current life. As a teacher myself, I'm attempting to pass on those lessons to my students. As an actor, I realize that the superior training I received and the lessons I learned from Darryl have enabled me to work at the highest level, with the very best people on the very best projects in this industry."

—**Michael D. Simms**, President and CEO/MDS Productions Inc., acting teacher—former student

"My experiences as a student in Darryl's classes helped open a whole new world for me, and I will be forever grateful to him. He was patient, kind and, most of all, a teacher of not only acting skills but of self-understanding and personal awareness."

—**Carol Stein**, co-owner and President/CCS Property Management—former student

"In his brilliantly realized book, Hickman suggests that fine acting—and any creative endeavor—emerges from a marriage of right and left brain activity. Having worked as an actor, writer, producer, director, entertainment executive, and now sought-after teacher, Darryl Hickman brings the most complete knowledge of craft, art and business that you'll find in a book about acting. For someone hoping to break into acting, Hickman's book is a crowbar."

—**Peter Barsocchini**, Emmy Award-winning producer/ screenwriter—former student

"When I advise my college students about the art of acting, I point to Darryl's picture above my desk as my greatest teacher and the primary source for the creative process that I utilize as an educator. His techniques and inspiration have served me for more than twenty years. On this dynamic journey toward authentic emotional expression and self-realization, Darryl leads us with total compassion; his sharp intellect cuts precisely through our illusions about ourselves and guides us masterfully toward the very thing we desire —creative freedom!"

—**Doug Kaback**, Professor of Theatre at California State University, Northridge, director, playwright, actor—former student

"I cannot imagine an acting teacher with more experience, expertise and infectious enthusiasm than Darryl Hickman. By offering specific, well-defined guidelines toward a *living in the moment* acting approach, Darryl helped me solidify my technique, unleash my emotional life and infinitely boost my ability and confidence out in the workplace."

—**Dan Frischman**, actor, writer—former student

"The Process that I learned through Darryl Hickman has been incredibly useful in my professional and personal life. I first studied with Darryl as an actor, and the Process was mind-expanding. When I changed careers to Casting, I was able to use much of the same Process in evaluating and connecting with the actors I was auditioning. In terms of my personal life, I feel more aware and connected due to what I've learned from Darryl. His Process is no less than awesome."

—**Jeff Greenberg**, casting director, Jeff Greenberg and Associates/ Paramount Studios—former student

"This book is powerful, clear and concise. The work that has gone into this actor's 'bible' is staggering. If you're an actor, writer, director, producer or simply an artist of any kind, you will take something away from this book that will not only help further your career, but it will help you in your day-to-day life. I LOVE THIS BOOK!"

—**Tony Griffin**, actor, screenwriter, filmmaker—former student

Out of Control, In Full Command®

the UNCONSCIOUS
ACTOR®

The Art of Performance in Acting and in Life

DARRYL HICKMAN

SMALL MOUNTAIN PRESS

THE UNCONSCIOUS ACTOR®
Out of Control, In Full Command®
by Darryl Hickman

First Edition.

Library of Congress Control Number: 2006930612

Publisher's Cataloging-In-Publication Data
(Prepared by The Donohue Group, Inc.)

Hickman, Darryl.
    The unconscious actor : out of control, in full command : the art of
performance in acting and in life / Darryl Hickman. —1st ed.

    p. : ill. ; cm.

    Includes bibliographical references and index.
    ISBN-13: 978-0-9776809-2-4
    ISBN-10: 0-9776809-2-4

    1. Hickman, Darryl. 2. Actors—United States—Biography. 3. Acting
teachers—United States—Biography. 4. Performance. 5. Acting—Study
and teaching. 6. Creative ability—Study and teaching. I. Title.

PN2287.H53 A3 2007
792.02/8/092   2006930612

Small Mountain Press
1187 Coast Village Road, Suite 286
Montecito, CA 93108
Phone: (805) 969-1865
Fax: (805) 969-5379
E-mail: smallmountpress@aol.com
Web site for the book: www.TheUnconsciousActor.com

Printed in Canada

0 9 8 7 6 5 4 3 2 1

For Lynda . . .

Without whom there would be no book.

*"Every child is an artist. The problem is
how to remain an artist once he grows up."*

—Pablo Picasso

Acknowledgements

I wish to express my deepest gratitude to the amazing artists I've had the privilege of working with in the drama business over the decades. Being an expression of what they taught me, this book is first of all a tribute to them. But I must also acknowledge the many gifted, hard-working actors who have been a part of my workshop over the last thirty years, on both coasts, and the huge contribution they made to the unique teaching methodology described in these pages. You know who you are, and I thank you all from the bottom of my heart.

Contents

To the Reader xv

ONE   Movie Star or Monk? 1

TWO   What is Acting, Anyway? 22

THREE   The Method or Else! 58

FOUR   Beyond Box Office: Performance as Art 82

FIVE   Zen in the Art of Acting 115

SIX   Out of Control, In Full Command®:
        The Process 152
            Sitcom City 153
            Debbie Reynolds Has Her Own Studio? 164
            The Mechanics of Creativity® 171
            Exercises: Flow 190
            Scene Study: Form 216
            How to Rehearse 220
            Performance 257

Recommended Reading List 276
Index 280

To the Reader

Part memoir, part historical record and filled with probing analysis of master teacher Constantine Stanislavsky, Darryl Hickman's *The Unconscious Actor* is the result of a lifetime of real-world Hollywood, Broadway and teaching experience. After decades of work, study, personal reflection and thoughtful laboratory experimentation, Darryl carefully coaxes his students to be *out of control* but *in full command*.

What results on these pages is an approach to acting that is vital, immediate, spontaneous, personal, accessible and healthy. It is a proposition that dares one to discover structure through imagination and intuition and to risk what is familiar for the wordless, spontaneous, emotional energy that informs all honest communication and is the bedrock for human relationship.

To do this, Darryl asks journeymen and professional actors alike to consider both rehearsal and performance as a fluid, emerging *Process*. The uncomfortable implication is that results and mastery are perhaps irrelevant, except as the fuel that keeps the artist ever reaching for a deeper experience of personal truth.

But in the end, *The Unconscious Actor* is about far more than just learning how to act. It is about an approach to living informed by a life fully lived. It is a joyful meditation on de-constructing and understanding the human condition while combining life experience with imagination. The confluence of the principles here lead one to gently and humbly accept what is both illusive and true: that infinite, undeniable poten-tial slumbers in each of us, waiting to be released.

Todd Robinson
Emmy Award-winning writer/director and former student
Malibu, California

◇ ◇ ◇

ONE

Movie Star or Monk?

When I was in my thirties, I asked my mother, "Mom, how come I was out at the studio making movies when I was three years old?" Without hesitation, she replied, "It's something you always wanted to do." I laughed. She didn't; she was serious. The fact is, my mother, like many attractive young women of the era, aspired to a career on the silver screen, but she was so shy and lacking in self-esteem, just getting her picture taken freaked her out. She was ambitious though, and didn't give up, biding her time until her first child was born.

At three, I found myself following in Shirley Temple's hallowed footsteps, learning how to tap dance and "sell" a song as a Meglin Kiddie. I hadn't gone to a regular school yet, but I would soon be making a good living and functioning as a breadwinner of sorts, embarking on the career my mother had dreamed of when she was a Mack Sennett Bathing Beauty in the 1920's.

My career would be her career; it was as simple as that.

I didn't know any better. The operative word in that sentence is *know*. The truth is, I didn't know what I was doing when, at the age of six, I found myself in front of a camera begging "alms for the poor" from Ronald Colman in *If I Were King*. Whatever I did, I did instinctively, which has nothing to do with knowing anything. I was a primitive unconscious actor before I could read or write.

By the age of seven I was at home on a film set, but I still didn't know—or care—where the camera was. Bing Crosby, who took me under his wing in a film called *The Star Maker*, would say to the director, "Can't we give Darryl a line here?" When I'd been given added dialogue, he would turn me towards the camera with the admonition: "The camera's over here. Say your line to the camera."

Bing's nickname for me was "Yes-sir-ee" from a line in my audition song, "Franklin D. Roosevelt Jones." While we were rehearsing the musical numbers for *The Star Maker*, Y. Frank Freeman, the head of the studio, and other big-wigs at Paramount would come by to visit Bing in the rehearsal hall, and he would inevitably call me over to sing my song for his visitors. "C'mon, Yes-sir-ee, do your stuff." Everybody cracked up, and nobody clapped louder than Crosby.

Nonetheless, it came as a surprise when Bing approached

my mother at the end of the shoot. He said, "Mrs. Hickman, I know Yes-sir-ee doesn't have an agent, and, if you don't mind, I'd like to call my brother and set up a meeting for you." She was floored. Everett Crosby ran one of the most prestigious talent agencies in Hollywood. "Why . . . no . . . I don't mind . . . at all," she stammered. And a week later we were both sitting across from the other Mr. Crosby in his opulent office on the Sunset Strip.

He looked down from what seemed like a throne, staring at me for a moment before he spoke, "I don't know who you are, Darryl Hickman, but if Bing says I should handle you, I'm going to handle you."

With those words, I was granted credibility in the motion picture industry. Within a few weeks, I was acting in *Untamed* with Ray Milland and Patricia Morrison. No singing or dancing in that movie—I was the child of a backwoodsman, troubled and insecure. Though I was flying blind, fearlessly dependent on urges from somewhere inside, I pulled it off and went right into *The Farmer's Daughter* with Martha Raye. In a matter of a few months, I had been cast in three pictures in a row at Paramount. I was off and running.

Within a year, I found myself in the casting office at Fox with at least fifty other kids my age on a cattle call auditioning for a plum role in *The Grapes of Wrath*. In the early stages of a career, an adult actor reads for a director, but since a child actor hasn't learned to read, he or she simply meets with the casting director, the director, sometimes the producer, and has a conversation. In effect, it's a job interview.

Despite the fierce competition, after an interview I almost

always walked away with the role. *The Grapes of Wrath* was no exception.

While shooting the film, director John Ford told my mother he had hired me because I was a normal kid and "not like an actor." I didn't impersonate anybody; I was just myself. She told me that I loved being in the movie business, and I never questioned it. Apparently, I brought enthusiasm, an openness and willingness not to act like Winfield Joad but to *be* Winfield Joad at the audition. I found out later that's why I had been chosen over several hundred other children who were up for the part.

There's a lesson here. I never competed with the other kids on a job interview. The ones who didn't get the job competed with me. Even as children, the pressure they felt to get approval, to win the competition, to become a success, made them try too hard to make an impression. I didn't care about the salary, or the prestige, or becoming rich and famous. All of the nonsense that motivates most actors, young or old, meant nothing to me. It wasn't conscious on my part, but I now realize I was successful at the age of eight because I wasn't trying to prove something. I was just having a good time.

Fun. We should all bring more of that "F" word to the work place. Fun. Especially those of us who tend to take ourselves too seriously; actors and other professionals need to have a light heart about auditioning. It's not, or it shouldn't be, a matter of life or death. A smart job seeker doesn't go to an audition to *get* anything. One goes to *give* something and to bring a compelling lightness of being that is most always irresistible to a prospective employer. In any field, it's the relaxed interviewee who gets the job.

Mr. Ford encouraged me to have fun on the set as well. In *The Grapes of Wrath*, I had fun being an Oakie, the youngest member of the Joad family. I had fun riding all over the countryside perched on top of the dilapidated truck that was bringing us from the dust bowl to the greener pastures of California. I had fun being on the set with the other cast members, a dozen or so of the most highly-respected members of the acting profession.

I also had fun learning from the wonderful actors I was working with. The most memorable moments from *The Grapes of Wrath* came at the tail end of the production, while we were shooting interiors at the Twentieth Century Fox studio in Los Angeles. I was able to stand behind the camera watching big brother Hank Fonda play a heart-wrenching farewell scene with Oscar-winner Jane Darwell. I was enthralled. It was the beginning of my education as a real actor.

What was the nature of acting being practiced by Fonda and Darwell under the guidance of legendary filmmaker John Ford? The first lesson was unmistakable: acting was simple, honest, being open to your scene partner, and more importantly, believing you were Tom Joad and Ma Joad saying goodbye forever. Standing there on that darkened sound stage, I could feel their love for each other, and tears came to my eyes. Oddly enough, tears still come to my eyes as I write these words some sixty years later. That's the depth of the impression these two wonderful actors made on me as a child.

I have always been grateful for the experience. With Bing

in *The Star Maker*, I had been taught to *perform*; as Winfield Joad, I was required to *act*. In a little more than a year, without being fully cognizant of it, I had gone from a pint-sized song-and-dance man to a serious actor, solely dependent on unconscious forces to get me through.

Crosby, the consummate performance artist, had shown me the way; be yourself, have a good time, and reach out to the audience through the camera.

Fonda and Darwell, on the other hand, were demonstrating the art of being a character in the context of a scene, involving relationships and situations in a dramatic story while the camera eavesdropped from a few feet away. The realistic actor imagines a "fourth wall;" eating in the kitchen, sitting in the drawing room, riding on the prairie, impersonating a character while pretending the camera or the audience isn't watching. This kind of actor must, as the poet Coleridge said, embrace a "willing suspension of disbelief." He or she must believe the make-believe or fails miserably.

Thankfully, the seeds of this commitment had been sown by the time I finished *The Grapes of Wrath*, because my next assignment was the role of Flip, the cocky, tough-talking runaway from a reform school in *Men of Boys Town* at MGM. A sequel to the box-office hit *Boys Town*, the film once again starred Spencer Tracy as Father Flanagan, the Catholic priest who started a home for what used to be called juvenile delinquents in Omaha, NE, and Mickey Rooney, who played Whitey, the young mayor of the institution.

Flip was the premier delinquent in the story—an orphan, a wise-ass punk who, at nine years old, was a semi-hardened

criminal. How in the world would I be able to portray a character whose life experience was so different from my own? At
least as Winfield Joad I had a mother and a father to relate to;
in *Men of Boys Town* I was on my own. And for the first time,
I had a ton of dialogue written in "gangster-ese," a totally unfamiliar speech pattern I was being asked to make my own.

Thank God for Rooney, Tracy, director Norman Taurog,
and, most of all, the wardrobe department which, as I would
soon realize, was a magical resource for an unconscious actor.
The minute I put on the costume, I put on the character of
Flip. The tacky reform school uniform smelling of disinfec-
tant, with scuffed work boots and an ill-fitting cap, made me
feel like a precocious convict. The costume was a passageway
to the part.

Physicalizing the character, as I was discovering, is a fundamental aspect of craft. Whatever gets actors out of their
heads and into their bodies is valuable, which is why the
wardrobe man seemed like my best friend in those early days
in filmland. Choosing the right costume was the first and, in
some ways, the most important step in defining a character. I
found Flip in the huge wardrobe department at MGM, so Flip
was in me when I took his clothes off the hanger, got dressed,
and walked on the set.

In the first scene we played together, Rooney, angered by
Flip's obnoxious attitude, grabbed my shirt; we were physicalizing our relationship before I knew what was happening.
Rooney was teaching me that on the screen, the most effective behavior is physical and therefore visual. The number-
one box-office star of the day knew that film acting—all

acting, for that matter—depends on a basic fact of dramatic communication: the audience reacts first to what it sees, not to what it hears.

Why is this always the case? Because light travels faster than sound, visual information trumps the dialogue every time. This is a scientific law, and every great cinematic artist is aware of its importance in making films. Jimmy Stewart once quoted John Ford as saying, "If you can't tell the story without words, you've failed the audience." I'd be willing to bet that my illustrious scene partner, Mickey Rooney, knew nothing about Einsteinian physics, but he had made his film debut at the age of six, and he had acted in fifty-five movies by the time I worked with him in *Men of Boys Town*. He was twenty-one, an artist of unsurpassable skill, and I, a neophyte, was soaking up the lessons he taught me like a sponge.

Rooney's remarkable physical energy was an important attribute of his screen persona. Working with him in the flesh was akin to absorbing a high voltage jolt of electricity. In contrast, playing a scene with Spencer Tracy was like playing a scene with Mount Rushmore. As Father Flanagan he was majestic, solid as a rock, if you'll pardon the pun, and present in a way that was astonishing. Tracy's presence suggested a deep, still, unperturbed pool of inner truth. He listened. My God, how he listened, focusing on his fellow actor, even one nine years old, as if there were nobody else on earth worth paying attention to at that moment. "Acting is reacting," he said, and he proved the value of that axiom to me more than once in *Men of Boys Town*. A silent reaction from Tracy was worth all the words in the script.

The director of *Men of Boys Town*, Norman Taurog, was known as an expert in handling children on a film set. He had won an Academy Award for directing his nephew, Jackie Cooper, in *Skippy*, which made young Jackie a star. Taurog had also been nominated for *Boys Town* a few years earlier, which once again recognized his genius for helping young actors turn on the tears.

A kid actor in those days was either a good crier or standing in line at unemployment. I faced the challenge right off the bat in *Men of Boys Town*, and Taurog came to the rescue. He went to my mother and asked her who I loved most in my immediate family. Then, when we were ready to shoot, he said to me quietly, "I want you to imagine going home tonight and discovering that your grandmother passed away today." When I started to weep, Taurog said, "Roll 'em," and we got the scene in one take.

I was aware of the director's response immediately: respect. "The Mick," as Rooney called himself, was very complimentary, and I could feel admiration being showered on me from cast and crew alike. Fortunately, I had passed a litmus test for accessing my emotional life, and the confidence it gave me would sustain me throughout my childhood. As a sign that I had been initiated into the close-knit family at Metro, Taurog said, "From now on, I want you to call me Uncle Norm." At that time, only Jackie Cooper and Mickey Rooney had been accorded this privilege.

I was walking on air.

MGM signed me to a long-term contract before principal photography on *Men of Boys Town* had been completed. This meant I would be attending school with classmates Elizabeth Taylor, Jane Powell, and Margaret O'Brien on the lot for the next few years. I was the only male student in a schoolroom full of girls, budding starlets mostly, who teetered on their newly-acquired high heels and disdained my passion for football as gross and barbaric. Elizabeth, a tomboy, was the only one who took me seriously. She learned how to throw a spiral, block, and tackle. The two of us would often scrimmage on the small plot of grass outside the schoolhouse. I hate to admit it, but at that age, Elizabeth was as good a tackler as I was.

But I had little time for football, or sports of any kind, while I was at MGM. I was always working on a movie: in quick succession, I was a frontier lad in *Jackass Mail* with Wallace Beery; a musical prodigy in *Song of Russia* with Robert Taylor and the eminent alumnus of The Moscow Art Theatre, Michael Chekhov; an underground resistance fighter with a French accent and Jean-Pierre Aumont's sidekick in *Assignment in Brittany*; a mentally deficient child in William Saroyan's *The Human Comedy* (my second film with Rooney); and an emotionally fragile gatekeeper's son in *Keeper of the Flame*, once again with Tracy and his long-time screen partner, Katharine Hepburn.

While the ingénues under contract were studying acting with the resident acting teacher, Lillian Burns, and being groomed for stardom, I was polishing my craft under the tutelage of some of the top directors at the studio: Norman Z. McLeod, Gregory Ratoff, Clarence Brown, Richard

Thorpe, Vincente Minnelli, and George Cukor, to name a few. Each director had his own way of dealing with actors, his own strengths and weaknesses, his own approach to running a set. I learned something new from every director I worked with at Metro. Since the relationship between actor and director is the most crucial interaction in filmmaking, I came to depend on the staff directors at Metro-Goldwyn-Mayer, who were some of the best in the business.

Norman Z. McLeod had a wry sense of humor and knew how to get the laughs out of the script and onto the screen. Forget jokes. It was all about bent characters reacting to the pressures of everyday life. Gregory Ratoff, a "mad" Russian, was an actor himself; enthusiastic and expansive, he showered each member of his cast with abundant affection. His secret was love the actor, and the actor would automatically give the director his or her all. Richard Thorpe was a quiet, unimposing man who essentially left actors to their own resources. I never remember him giving me verbal feedback. He got the job done by silent indirection.

Clarence Brown, though, would say just the right words at the right moment to guide an actor's performance. Before we began shooting *The Human Comedy*, he had made a decision that unlocked Lionel for me. A dentist fitted me for removable buck teeth, and the prop department provided a pair of thick glasses. The moment I put on the teeth and the glasses, I was the slowwitted boy Saroyan had created so sensitively on paper. Then Brown helped me with explicit, succinct direction before every take. "Blink a little less the next time," he'd say, and I would zero in on the characterization. Lionel was living in my teeth, my bad eyesight, my whole being.

Character acting, I was learning, was not just the right wardrobe. I was dependent on the right make-up, the right walk, the right props, the right speech pattern, the right physical mannerisms. In other words, I had to find specific, idiosyncratic behavior that would suggest I was someone other than who I was in everyday life. Character actors use their imaginations to form an image of the character they are going to play and then set about recreating that image in the body and voice. Thanks to Clarence Brown and the many other wonderful directors I worked for, I knew all this before I had a chance to take an acting lesson.

I've saved George Cukor for last because he turned out to be the best acting teacher I ever had. In *Keeper of the Flame*, working with Tracy one more time, I had to play an unusually long, emotionally charged scene in which I was asked to make a number of difficult transitions. Only one wrinkle: I didn't know what a transition was. When it came time to shoot my big close-up, Cukor sat me down in front of the camera and explained how the progressive changes in the relationship between Tracy's character and my character, Jeb, were transitions connecting the subtextual beats which made up the arc of the drama.

Of course, the great director wouldn't use words like "transitions," "arc," "beats," or "subtext," because he was dealing with an eleven-year-old child who didn't have a clue about this technical way of structuring a scene. Cukor, who had an incredible knowledge of technique, did the subtextual work for me and patiently helped me get that subtext into my performance. My contribution was to believe what he told me to believe; Cukor (and Tracy, too) supplied the craftsmanship, and I contributed the belief and the emotion. I remember Tracy, who was normally stingy with words, saying, "Why don't you pause there . . . it'll help you make the transition."

In other words, "Take your time." He knew how difficult it was to play this scene, and he knew why. The script demanded a lightheartedness in the first two or three beats, but the fourth beat demanded tears of guilt and remorse, and they had to come spontaneously. Want a challenge? Try starting a pleasant conversation with someone, then burst into tears in the middle of it—on cue. Actor or not, this isn't an easy thing to do at any age.

Before *Keeper of the Flame*, directors like Norman Taurog had helped me cry by asking me to think of something sad from my own life and rolling the cameras when the tears came. I was totally unaware that this prep was a version of Lee Strasberg's *affective memory* exercise and a staple of Method acting. My debt to George Cukor for introducing me to a Stanislavskian approach to acting cannot be overstated. Happily, I was System-oriented before I knew what the Stanislavsky System was. Cukor was employing "the magic If," programming my unconscious and trusting me to play the given circumstances from my own sense of truth. A masterful director, he knew that this particular scene with Tracy could only be played from my imaginative point of view, discovering the beats as I went along.

I'll talk more about Stanislavsky later and how crucial his

ideas would be in the evolution of The Unconscious Actor. At the moment, though, this much should be clear: craft can be taught, but the innate willingness to embrace a dramatic situation, to invest one's imagination in a set of given circumstances, and then to feel deeply about those circumstances is what some people call talent. Craft is an attribute of a mature, conscious, analytical mentality, but no amount of thoughtful analysis will help an actor *believe* anything; the thinking mind usually gets in the way. Belief is a childlike gift from the heart and soul.

Over the years, when people ask me questions about my childhood, I tend to draw a blank. In a sense, I really didn't have a childhood. I had forty or fifty of them. In a way, I lived forty or fifty lives in the movies; riding horses, driving cars, getting drowned by a jealous stepmother, going to the gallows for a crime I didn't commit, conducting a symphony orchestra, and tap dancing with Shirley Temple in *Young People* at Fox was all in a day's work.

I didn't have much of a personal life because I didn't have time for it. Elizabeth Taylor was the closest thing I had to a friend in grammar school. We used to go out to the back lot where we worked as if we were stable hands, cleaning out the stall of the horse she rode in *National Velvet*. Liz had a crush on the horse; I had a crush on Liz. Being twelve years old, I didn't have much experience dealing with girls, and I certainly didn't know how to compete with a horse. But our boy/girl relationship was out of my hands. Sadly, our friendship and our scrimmages on the grass in front of the schoolhouse would soon be a thing of the past.

We were about to be teenagers. For a majority of child actors, growing up—becoming a teen—is not a coming of age, it's a death sentence. Professionally. Of course, Liz Taylor didn't have to worry. She never went through what my mother used to call the "awkward age." One day Liz was a beautiful little girl, and the next she was a gorgeous, sensual woman on her way to becoming an admired movie star. She never had an "awkward age."

I did. For me, one day I was a kid, and then I grew eight inches in a year, fighting a case of adolescent acne, scraping facial hair off sensitive skin with a safety razor, stifling a crack in my voice, and feeling pretty inept at playing the dating game. I was as unprepared for the role of a macho male as Liz was comfortable with being an internationally-known sex goddess. A very confusing turn of events, indeed.

I was going through an identity crisis. On the one hand, I was a charter member of the young Hollywood inner circle, a nationally known actor with several fan clubs, and photo layouts in popular movie magazines appearing on a regular basis. On the other hand, I was deeply religious, a former altar boy, a daily communicant, totally devoted to living the life of a model Christian. Outwardly, I was a young man about town; inwardly, I was more spiritual seeker than movie star.

No longer under contract to a studio where I attended school on the lot, I was enrolled at Cathedral High School in downtown Los Angeles. Run by the Christian Brothers, Cathedral was on North Broadway in the heart of the industrial section and in a primarily Chicano neighborhood. Whereas before, my classmates were starlets in frilly dresses and high-heeled pumps, I was now in an all-male environment of tough-minded *Pachucos* who sported duck-tail haircuts and tattoos. For a while I was in culture shock, but the Brothers were very understanding, ignored my celebrity and treated me as if I were just another student. When the novelty of having a film actor in their midst wore off, it was good to hang out with the guys, go to the prom, and, temporarily at least, live like a normal teenager.

My faculty advisor, Brother Edward, was the kind of man who inspired trust, and I was able to discuss my spiritual aspirations out loud for the first time. I told him my goal was to serve God, but how could I do that being caught up in the Hollywood scene? Brother Edward reassured me, "You can be a Christian and a film artist at the same time." He gave me several books by Graham Greene, one of which, *The Power and the Glory*, made the point that a Catholic writer, a famous one at that, can use faith as the source of creativity. Why couldn't an actor do the same thing?

Brother Edward also introduced me to the fiction of Leon Bloy and François Mauriac—like Greene, successful novelists of the day whose sensibilities were similar to my own. They were artists, they were devout Catholics, and they were anything but disadvantaged by their religious convictions. In fact, their books were all about the struggle between good and evil, the essential element of every dramatic story. I began to realize that the internal conflict I was describing could be the stuff of a more informed, more satisfying approach to the acting business.

My religious understanding broadened as well when I read *The Seven Story Mountain*, Thomas Merton's best-selling autobiographical account of his decadent life before his conversion to Catholicism and his decision to become a Trappist monk. What could be more compelling and dramatic than a sinner-to-saint theme being played out in a man's life? The possibilities for marrying religion with the art of dramatic storytelling were apparent in his writing, but I couldn't figure out how to emulate him by bringing similar convictions to a career in Hollywood.

Reading Merton's *Seeds of Contemplation*, another unlikely best seller written in the monastery, opened my eyes to a deeper appreciation of Christ's message beyond the dogma, the moralism, the legalese of the institutional Roman church. A contemplative doesn't worry about obeying manmade laws; he or she is too busy tuning in to a higher vibration, seeking union with the greater Self. From Merton I learned that "it takes heroic humility to be yourself and to be nobody but the man, or the artist, that God intended you to be."

Merton opened my eyes to a more mystical religious experience, which set the stage for meeting a living, breathing mystic—Cora Evans. Like Merton, she was a convert, but the similarities ended there. Cora was a mother and homemaker whose husband, Mack, sold ice cream from a Good Humor truck. She wore stylish dresses, costume jewelry, and could hold her own with Julia Child in the kitchen. Unlike Ms. Child, however, she spent hours each day in a trance-like state in front of an electric typewriter, typing books so fast that she didn't have time to change the paper. Cora used rolls of shelf paper cut to the width of the typewriter; at the end of a day's work, her output was twenty or thirty feet long!

Visiting Cora at her home in Boulder Creek, CA, was a trip into a fantastic world of higher consciousness. While I was in the other room, she would type without so much as a pause to rest her fingers, spilling phrases, sentences, paragraphs, chapters nonstop onto her shelf paper. A form of automatic writing, there was no thought, no analysis, no editorial interruption to stop the flow of language coming through her fingers.

I was too young to fully comprehend it at the time, but I now realize I was witnessing a demonstration of extraordinary creativity that simply bypassed the conscious mind. Cora was an unconscious writer, and she had no idea how she did it. She had been raised in rural Utah and had never gone to high school, so it came as a surprise when a professional screenwriter who had been asked to edit one of her manuscripts exclaimed: "My God, this is blank verse. Where did you learn to write like this?" Cora replied: "Blank verse? What's that?"

According to her, the books were being dictated by her guides, usually St. Aloysius of Gonzaga. Incredible data about the life of Christ, the meaning of symbols in the Old Testament, the real reason for the Protestant Reformation, the transformative power of death, the three levels of mind, soul, and spirit intrinsic to human nature—Cora's words, written or spoken, were a feast for an inquiring mind. Cora willed her writings to the diocese where she had spent her childhood, and when she died I had the privilege of delivering them personally to the Bishop of Salt Lake City.

Cora Evans was my "spiritual" mother; her influence on me was profound. She saw no distinction between *the art of sanctity* and *the sanctity of art*. In her view, there was no incompatibility between my search for spiritual fulfillment and my success as a professional actor. If I had been able to fast forward to the time when I would be teaching unconscious acting (the Process that would unite mystical perception with the mechanics of craft), I would have been more patient about the future and, probably, made a less abrupt choice to give up acting and enter the priesthood.

But I was young, and the divided self walking around inside my skin had taken over my psyche. I felt like Humpty Dumpty who had fallen off his wall and lay helplessly fragmented with no apparent means of putting myself back together again. Unless, it occurred to me, I could utilize my abilities as an actor to follow Christ in a new vocation as an ascetic and, at the same time, a messenger spreading the gospel to my fellow man. The monastic life was calling as never before.

From my early teens, I had been attending annual weekend retreats with my father and the men of the Immaculate Heart parish at a nearby Passionist monastery. Father Isidore, the retreat director, had become a confidante who advised me to pray for guidance about my future. The life of a Passionist monk was a hard one, he reminded me; if I did decide to enter the priesthood, why not enter a diocesan seminary and become a parish priest? I would be living in the everyday world instead of sleeping on straw in a cell, eating in silence with one's fellow monks, and chanting four or five hours in the chapel, day and night, as a member of the Congregation of the Passion.

I tried to explain to Father Isidore why his order was perfect for me. A Passionist lives a part-time rigorous monastic life, which appealed to me, but also leaves the monastery to preach missions and retreats in local parishes. I wanted to use my communication skills on a regular basis instead of delivering a brief homily at Sunday mass. He saw the wisdom in that reasoning, again counseling me to pray for an answer to the question: did I have a calling to the priesthood.

Finally, at age twenty, I made the decision. I would become a Passionist monk. When I told my family I was going to enter the novitiate in St. Louis and become a novice, my mother was stunned. Though she had always encouraged my religious piety, this was not what she had in mind for her movie-actor son. "How could you?!" she cried. "How could you give up the career we worked so hard to build?"

When I tried to explain that I was no longer happy being an actor, that living in Hollywood's fast lane had lost its magic, that I was convinced I was meant to be a priest, her only response was copious tears. She begged me to reconsider.

Heartrending as it was, I stuck to my guns. I sold my car, told my agent to take my name off his client list, said goodbye to my friends in the film community, booked a flight to St. Louis and, not yet twenty-one, left Los Angeles for a better future. As the plane roared eastward, I looked down at the city where I was born, doing my best to leave memories of youth behind. I was sure that my true destiny lay before me. I was about to get some training at last—and learn how to play the most important role of my life.

TWO

What is Acting, Anyway?

Culture shock overwhelmed me at the novitiate in St. Louis. Instead of inner peace, I found only desolation. My fantasies about the safety and consolation of the monastic life disappeared when I was faced with playing the real-life role of a Passionist monk. I would never make it to ordination. The novice master knew it, my fellow novices knew it, and before long, resist as I might, I knew it. My career as a monk lasted thirty-two days.

As I write, I don't understand how or why it all happened. I have long since given up trying to figure it out. One thing was for sure—I was twenty-one years old, and the curtain had fallen on my childhood: Act One of my acting career was over. Some time would elapse before I would find a way to raise the curtain on Act Two.

While I was pondering my future, I opened my mail one day and suddenly realized I had a bigger problem than becoming a grown-up actor. I had been classified 1-A in the draft. Now what? Would fate, and the draft board, make my future plans for me? Time was of the essence. I needed a breather so I could figure out how to begin the second act of my life.

When I explained my predicament to a not-very-sympathetic lady at the draft board, she shrugged and said: "You're only an actor. That's no reason for a deferment. Now, if you were a full-time college student, I could defer you till you graduated."

Within the month, I had enrolled at Loyola University, a Jesuit liberal arts school in Playa Del Rey [a suburb of Los Angeles] majoring in English. So immature was I that I saw higher education as a detour from the pathway to becoming a successful *adult* actor. At the time I reasoned that it was either college or basic training and, as I saw it, I didn't have any alternative.

If the university had offered a degree in drama or acting, I would have gladly opted for theater arts. I chose English as a major rather than psychology, history, or philosophy, because I was so inspired by the great novelists I was reading— Greene, Hemingway, Thomas Wolfe—that I had begun to write short stories in my spare time. At Loyola I ended up editing the literary magazine and entering an intercollegiate one-act play contest; I was delighted to win first prize.

For a while, I wasn't sure if writing was my first or second love. But when I joined the campus drama club, The Del Rey Players, and acted in a couple of plays—not for money, just because I wanted to—I knew that the need to act was still an essential part of my nature. I would be an actor as long as I lived. On-the-job experience aside, however, I was alarmingly ignorant about acting technique: where acting came from, how it had evolved, who had been the great actors, teachers, and practitioners of acting throughout history.

Like so many of my colleagues young and old, I had no sense of heritage, and it became painfully obvious that I had never so much as questioned who I was, what were my artistic origins, what kind of actor did I want to be when I grew up? Silly as it sounds, as a kid I had assumed my only ancestors were the likes of Bing Crosby, Henry Fonda, and Spencer Tracy; since the movies were my only frame of reference, I was unaware there had been quite a bit of significant acting done prior to talking pictures.

I was hungry for information. Staking a claim on a chair in a remote corner of Loyola's library, I began my research by asking, "What is acting, anyway?" Recorded history, I soon discovered, only went back so far. I had to use my imagination, a limited knowledge of anthropology gleaned from a few books, and enough curiosity to simply conjecture—were there actors, or performing artists, in ancient societies? If so, who were they, what kind of performing did they do, and for what purpose? As I got more and more data, I kept a journal, writing it all down as I went along.

On the first few pages, I speculated about that magical moment, lost in the mist of pre-history, when one of our earliest ancestors obeyed a primal impulse, grabbed a torch from the campfire around which the tribe sat huddled for warmth and created performance art.

I imagined that first improviser (could he have been the original stand-up comic, too?) rolling back on his haunches, wailing eerily, while contorting his body in a symbolic re-creation of the day's successful hunt. No critics being present, the response of the startled cave dwellers who made up the first audience is unrecorded. Let us assume they pounded their hairy mitts together in approval.

Applause! We all know how addictive that can be. No doubt our Stone-Age Laurence Olivier was hooked for the rest of his short life. Sans the benefit of text, make-up, costume, props, scenery, or rehearsal time, he had become the first member of the world's oldest profession in a nameless cavern somewhere near the dawn of time.

Acting, as I saw it, came before civilization. Acting in its purest form is an urge from deep in the human psyche to celebrate our aliveness, to act out our dreams and fantasies in a public display of our most private selves. It is chant, and movement, and rhythm, and mimicry, and laughter, and tears; it is a crude mix of theology, fertility rite, magic, and folklore; it is more physical than mental, more emotional than brainy, more spontaneous than a result of analytical skills.

Acting comes from an innate necessity to explore our relationship to the world around us. Humankind knows it is separate from the animals on whose flesh it nourishes its body, yet it acknowledges a deep-seated commonality with the flora and fauna who share the planet. From the beginning, aboriginal peoples painted, sculpted, carved, sang, danced, and acted out their religious beliefs, social history, the saga of their survival, creating a more lasting record of their all-too-brief presence on the earth. The artistic spirit, that quality which differentiates human from beast, is the wellspring from which acting was born. This peculiar creativity prompted the magnificent murals on the walls of the cave at Lascaux some 20,000 years ago. It sustained the early Egyptians as they labored on the pyramids, the Etruscans as they molded their magnificent pottery, and the Mayans as they carved their innumerable *stelae* in the jungles of the Yucatan.

Webster defines art as the "human effort to imitate, supplement, alter or counteract the work of nature, the conscious production or arrangement of sounds, colors, forms, movements or other elements in a manner that affects the sense of beauty." If the production of something beautiful is the result of conscious choices being made by the artist, its origins are in the unconscious, the voice of which is the series of a mysterious flow of impulses called *instinct*. True actors instinctively mimic their fellow humans, re-create the everydayness and the oddities of the natural world, fashioning their own statements, not only about how life is, but how it could ideally be.

That is why acting must be an ancient profession. Mimicry is a primitive expression of art. The earliest drama was pre-literate; the earliest performance artist had little more to work with than awareness, observation of life on planet

Earth, and an emotional response to the battle for survival. The primary tools were voice and body. The entrance on the stage, the hard floor of a drafty cave, must have been a courageous act of self-expression. If that intrepid Stone-Age Olivier didn't get a standing ovation, he should have. He deserved it.

Actors have always expected applause and, most of the time, they've gotten it. Drama elicits a strong social response. Since acting is the art of telling us about ourselves, the actor personifies the myths of the culture inhabited. He or she is a hero or a villain, depending on the role assigned by the audience being served. Whether witch doctor, comedian, or simple raconteur, the prehistoric performer served the unwritten code of the clan, symbolizing its fears and aspirations, describing the tribal sociology in a personal way. The actor was the essential dramatist for millennia, dominating theater with skills that became a language of their own.

Then, after thousands of years, came the written word.

My solitary introspection into the origins of the actor's art soon collided with the information I was absorbing from my academic studies in the English department. A survey of Western drama was the first eye opener; in Judeo-Christian culture, theater as we know it began with the Greeks. Aeschylus, Sophocles, Euripides, and Aristophanes defined the European dramatic form. Language was imposed on acting for the first time, and the primacy of the actor's creative imagination came to an end. In the Athens of the fifth century before

Christ, Aeschylus & Co., having introduced linguistic structure to theater, transformed an instinctual, ancient liturgy
into what we now call the drama of Western civilization.
Once plays were being written, acting by definition became
an interpretive art.

Originating in the popular Dionysian festivals—orgiastic
spectacles that blended tragedy with comedy in alternating
presentations—our drama was born in an era of extreme
competitiveness where the playwright vied with the actor to
take control of the theater. The cards were stacked against
the actor. Sophocles, arguably the most distinguished of the
great Athenian dramatists, was also an actor, but who remem-
bers or cares about that? An actor's performance lives and dies
in the moment. Words, on papyrus or a stone tablet, live forever. A play is a documentation, a record which can be
handed down from generation to generation. A play has per-
manence. Before the advent of motion pictures, an actor's interpretation was something like a Buddhist sand painting; it
lived vividly for a brief moment then vaporized into thin air.

The failed monk in me was somehow comforted when I
learned that there is a priest in every actor's genes. Why? Because the Grecian citizens' major concerns were humanity's
relationship to the gods. Greek theater explored cosmic
themes, and the actor was a spokesperson for the characters
in this mythological cosmos. Invariably a priest or high-born
citizen [most commonly male], the actor entered into a hallowed compact with the citizenry. Costumed in *cothurni* (high
boots) and *onkos* (a tall headdress), colorfully clothed, and
padded to amplify his size on stage, the actor in the Greek

theater was larger than life. Masks, a carry-over from primeval rituals, were likewise employed to heighten dramatic impact.

Highly trained and demanding large salaries, the first classical actor's most important attribute was a booming voice. Movement limited by an unwieldy costume and the large mask enveloping his face, the actor/priest needed all the vocal power at his disposal in the huge, stone amphitheaters in which he performed. (Of course, as always, there were exceptions to the rule. Aeschylus is said to have favored a performer who was expert at using only his body to make a powerful dramatic statement.)

It was Thespis, the common namesake of contemporary actors, who downscaled the social status of acting and made it accessible to the lowborn. A commoner, but stubbornly ambitious, Thespis was an itinerant player from the provinces who daringly separated himself from the chorus, thereby creating a dialogue between the chorus and the gods or noble personas who were the major characters in a play. It was a first, and marked the beginning of the end for the actor/priest with a social pedigree. His function as a pipeline to the sacred realm of mythological beings was impossible to maintain ever after.

The lofty Athenian ideal of acting would change drastically over time. By the end of the fourth century B.C., a gradual secularization was spreading across the theater world. The age of the great playwrights was only a memory. Aeschylus, Sophocles, and Euripides, who had created immortal characters for actors to play—Agamemnon, Oedipus, Medea, to name a few—were being performed less frequently. The drama was losing its majesty and religious significance. No longer a way of communicating with the gods, it was at its best a means of artistic expression, and at its worst a debased pop entertainment.

Audiences like to cry, but they love to laugh. The Greek citizenry was no exception. Tragedy was not selling, but comedy was. Aristophanes, the master comedian who invented comedy, had written the first *comedy of manners* and was becoming more box office by the day. This social commentary and political satire was meant (in the age of Socrates) to encourage the masses to think for themselves. His comic heirs, most notably Menander (342–291 B.C.), adapted the Aristophanic formula into a new comedy. Devoid of any sacred intent, its primary purpose was to provide amusement for the commoner in the cheap seats.

Needless to say, the actor continued to lose status in this society. As the tentacles of the Roman Empire encircled the Hellenistic peninsula in the third century B.C., absorbing the best of Grecian culture in the wake of its conquest, laughter became the principal theatrical export from the conquered lands. Acting was becoming little more than "a talent to amuse." In the second century, Plautus, the first important Roman playwright and a former actor, brought his own version of farce to select Roman audiences. He was streetwise, a bit crude, but a gifted interpreter of the comic inventions imported from the Greeks. Terence, the other major writer of his day, was a more sophisticated, literate man, who disdained the crudity of burlesque and developed an approach to high comedy which would later influence European theater when interest in classical comedy was rekindled in the 16th century.

Neither Plautus nor Terence, however, would appeal to the average Roman citizen worshipful of secular power and titillated by the sins of the flesh. The masses flocked to bawdy mime shows featuring semi-naked dancers, pratfalls, and obscene behavior, filling theaters with raucous laughter at every sold-out performance. When vulgar taste breeds vulgar entertainment, a diminished respect for the art of acting can't be far behind. Actors shared a divided image by the first century B.C.; to the cultured few in Roman society, acting was respected as a means of artistic expression, but the lower classes viewed the actor as little more than a buffoon.

This double standard permeated the Dark Ages when Christianity ruled the European landscape. While the theatrical tradition of antiquity was being suppressed by the Roman Church, the actor was either a cleric or a clown, depending on the audience he attracted. The miracle plays or morality spectacles took place in the cathedral and were attended by believers intent on saving their souls. They were performed by priests and their acolytes acting out biblical themes. Simultaneously, in the local pub or public square, a wandering minstrel, an acrobat, and a jester or two were cavorting shamelessly to the delight of a ragged throng. It was virtue versus belly laugh, homily versus dirty joke, highbrow moral

vision versus the low comedy of the streets. The truly classical actor had been interred with the bones of the Greco-
Roman dramatists, and the transcendent theater of Calvary
would pre-empt any attempt by medieval playwrights to create a comparable tragedy on the stage for at least a thousand
years.

Nonetheless, while the legitimate actor was on hiatus for a
millennium, street theater was alive and well underground.
Tomfoolery never goes out of style. Jugglers, troubadours,
mimics, monkey trainers, wrestlers, and "tellers-of-tall-tales"
kept show business alive until interest in the classics revived
the actor's art during the Renaissance.

Sixteenth century Italy was the cradle of a resurgence in classicalism. The drama of Greece and Rome was rediscovered
and, liberated from ecclesiastical control, the Italians rein-
vented secular theater with a gusto that was characteristic of
the age. Italian artists were responsible for the proscenium,
painted scenery, opera, ballet, and a new, ornate style of
building in which to house their innovations.

Most important to the actor's tradition in this flurry of
creativity was the origin of *commedia dell'arte*. This comic theater, which evolved in the mid-1500's, combined improvisation, song, dance, acrobatics, and the use of musical
instruments, weaving folk tales and familiar imagery into a
highly successful form of dramatic presentation.

Traveling across Europe until the middle of the 17th century, *commedia dell'arte* established a number of theatrical conventions that are alive and well today. They include a zany approach to comic characters which captured the public's imagination (Harlequin and Punchinello among them), the integration of music, movement, dance, and mime into a dramatic story, and the tradition of a company of players managing themselves and using box office receipts to maintain their autonomy.

The success of *commedia dell'arte* was a milestone in the history of acting in the Western hemisphere. The actor as creator of the drama was not dependent on a playwright to write a role to play or a producer to offer a job. It may have been the only true actor's theater in history; members of a *commedia dell'arte* ensemble devised their own characters improvisationally, and usually played them for a lifetime. There was no casting director to worry about, no play to be cast in, no writer to dictate what to say or do in performance. Actors could sing, dance, or play musical instruments, using their imagination, voice, body, and emotional life as they pleased. The final arbiter of success or failure was the audience, not a gaggle of amateurish critics who had decided how a play should be interpreted before they arrived at the theater.

For actors, it was the best of times while it lasted. By the mid-1600's, forces were at work in European society that would make it difficult for troupes of wandering players to survive. Political boundaries were being solidified, regionalism was a growing trend, and theater would thereafter be centered in large urban areas, usually a nation's capital such as Paris, London, or Madrid. Permanent national companies came into being, with resident playwrights writing plays that reflected the social mores, local controversies, or moral dilemmas of their fellow citizens.

As a result, the actor was forced to settle down. The free spirit pulsing in the *commedia dell'arte* movement would be replaced by the medieval version of a mortgage commitment. Roots had to be established, obligations assumed, civic responsibility accepted. Living next door to a member of the audience brought a new pressure to conform, a new appetite for respectability unnecessary in the days of the nomadic player. Four hundred years later, respectability still eludes many in the acting community who are suspected of being rogues and vagabonds, much as they were in the 17th century. Even as illustrious a thespian as Molière was hurriedly buried at night in what was unconsecrated ground. (He was reburied in Versailles secretly in the middle of the night at the insistence of his patron, Louis XIV.)

Respectable or not, with the wide popularity of *commedia dell'arte*, the actor contributed to the new vitality of secular theater in Spain, France, Germany, Russia, and most of the countries of Eastern Europe. Nowhere, though, did dramatic art flourish more eloquently than in Elizabethan England. When actor Richard Burbage and his brother, Cuthbert, built the Globe Theatre in London in 1599, the longest-running theatrical tradition in the Western world would find its original home.

The building didn't matter. The people did. Burbage, one of the most famous actors of his day, was the original Hamlet, Lear, Othello, and Richard III, but it would be another company member who would achieve lasting immortality by writing these plays for his fellow actors to perform: William Shakespeare. A towering genius, the Bard of Avon was, surprisingly, not fully appreciated in his lifetime. (Was he too popular with the groundlings?)

Notwithstanding the petty jealousy of his rivals, Shakespeare's gifts are evident on the page. He did it all: tragedy, comedy, farce, romance, pastoral, history, and social criticism. Moreover, he had no compunction about entertaining the *hoi polloi* in the cheap seats. He loved bawdiness, double entendre, tabloid sensationalism, melodrama, violence, blood and guts—you name it, he wrote it, and with awesome versatility.

Working in an age devoted to classicalism, Shakespeare was his own man. Having been influenced by *commedia dell'arte*, he ignored the Aristotelian unities of time, place, and action, writing sprawling masterpieces and great roles for actors to play. With his cohorts Christopher Marlowe and Ben Jonson in England, Corneille and Racine in France, and Lope De Vega in Spain, Shakespeare was *numero uno* in the generation that put the national theater movement on the map to stay.

Only Molière, who was born six years after Shakespeare's death, would achieve the same recognition as his counterpart across the channel. Another actor-turned-author, Molière popularized the traditional Aristophanic *comedy of manners,* borrowing once again from the best of *commedia dell'arte* to form his own comic style. His legacy, aside from the

Comédie-Française, established by his widow after his death, was a body of work providing wonderful, extravagantly humorous characters for actors dedicated to recreating classic comedy on the stage.

Shakespeare and Molière were masters of their craft, considered by many to be the twin colossi astride the Western theater. Under the weight of their genius, the drama of improvisation, spontaneity, physical dexterity, and one-dimensional characters collapsed, giving way to textual drama providing stimulation for the intellect as well as the imagination. Punch and Judy, both of whom had degenerated into cartoon characters over the years, would be replaced by Lady Macbeth, Lear, and Tartuffe, characters of greater depth and dimension who would become a part of the literature of the theater forever.

With the exception of Johann Wolfgang von Goethe (1749–1832), the widely-known German poet-philosopher (also an amateur actor who wrote for the theater), no major playwright would appear for nearly two centuries. For most of the 18th and early 19th centuries, provincialism dominated the theater. As a result of the reorganization and consolidation of national boundaries, cultural separatism was the order of the day, and even the better playwrights did not travel well. Potboilers and hack writers abounded; the more skillful work being produced was mostly derivative. Shakespeare, for example, was translated, plagiarized, imitated, parodied, and sometimes mutilated beyond recognition. One unscrupulous adapter had Hamlet walk off into the sunset with Ophelia to give the play a happy ending.

In this climate, the art of interpretation assumed a new importance, and the *literary* actor came into his own. In England, John Philip Kemble, David Garrick, Edmund Kean, and Henry Irving [the first actor to be knighted by the crown] had worldwide success in their lifetimes, and their status in theatrical history was assured for close to 200 years. The continent, likewise, had its share of respected interpretive artists. Among them was Henri-Louis Lekain, the renowned protégé of the philosopher Voltaire, who himself was enamored of the theater, writing plays for amateur theatricals that he presented in his home. Lekain became a leading player at the Comédie-Française, distinguishing himself as a tragic hero until his untimely death in 1778.

Actors, actors, everywhere—but what about the talented women who successfully plied the craft? It's no secret that the male chauvinism which animated the Greeks was shamefully alive as late as Elizabethan England, when boys were recruited to play female roles at the Globe. In the 18th century, however, "the times they were a-changin'." Having been upstaged for almost 2500 years, women would, at last, take their place in the spotlight.

Not that women hadn't always been unsung contributors to the art of drama. The Empress Theodora, for example, was a mime player before she married the Roman Emperor, Justinian. We know that Isabella Andreini was a much-admired player with the *Gelosi*, a *commedia dell'arte* troupe touring Europe in the 16th century. And Armande Béjart, Molière's wife, for whom he wrote a number of juicy parts, was a co-founder of the Comédie-Française, successfully managing it for years with her second husband.

Recognition was slow to come, but when it did, the fairer sex had its fair share of prestigious actors. An English ingénue, Nell Gwynne, achieved fame in the late 17th century before retiring from the stage to become the consort of Charles II. Peg Wolfington, another British star, turned the tables on the Elizabethans by playing young men's roles in several notorious productions. Kitty Clive was a popular comedienne of her day, Sarah Siddons (John Philip Kemble's sister) played opposite David Garrick, and Ellen Terry carved out her own niche as Henry Irving's leading lady in the late 1800's.

Likewise, across the Atlantic, a number of accomplished women were making their mark, among them Lotta Crabtree (famous for her portrayal of Little Nell), Maude Adams, Julia Marlowe, and Mrs. John Drew—who, as Louisa Lane, enjoyed a long career which spanned most of the 19th century. A dynasty of actors followed in her footsteps, including her grandchildren Lionel, John, and Ethel Barrymore, all of whom became household names early in the last century—not to mention her great-great-grandchild, Drew Barrymore, who represents the family on the screen nearly a century later.

But I'm getting ahead of the story. Even if actors, male and female, were largely responsible for keeping playhouses open in
the mid-1800's, drama's pulse was growing fainter by the day.
The Western hemisphere was in ferment politically and socially, while at the same time, theater owners were filling
their stages with trivial comedies and melodramas to pay the
bills. A vacuum existed, and a dynamic, new drama reflecting
societal values was needed to restore the theater's vitality and
improve its vital signs.

Henrik Ibsen was just what the doctor ordered. Ibsen
(1828–1906), credited with being the first major realistic
dramatist, turned his back on the frothy romanticism so popular in his day and set the stage, literally, for a theatrical revolution across the boards. August Strindberg, another
Scandinavian playwright, would also make an important contribution to the movement, as would George Bernard Shaw in
England and the great Russian writer of short stories, Anton
Chekhov, who turned his attention to the theater on the cusp
of the 20th century. When *The Seagull* premiered in Moscow
in 1899, Chekhov established not only himself but the theatrical style he represented as the drama of modern times.

By the late 19th century realism was in, romanticism was
out. Fanciful, overblown discourse on the stage became old-
fashioned overnight. After Ibsen, characters were expected to
talk the way average people talked in everyday life. Elitism
was dead, the problems of the middle class were being dram-
atized with more honesty, and a social conscience was becoming as essential as interesting characters and a well-made plot.
In the words of critic Alexander Bakshy, modern playwrights

were expected to *represent* human behavior dramatically, whereas the playwrights of yesteryear *presented* it. True-to-life was becoming the norm. Writers were encouraged to show the audience a photograph of itself without embellishment, comment, or heightened effect. This theatrical style would prevail until the latter half of the 20th century.

To accommodate this radical statement, a bold reconstitution of the dramatic environment was necessary. Visionary producers and directors sought more naturalistic stagecraft, not only from the *dramatis personae*, but from the architects, scenic artists, designers, and costumers responsible for the physical, visual aspects of the work. First among these modernizers was the Duke of Saxe-Meiningen, who turned his small European duchy into a laboratory researching these basic elements. Touring the continent with missionary zeal from 1874 to 1890, his productions featured a box set that resembled a room (necessitating a symbolic fourth wall), and real scenery with real objects on the stage. In addition, the actors were instructed to look at each other when they spoke instead of declaiming their dialogue directly to the audience in the customary way.

André Antoine, an actor-turned-director-turned-drama critic, saw a performance of the duke's company in Brussels in 1888, returned to Paris and promptly formed the Free Theater to experiment with his own brand of naturalism. A year later in Berlin, Otto Brahm picked up the idea, inaugurating his Free Stage's first season with Ibsen's *Ghosts*. Again, the sets were realistic and the acting was self-contained. The Independent Theater, founded by Jacob T. Greim in 1891, brought re-

alism to London providing George Bernard Shaw his first opportunity to have a play produced when *Widower's House*
opened in 1893. Finally, Constantin Stanislavsky and his colleague, Vladimir Nemirovich-Danchenko, completed the
trans-European revolution when they formed The Moscow
Art Theatre in 1897, creating a modern theatrical company
that would introduce organic acting into the theatrical mainstream.

A different kind of dramatic writing demanded a different
kind of actor. No more declamatory speechifying, no more
broad gesticulation, artificial facial movement, or bombast
would be acceptable for the serious actor at the beginning of
the new century. Henceforth, realistic acting would demand
greater fidelity to the truth of human behavior, a more natural way of speaking the text, movement closer to the body
language of daily life, and, especially, internal, emotional ve-
racity hitherto unknown on the stage.

No one exemplified the transition from the old acting to
the new better than Eleonora Duse (1859–1924). It was Ibsen
the playwright, Stanislavsky the director-teacher, and Duse
the actor who mapped out the road for future generations to
follow. Duse began her career humbly in her native Italy, but
she toured Europe and America in the late 19th and early 20th
century to near worshipful acclaim. She was the mistress of
understated power, possessing an inner reality which traveled
across the footlights in some mysterious, telepathic way. Her
work, as we shall soon document, was a prelude to unconscious acting.

Her only rival during her reign was the French idol Sarah

Bernhardt (1845–1923), whose expansive theatricality was in direct contrast to Duse's understatement. An eccentric—she periodically slept in her coffin—Bernhardt was a throwback to the larger-than-life *grande dame* of yesteryear, a breed of player that would not survive the Spartan demands of realism. She would prove to be the last international star in a dying tradition.

Revolution inevitably foments counter-revolution, and, being a living organism, theater is no different from the body-politic. Call it counter-realism or whatever, no sooner had the triumvirate of Ibsen, Duse, and Stanislavsky set up shop in the European neighborhood than an alternative product was available across the street. While *Ghosts* was drawing a crowd in one theater, down the block other theatergoers were puzzling over Luigi Pirandello's *Six Characters in Search of an Author*, a non-realistic play with grotesque overtones and an early example of the Theater of the Absurd. Soon, across town, Ferenc Molnar's *Liliom*, a neo-romantic fantasy, was capturing the public's imagination. It wouldn't be long before epic-realism would have its day; Brecht's *The Private Life of the Master Race* typified this unique dramatic style.

Labels proliferate. *Neo-classicism, Symbolism, Expressionism, Formalism, Surrealism,* and other anti-realistic means of expression have inundated the hardcore audience since 1900. The various "isms," always difficult to define, are less compelling for a practicing craftsman than the academically inclined. One thing is clear however, so many diverse dramatic statements spelled T-R-O-U-B-L-E for the aspiring actor. After 1875, the *literary* actor had to be either versatile or out of work. Every important playwright, every innovative director, every original dramatic point of view required a specific acting style. Classical, naturalistic, farcical—how does one prepare an aspirant to play so many different styles with expertise? It's enough to make a young actor emigrate to Japan, where Kabuki training is dogmatic, immutable, and passed down from father to son.

The theater of the Western world has no such tradition, and it never will.

The *literary* actor was in search of an American dramatist throughout the 19th century and would have to wait until the 20th century for one to appear. Meantime, sowing the seeds of a grassroots drama was left to a group of talented actors, among them Edwin Forrest, Richard Mansfield, and Joseph Jefferson. Edwin Booth (1833–1893), the most celebrated member of the prominent performing family, was the first native-born actor to achieve international fame.

He made his reputation, however, in plays written by European playwrights. Being an offspring, our indigenous theater lagged behind its continental relative well past 1900. Artistic experimentation was slow to take hold in the colonies. The dramatic revolution or, more precisely, evolution, so widespread in Europe was a late arrival in the States.

Let's face it, on the main we Americans are not impressed with dramatic "artists," nor are we devoted to a faithful observance of changing theatrical traditions like our brethren across the Atlantic. Classicalism, realism, surrealism—they are words residing in the dictionary. Our favorite "ism" is— what else—commercialism. In the earliest days of the last century, the conflict between *art* and *what sells* was as much a part of our national mindset as the Bill of Rights, Mom, and Apple Pie. Art is okay, as long as it makes a buck. That's the American way.

A gentle probe of our theatrical consciousness will reveal a schizoid personality, two combative alter egos engaged in an ongoing struggle for control of our dramatic soul. At one extreme is a version of Robert Lewis Stevenson's Dr. Jekyll, an idealist, pure of spirit and more than willing to starve in a garret to preserve his artistic integrity. At the other end of the spectrum is Mr. Hyde, a huckster without scruples who lives by a twisted paraphrasing of the old adage, "trendiness is next to godliness." Neither of these obstinate sub-personalities has ever been willing to compromise, so the battle goes on to this day.

During the first two or three decades of the 20th century there was a standoff between the extremes, with a slight edge going to moneymakers over proponents of serious "the-a-tah." Frothy musicals, hackneyed melodramas, vaudeville shows, operettas, lightweight comedies—the litany of unabashed entertainments drew the bigger crowds. The star system, defined as the exploitation of a personality for profit and developed into an art form of its own by a host of energetic American producers, carried the day. David Belasco, George

M. Cohan, Florenz Ziegfeld, Lillian Russell, Fanny Brice, Eddie Foy, Sophie Tucker, Ed Wynn, Victor Moore, W.C. Fields, Bobby Clark, and the Marx Brothers were only a few of the stellar names lighting up marquees. They were showmen, curvaceous singing stars, song-and-dance men, red-hot mamas, saloon singers, and burlesque comedians who made us laugh until we cried uncle. Performers rather than actors in the traditional sense, they used beauty, charm, a throaty singing voice, the waltz clog, or zany physical comedy to delight audiences, raising vaudevillian hi-jinks to a high level of performance art. And commercial success.

It should be noted that the true artist is no less worthy of our admiration and respect just because he or she is a crowd pleaser who takes huge sums of money to the bank. Artistry, for the interpretive artist at least, is measured by how well performance skills have been mastered, not the material being performed. In my view, an accomplished tragedian has no inherent superiority over an equally accomplished *farceur*. A flood of tears is no more valuable than a double-take. Hamlet's duel with Laertes is no more impressive than Cohan's soft-shoe routine, regardless of what pedants say. The opinionated Dr. Jekyll among us needs to acknowledge the legitimate achievements of all those entertainment specialists who ply their trade with uncommon expertise.

Devotees of "the-a-tah" never allowed their high-blown status to threaten their appetites for creature comforts. During the

early 1900's, the star system also kept food on the table—
champagne and caviar, at that. In the absence of a native-born
playwright with the stature of Ibsen or Chekhov, producers
were dependent on star vehicles, European imports, revivals
of the classics, and touring companies to recoup their invest-
ments. Recognizable names attracted customers; loyal fans
would return again and again to see their favorites, whether
or not they had seen the identical performance on a previous
occasion. Otis Skinner, George Arliss, Douglas Fairbanks, Alla
Nazimova, John Drew, Eva Le Gallienne, Alfred Lunt, Lynn
Fontanne, Katherine Cornell, Helen Hayes, and the illustrious
Barrymores were all lionized by loyal followings and adored
by critics at home and abroad.

The truth is that, whether in the frothier world of show
biz or the theatrical arts, producers have always cultivated the
cult of personality. As a consequence, even bona fide artists
can be seduced by the bitch goddess, Success. Sometimes,
constant ego massage erodes artistic integrity, but once in a
while, an actor of Eva Le Gallienne's stature is able to use
popularity in the service of art. In the late 1920's and early
1930's, her Civic Repertory Theater proved that a Broadway
star could thrive in an ensemble dedicated to a value system
other than a tally of box-office receipts. Actor, director, de-
signer, manager, translator, and author, Ms. Le Gallienne was
one of those rare people able to survive the star system without compromising her artistic values.

The contrast between the empty façade of the clever, old-
fashioned actor and artists like Le Gallienne was heightened
by the advent of motion pictures. "Mugging" and "chewing

the scenery" is harder to detect from the back row of the Winter Garden; on camera, the dynamic that used to work on stage is less effective. With the advent of sound in the movies, underplaying would slowly replace overacting in theater and in film. But a different acting technique, old versus new, would not be the schism that divided the acting family in this country throughout most of the century. The soul of the actor would be torn between the traditionalism associated with the theater and the upstart, crass commercialism represented by the movies.

When the film industry came of age around 1915, the traditionalists attached to live drama suffered a body blow from which they have never fully recovered. Chief among these early filmmakers was D.W. Griffith, who was the first—in this country at least—to demonstrate the potential power of the new medium. Griffith's epic silent film, *The Birth of a Nation*, drew mass audiences away from live theater to movie houses where, for a nickel, they were transported into the magical kingdom of the nickelodeon. My God, the diehard purists could be heard grumbling, what will the money-grubbers think up next?

The motion picture, as we all know, captured the public's imagination in an extraordinary way. Not only was the audience entranced; by the 1920's, writers, directors, and especially actors had begun a mass exodus from the Broadway stage. The old adage "Go west, young man" took on new meaning. Al Jolson, Mae West, Douglas Fairbanks, and a host of talented actors followed the Gish sisters, Lillian and Dorothy, to movieland. Within a few years, the screen's biggest stars would be émigrés from New York: Gable, Tracy, Cagney, Fonda, Bogart, Bette Davis, Cary Grant, and Fred Astaire had all deserted the theaters clustered in the west 40's of Manhattan for the drafty sound stages of Hollywood. In hindsight, we now know it was only the first wave of what would become a hemorrhage of talent flowing to the film capital, not only from New York but from every other dramatic center in the Western world.

Despite the rupture through which its finer young artists were swept away, the theater held its own. Circa 1920, American drama, formerly a gawky teenager, was growing up, flexing its muscles and displaying new maturity. By the end of the Roaring Twenties, it was no longer necessary to apologize for its European roots. There were, in my opinion, three factors contributing to this welcome maturation: the emergence of the book musical, the plays of Eugene O'Neill, and the success of the Group Theatre.

What would our theatergoing experience have been like all these years without *Showboat*, or Jerome Kern, or George and Ira Gershwin, or Cole Porter, Rodgers and Hart, and Oscar Hammerstein? Imagine a world without *Girl Crazy*, Ethel Merman, Bob Hope, Gertrude Lawrence, Danny Kaye, Bea Lillie, or Gene Kelly. When the Gershwins' *Of Thee I Sing* became the first musical to win the Pulitzer Prize in 1931, it was a sign that musical theater had arrived. The book musical was then, and is now, a distinctly American contribution to the art of drama, more original, more expressive of our Yankee spirit than any other art form. *Showboat* dramatizes our history in song and dance, *Oklahoma!* is a paean to our inherited love of the land, and *Guys and Dolls* is our unique urban mythology celebrated on the stage.

With all due respect for Andrew Lloyd Webber's success, his American predecessors did it first and did it better. Gershwin's jazz idiom captured the pulse, the rhythm, the energy and restlessness of the multi-racial pioneer spirit and exported it to the rest of the world. With the exception of Stephen Sondheim's best work, the splendor of those earlier productions is missing in today's musical drama, but we should be reminded once in a while of the debt we owe the creators of the book musical for putting American theater on the map.

We should be grateful to Eugene O'Neill, too. When O'Neill won the Pulitzer Prize in 1920 for *Beyond the Horizon*, it would signal the beginning of a golden age of American dramaturgy. Elmer Rice was a talented playwright who won the Pulitzer for *Street Scene* in 1929, but no one captured the deep-seated ferment in the American psyche better than the tortured son of actor James O'Neill, a journeyman who never lived up to his potential. Writing in a variety of styles—realistic, tragic, comic, expressionistic—the younger O'Neill fashioned a body of work that brought him an international reputation, wealth, and the ultimate in recognition. He was the first American writer to win the Nobel Prize for literature.

Countless actors have feasted on a smorgasbord of roles concocted by the prolific O'Neill, whose work is constantly being revived decades after his death. Jason Robards, Jr., a veteran of both stage and screen, made his reputation with a critically-praised portrayal of Hickey in Jose Quintero's off-Broadway production of *The Iceman Cometh* in 1956. Later that same year, he joined Frederic March, Florence Eldridge, and Bradford Dillman in the premiere of O'Neill's masterpiece, *Long Day's Journey Into Night*, which won both the Critics Circle Award and the Pulitzer Prize.

O'Neill was a prime source in the surge of theatrical vitality during the third decade of the century. But other writers were part of the movement: the aforementioned Elmer Rice, Robert Sherwood, Philip Barry, Maxwell Anderson, Thornton Wilder, and the irrepressible actor/writer/composer Noel Coward, who transported his unique British comic sensibilities to the New York stage.

Ah, Wilderness, O'Neill's Pulitzer Prize-winning comedy (starring, of all people, George M. Cohan) proved that the tragedian had a sense of humor. During this period, comic invention was raised to new heights by S. N. Berhman and George S. Kaufman who, with Moss Hart, wrote crowd-pleasing versions of the comedy of manners in such plays as *Once in a Lifetime, You Can't Take It With You,* and *The Man Who Came to Dinner.* The argot of Ben Hecht and Charlie MacArthur, which brightened *The Front Page* with fast-paced, rapid-fire dialogue, expertly utilized the hard-edged rhythms of our natural speech patterns to sustain farce in a typically American way.

The actors who played this comedy well invariably ended up in motion pictures, as did Monty Woolley, who originated the role of Sheridan Whiteside in *The Man Who Came to Dinner* on stage. Fred MacMurray, Clifton Webb, Spring Byington, Jean Arthur, Ray Bolger, Bert Lahr, Margaret Sullavan, Walter Abel, Sam Levene, Eddie Albert, Louis Calhern, Martha Raye, Katharine Hepburn, and many more gifted comedic artists honed their skills in front of live audiences before making their reputations on the screen.

Though by 1931 the book musical had established a solid beachhead and O'Neill, along with his fellow playwrights, had revitalized a hand-me-down European drama, the social repercussions of the Great Depression were not being reflected on the stage. Nor were the cultural disruptions brought about by the changing mores of modern times. Freudian theories had pierced the puritanical curtain in the field of psychology, and psychoanalytic jargon was being spouted by the cognoscenti at Fifth Avenue soirées. The libido had been liberated, and sexual freedom was replacing Victorian restraint. Confidences formerly restricted to a psychiatrist's couch were finding their way into casual conversation. People were discarding, or attempting to discard, neuroses like soiled underwear. Tried and true values were of little use to a sophisticated man or woman on the move. Somehow, this questioning, this turbulence would seek a voice in the living theater.

So would the political tumult of the times. Karl Marx had become a prophet for a disenchanted group of left-wing intellectuals who were reacting to the social and economic malaise caused by hard times. In the early '30's, unemployment was widespread; soup kitchens, bread lines, and later Roosevelt's WPA sought to alleviate not only physical hunger but the psychological depression affecting the masses. The disaffected were seeking a soap box where their socialistic fervor could be expressed. What better platform than the stage?

In playhouses across the land, audiences had been given an opportunity to shed purgative tears as characters in *Desire Under the Elms*, *Mourning Becomes Electra*, and other tragedies mined the riches found in Freud's interpretation of classic themes. But attending such productions had its dangers. One could leave the theater having contracted an Oedipus complex when the only reason for buying a ticket in the first place was to have a good cry. Escapist entertainment was safer because it dulled the pain without exacting an emotional toll. But once outside the theater, the truth remained; many of our citizens had lost confidence in the American dream. A radical dramatic response was in the offing.

The Group Theatre was that response.

Founded by Harold Clurman, Lee Strasberg, and Cheryl Crawford on June 8, 1931, the Group would become the most important theater company in American history. No band of artists has ever had such an impact, been as controversial, hatched as many significant actors, writers, directors, and teachers, or given the "fabulous invalid" a more timely transfusion. Clurman, a youthful play reader for the Theater Guild, spearheaded the fight for truer, more relevant drama on the Broadway stage. He commissioned a number of playwrights—among them Sidney Kingsley, John Howard Lawson, Maxwell Anderson, Irwin Shaw, and William Saroyan—to convey his principles in dramatic terms. It would be his friend, the less than eloquent, out-of-work actor

Clifford Odets, who would prove to be his most successful but unlikely mouthpiece. Writing from his own turmoil, Odets provided the Group with such plays as *Waiting For Lefty*, *Awake and Sing*, and *Golden Boy* for a series of groundbreaking productions.

Clurman worked with the writers while Strasberg trained the acting company. Strasberg taught classes at the Group's first summer residence at Brookfield Center, CT, where he started rehearsals for Paul Green's *The House of Connelly*, scheduled to be their premiere presentation. More than a director, he was a natural-born teacher. The many fine actors under his tutelage during the Group years are testimony to the effectiveness of the training: Franchot Tone, Sanford Meisner, Stella and Luther Adler, Phoebe Brand, Lee J. Cobb, J. Edward Bromberg, Morris Carnovsky, Elia Kazan, Margaret Barker, Jules (later John) Garfield, Art Smith, Ruth Nelson, Lloyd Nolan, Roman Bohnen, Leif Erickson, and Van Heflin, to name a few.

Ultimately, when the Group Theatre folded most of its members went on to successful careers in stage and film. Sadly, the idealism which had held them together dissipated before this country entered World War II. Perhaps the nation was facing greater perils than social injustice, empty pocketbooks, and superficial art on the Broadway stage. But theater would never be the same again. Neither would acting in America nor our standards for judging an actor's performance be quite the same either.

After dipping into Sophocles and Euripides in a course on Greek mythology, reciting Shakespearean verse out loud in Dr. Frank Sullivan's required course in Elizabethan drama, comparing translations of Molière, Ibsen, and Strindberg during a survey of European drama, and being introduced to the compelling plays of O'Neill, Arthur Miller, and Tennessee Williams in a study of 20th century American literature, I finally understood that an independent history of acting was impossible if separated from a playwright's text.

The playwright has proven to be the mind of the Western theater; the *literary* actor would turn out to be the heart and soul and voice and body of the theater created in performance. Being an interpretive artist, the actor is traditionally dependent on a dramatic literature which demands the best from within. I was starting to put the acting I had done as a child into perspective. A film actor's primary job boils down to taking words off the page of a script and living them in front of a camera. Having done this research and gained this insight, I had a sense of my place in the scheme of things and a clarity about what it meant to be a *literary* actor. As the wags used to say, "If it ain't on the page, it ain't on the stage."

The intermission between Acts One and Two of my life had lasted almost four years, and my sense of self had changed, not for the worse, but for the better. I was almost ready to put my career into second gear with a heretofore missing maturity. My studies brought the realization that the instinctual acting I had done in childhood had built-in limitations; I was only able to exercise one half of my brain—the right side. Instinct and imagination (overlaid with a superficial patina of second-hand craft) had sustained me while I was growing up. An adult actor, on the other hand, has to engage the left hemisphere, too, adding intellect, analytical prowess, and the most powerful tool of all—the ability to make conscious choices—to the mix. A mature unconscious actor must *feel* deeply but must also *think* skillfully, and that's exactly what I was learning how to do.

My grades were good enough that I was allowed to miss classes and make four or five films while I was at the university. Among them were *Lightning Strikes Twice* at Warner Bros., playing Oscar-winner Mercedes McCambridge's crippled brother; *Destination Gobi* with Richard Widmark at Fox, the second of two films I did for director Robert Wise; and *Island in the Sky* for John Wayne's Batjac Productions, working again with directorial legend William Wellman.

Making movies is a team effort, and for the first time I felt like a full-fledged member of the team, a true collaborator who contributes to the joint effort. McCambridge and I discussed our complex brother/sister relationship over coffee, during lunch, and after dinner for weeks. During the shoot of *Lightning . . .* , the ageless director, King Vidor, paid us the compliment of asking us how we wanted to play our roles. There was no "do it this way" or "do it that way" or "do it my way" from Mr. Vidor. A full partnership between actor and director was established on the first day of production, and it didn't change until the wrap.

I definitely had a different relationship with Robert Wise the second time around. Wise, who had been a film editor [*Citizen Kane*] before he took the director's reins, was eager to answer my questions about his odd way of shooting a scene, which was always truncated, in bits and pieces. He showed me the final edit for *Destination Gobi* diagrammed on his script; he had put it together in his head before we rolled the cameras. For me, it was a reminder to be prepared, to come to the set with a point of view for each scene, an arc for my performance with a beginning, middle and end for each sequence. An editor-turned-director like Bob Wise, shooting the way he did, only hired actors who knew how to do their homework. An actor couldn't depend on Wise for an overview, because Wise depended on the actor to provide it.

John Wayne brought in a point of view, discussed his thinking with Bill Wellman, and often compromised if the director came up with a better idea. "Duke," as he was addressed by his coworkers, was amazingly unimpressed with himself; even though he was the producer *and* the star, he carried the camera up a steep mountain for a shot Wellman wanted to get, ate lunch with the crew, and asked his fellow actors for suggestions about how to improve his own and everyone else's performance.

No ego, no higher status, no bloated self-image for John Wayne. He was an amazing man. Players of stature such as Crosby, Fonda, Tracy, Hepburn, Gable, and Wayne, had been teaching me the same lesson for more than two decades. A cast of professional actors is, from star to bit player, a true democracy, each individual equal to his or her fellow players: interdependent, openhearted, a member of a team.

Naturally, an egomaniac shows up now and then, but they don't fare well; they cause trouble from the get-go because they are out of sync with everybody else. The bigger the ego, the less they belong to the family, and an acting ensemble *is* a family, united on the basis of mutual trust and respect. Actors are incapable of trusting or respecting anyone else if they don't start with themselves. The rule is, never walk on a set or into a rehearsal hall if you don't bring with you a healthy dose of self-respect.

Nearing the end of my senior year at Loyola, I was feeling good about my transition from childhood to adulthood, and I couldn't wait to go back to my career full-time. But Fate had an ace of spades up its sleeve. I had been so busy preparing for finals that I had forgotten all about the draft board. Of course, the draft board had not forgotten about me. My induction notice was in the mail before exams were over, and I was at Fort Ord in basic training when my classmates received their diplomas at our graduation ceremony.

I got my diploma in the mail.

For two years, I would be a member of the Sixth Infantry Division, stationed at Fort Ord, CA. In the movie business, out of sight is out of mind, and I wondered if I would ever be able to resuscitate my acting career after my discharge. That is, if I didn't die in combat first. As the reader might imagine, as a lowly private in Uncle Sam's army, my plans were very much up in the air.

THREE

The Method or Else!

At some point during the time I was at Fort Ord, I read Constantin Stanislavsky's autobiography, *My Life in Art*. Once I finished basic training and was stationed permanently at the base, I had time at night and on weekends to set up my own postgraduate program with a chance to choose the curriculum. *My Life in Art* is three inches thick and difficult to read, but it changed my point of view about acting more than any other book I've ever read.

Having spent nearly a quarter of a century in the movies, I had always seen acting as a business; I had never viewed acting as an art. I was aware of Stanislavsky's reputation as an actor, director, and teacher, but his enthusiastic, adventurous spirit, his relentless self-criticism, and most of all, his unwavering commitment to peerless dramatic artistry came alive on the pages of his wonderful book. His zeal for elevating the art of acting in the Russian theater was contagious, but I was especially moved by his hunger for spiritual transcendence, and his eagerness to blend spirituality with excellence in the dramatic arts.

Remembering what Cora Evans had told me years earlier, that there should be no distinction between the art of personal sanctification and the sanctity of true art, I had found a role model at last. In both his life and his teachings, Stanislavsky was telling me not to despair; not only were my two selves—movie star and monk—reconcilable, but they were two halves of the same whole. The trick was to ignore the apparent dichotomy and to elevate my acting in a fusion of personal and professional aspirations. The master was adamant. Great art and peerless spirituality could be one and the same thing: inseparable.

In *My Life in Art*, Stanislavsky catalogues a long list of trials and errors, successes and failures, and an exhausting litany of experiments he undertook on his way to an international reputation. To imitate him, must I follow the same path? Craving a formula to follow, I read *An Actor Prepares* hoping to find a *how* that would get me on the right track in my thinking. A year had passed since I had been in front of a camera, and all of my new insights would have to remain so much unpracticed theory, for the time being at least.

If *My Life in Art* is a manifesto laying out Stanislavsky's philosophy about theatrical artistry and what led him to his discoveries, *An Actor Prepares* is a manual designed to help an aspiring actor learn the craft. For me, there was a ton of valuable information in *An Actor Prepares*, but I found it less helpful than I had hoped for applying the System to my own work. The fictional format seemed clumsy, and the translation— often wordy, overly formal and unclear—did not do justice to what must have been Stanislavsky's original intent. Some basic elements of craftsmanship were in the book, but a truly systematic methodology for creating a performance was nowhere in those pages. I was more than a little disappointed.

It was not until I read *Building a Character* some time later that I realized what was missing—the other half of the methodology. *An Actor Prepares* was published in 1926, but *Building a Character*, which would complete the published version of the System, wouldn't appear in American bookstores until some twenty-four years later in 1950. For a complete understanding of Stanislavsky's practical guidance to training actors, one would necessarily need to read and digest both of his teaching manuals. Even celebrated Method spokesman Robert ("Bobby") Lewis says in his famous lecture series *Method—or Madness?* that *Building a Character* is " . . . the book nobody ever reads." As I would later come to realize, no teacher who ever claimed to be an interpreter of Stanislavsky's principles could do so without fully assimilating *Building a Character* and including it in the curriculum.

I was out of town, away from "the biz" for two years, and I used the time to take a step back and try to get a handle on what was happening to actors in contemporary America. One thing was for sure, the Method was fast becoming the fashionable acting style of the mid-twentieth century. Where had it come from? Just what was Method acting? And how had Method actors taken over the film industry in such a short period of time? Would the Method actor prove to be a role model for the actor I aspired to become? I went to the movies and continued reading voraciously. I was beginning to connect the dots.

In 1947, Bobby Lewis, along with Cheryl Crawford and Elia Kazan, had founded The Actors Studio in an abandoned church on midtown Manhattan's West Side. But it was not until Lee Strasberg became artistic director in 1951 and began supervising scene study classes every Tuesday and Friday that his teachings became a dominant force in contemporary American drama. An outgrowth of the pioneering work he had done with the Group Theatre, Strasberg molded The Studio's first freshman class (inherited from Mr. Lewis and comprised of Julie Harris, Montgomery Clift, Karl Malden, Eli Wallach, Mildred Dunnock, Jerome Robbins, Maureen Stapleton, and future megastar Marlon Brando) in his own image, stamping them with The Actors Studio seal of approval. When Brando, James Dean, and a host of other Studio alumni made the trek to Hollywood in the '50's, the Method went to the movies. Before long, this new crop of actors would own the film industry.

But why? From my vantage point as an outsider, tucked

away at an army post near Monterey, CA, I could ponder the phenomenon with a certain objectivity. Strasberg's methodology had somehow unlocked a deeper emotional truth in his students, accessing a power that was unavailable to most of the actors I had known or worked with over the years. There was a rawness, an explosiveness, an irreverence toward the social niceties that constrained actors caught in an old-fashioned, conventional mindset. It was as exciting for me to watch on the screen as it was compelling for the rest of the audience. But what *exactly* were these Studio-trained actors doing that was so different from what the rest of us had been doing in the movies for decades?

As I would discover, there isn't any easy way to define Method acting. The Method actor is elusive and hard to pin down. But there are clues to his/her identity; the Method actor stumbled into a transitional theater that was naturalistic rather than classical, American rather than European, tragic rather than comic, kitchen sink rather than drawing room, verbal rather than symbolic, left rather than right, Freudian rather than Jungian, and materialistic rather than metaphysical. God, heaven and hell, and biblical salvation had long since lost their appeal to the playwrighting intelligentsia, and the actor, in the role of interpreter, was more than a little disoriented.

Instead of togas, tights, or tuxedos, the Method actor would have to invent another set of costumes to take stage in the theater of the post '30's America. Arthur Miller's Willie Loman would wear a rumpled suit in *Death of a Salesman.* Tennessee Williams' patrician Blanche DuBois, reduced to riding public transportation, would require threads of faded elegance, and her nemesis, Stanley Kowalski, would fashion a uniform for a generation of impressionable young actors by sporting a pair of jeans and a torn t-shirt in *A Streetcar Named Desire*.

Marlon Brando created Stanley Kowalski in his own image. Intense, rebellious, sexually predatory, Brando's volcanic Stanley was a different kind of leading man, both in the theater and on the screen. No widely-known actor has been more imitated (or maligned) as an example of the self-indulgent, "torn t-shirt" school of the Method.

The media pinned that label on Marlon Brando, and it stuck like flypaper. From critics of the Method, he got most of the blame. Whether worthy of blame or praise, Brando was not really responsible for what happened after he exploded on the public consciousness in 1947. The man behind the scenes, Stanley's "godfather," was *Streetcar's* director, Elia Kazan. It was Kazan who turned a then-unknown youth loose on the stage. It was Kazan who recognized the daring young actor's superlative instincts and supported his invention to the hilt. A worried Tennessee Williams took his director aside during rehearsals and complained: "That boy is distorting my play. It's about Blanche, she's the heroine, and he's twisting it around to make it about Stanley Kowalski." Kazan reportedly replied: "True, Marlon is putting his personal stamp on the role, but what he's doing is brilliant. And that's the way it's going to be."

In mid-century USA, Stanley became the prototype for a new kind of anti-hero. He was alienated, a stud with a heart of gold, a sensitive Neanderthal with no social graces longing for a girl who would jump on the back of his motorcycle and ride off with him into the West. Brando did it to perfection in *The Wild One*. Our hero was by now an even more disenfranchised, socially inept outcast in an uncaring culture. No poetry here, no eloquence, just a biker on a trip to an unspecified social nirvana where everyone, even bikers and Neanderthals, are created equal.

Was this the prototypical Method actor—mumbling, slouching, fondling his crotch, and kicking his toe in the dirt as he romanced the leading lady? Of course not. No more than Jimmy Dean's misunderstood, love-starved *Rebel Without a Cause* was a replication of every American teenager's story in the '40's and '50's. But in many people's minds, Brando and Dean, being the most famous graduates of The Actors Studio, became more mythic than the characters they portrayed or the approach to acting they represented. If Willie Loman was a proletarian martyr in the Method's earlier incarnation, Brando and Dean, by sheer charisma, turned themselves into the Method's proletarian icons.

Recognizing mythological stature is one thing; discovering the essence of Method acting is something else, if it's possible at all. The fact is that the players we most admire have been "Method-ized" since Mr. Strasberg began his revolutionary experiment more than seventy years ago. Despite Brando and Dean's reputations as minor deities, a torn t-shirt was never the standard costume of Method actors, any more than monosyllabic nobility was the only thing they could play. Their range was broader and far more comprehensive than that.

But the hard core, Studio-trained actor of the '50's *did* have limitations. They assiduously avoided the classics, and for good reason. Speaking verse was an unfamiliar experience, fencing was for sissies squeamish about toting a gun, and wearing tights was for a guy who was willing to take a back seat to a ballerina. Unexpectedly, Brando acquitted himself admirably as Marc Antony in a long-ago film version of *Julius Caesar*, but his fellow players, British actors John Gielgud and James Mason, clearly demonstrated why the Royal Shakespeare Company resides in England rather than midtown Manhattan. Shakespeare was an Englishman writing in a classical style that could be considered downright un-American. Classicism is at home across the Atlantic, where princes, ladies-in-waiting, dandies, noble knights, and warrior kings abound in European history. A Method actor is more at home in work boots than velvet pumps.

A Studio actor doesn't usually sing and dance very well either. Or play comedy. To bring Irving Berlin to life, or to comfortably inhabit the worlds of Oscar Wilde, Kaufman and Hart, and Noel Coward, an actor must have the proper training. Comedy, musicalized or not, often tells its story with broad characterization bordering on caricature. We laugh at familiar kinds of people we all recognize, with familiar traits we find amusing. The heart of the character must be truthful, but that truth should extend to a new level of expression which, in musicals, causes the character to sing and dance. Singing and dancing is impossible until the actor bursts out of a naturalistic skin. Fred and Ginger were larger than life, and larger than life is what counts in musical comedy, straight comedy, and farce.

The comic actor deals with the outside world more than investigating the self. A comic actor cannot afford to be too introspective nor take the time to stop and think reflectively. If too much genuine pain rises to the surface, the comedian has to dismiss it with a joke. Traditional Method training tends to focus so much on the actor's internal mechanism, the true emotional response, that the external behavior is taken for granted, or even ignored. In comedy, the physical behavior more than the words conveys the truth in a visual, hyperkinetic way. Slipping on a banana peel, doing a good double take, or finding a funny laugh for the character are more valuable to a comic actor than probing for a deeper emotional experience.

Whatever the faults or inadequacies, by the mid-'50's Method actors ruled the acting business. Ironically, they were becoming a more valuable commodity than the one-dimensional commercial actors being reacted against. With a swagger and a reticence about discussing inner workings, Method actors were deliberately inarticulate when it came to explaining themselves. Not known for humility, the Method insiders were clubby to the point of snobbishness in their treatment of the uninitiated actor of yesteryear. Self-explanatory, self-effacing, self-critical they were not. Why should they worry? Everything seemed to be going their way.

After nearly two years of wearing a uniform to work every morning, I was about to get a discharge. My military obligation fulfilled, I would return to civilian life a free man. I should have been ecstatically happy, but I wasn't. Instead, I kept having a recurring nightmare that was especially bizarre: my longtime agent had died, and somehow, I was entombed with him in a Los Angeles cemetery, alive but trapped forever, never to act again. Was this an omen? Was it a warning that my on-again, off-again acting career might be over for good? And if I was able to get a job, would I fit in with the New York-trained Studio actor who was all the rage in filmland during the '50's?

I had read everything I could get my hands on about the Method while studying Brando and Dean's performances in films like *On the Waterfront* and *Giant*, and I had to admit that, from a distance, I knew more about what the Method wasn't than what it was. Powerfully effective, yes; fully understandable, no. Was this new breed of actor bringing a Stanislavskian slant to the profession, or did it simply represent another novelty, a cult of personality that would soon fade away? Was it just another radical idea that had snuck up on the acting establishment and seized the high ground, or was it the genuine article? I knew I had to get back in the trenches to find out, but I was increasingly glum about the chances of reviving a career in the movie business.

Then, a miracle happened. Out of the blue, I received a call from the head of casting at MGM, Billy Grady. He asked me if I could come to Los Angeles for a meeting with Vincente Minnelli about a film he was preparing. "Sure," I said, trying not to sound too excited, "I can get a pass and be there by tomorrow afternoon." Grady said, "Be in my office at three o'clock," and hung up.

Just being on the lot at Metro was like old times. I met with Minnelli and Robert Anderson, who had adapted his play, *Tea and Sympathy*, for the screen. I had worked with Minnelli in *Meet Me in St. Louis* years earlier; I expected him to be polite but taciturn, and he didn't surprise me. Anderson was more talkative. He explained that Dick York had played Al, the role I was up for, on Broadway, but he was busy in William Inge's *Bus Stop* and might not be able to join his original cast-mates Deborah Kerr, John Kerr, and Leif Erickson in the film version of the play. They were looking for a back-up in case they had to hire another actor.

I expected them to ask me to read: they didn't. Minnelli ended the meeting with his version of "Don't call us, we'll call you," and I went back to Fort Ord, praying every step of the way for a greater miracle—that I would actually get the job. I waited by the phone for two or three weeks on pins and needles. I knew they were going into production within the month, so a decision had to be made soon, and each day that passed I was a little more despondent. Finally, I decided the whole scenario was too good to be true anyway and put it out of my mind.

That was when the call came. It was Billy Grady once again, with another question, "Can you start shooting next week?" "You bet," I said, overjoyed. Fortunately, I had saved my leave time and, with sixty days left, I could make the movie. The gods had smiled. I was able to jumpstart my career once more, and I was grateful for the opportunity to return to the film industry in style.

One thing I couldn't understand: with all the available young actors in town eager to play a good role like Al in a major motion picture, why had they cast someone who had been out of the loop for a couple of years? I later learned that I owed my good fortune to Robert Anderson, the playwright I would meet once and never meet again. The casting department at Metro had set up scores of auditions for Anderson, and he had picked me because he said I was the only actor in Hollywood who "didn't look or act like an actor." My army crew cut turned out to be more of an asset than a liability.

And it seemed my skills as an interviewee were also intact. I found I was still able to be fully present, open, and responsive while avoiding the biggest pitfall of all, pressing to get the job. As much as I wanted to be hired, I remembered lessons learned in childhood—an actor compelled to sell himself is a turnoff. If the actor and the role are a comfortable fit, there is a good chance the actor will be cast; actors have to trust themselves *and* those who audition them. Go with the flow, always. Don't push the river. When I interviewed with Vincente Minnelli and Robert Anderson, I wasn't conscious of employing this proven strategy. I just did it.

But the time soon came to deliver a performance. Not having been on a sound stage for three or four years, I was apprehensive about my re-entry into the movies. Al was the best written character I had been asked to play in a long while, and I knew I was rusty. Reading about acting or watching other actors act and analyzing their performances is not a substitute for getting on your feet and doing it yourself. Theoretically, one could have enough expertise about Shakespeare's plays to write a book about the character Hamlet and never be able to put one of his monologues on the stage. Bottom line: performing is an experiential form of art.

Tea and Sympathy had been directed on Broadway by Elia Kazan, whose reputation as *the* Method director spanned the continent; he was not only the toast of Broadway, he loomed as an even larger presence in the film business. Actors hired by Kazan, earning his imprimatur, were considered the pick of the litter. Though I was not an original member of his ensemble, if I was able to step into Dick York's shoes in a high-profile project, I would earn my stripes by association. Sure, I had been in front of a camera many times—in close to a hundred films, actually. But being part of the cast of *Tea and Sympathy*, I could prove that I was enough of a Method actor, formally trained or not, to get the job done. This was not just an acting assignment; this was a chance to show the industry that I could hold my own with the best The Actors Studio had to offer.

I was surprised at how the attitude at MGM towards actors had shifted since I was under contract in the '40's. Then, actors who came out from New York, migrating from the theater, were often belittled by their West Coast counterparts for being too "broad" and overacting in front of a camera. But in the '50's, studio brass and filmmakers as eminent as Vincente Minnelli had changed their tune about the East Coast contingent. Using Kazan's nickname from his days as an actor at the Group Theatre, Minnelli would ask Deborah Kerr on more than one occasion, "How did Gadge do this scene?" Respect, even hero worship, was built into the question. I saw firsthand how much Kazan was a formidable presence on the set of *Tea and Sympathy*, in the same way that Studio actors were a formidable presence in the film community.

I alone would reflect Minnelli's directorial contribution, and for the entire shoot he was on my case. "Rehearse, rehearse," he would say incessantly, picking at my interpretation until I was the Al he had in mind. In one scene with Deborah Kerr, his "rehearse, rehearse" began to get on her nerves, too, and when he asked us both to go to her dressing room to continue rehearsing while the cinematographer was lighting the shot, she closed the door and said: "Sit down. Relax. You're doing fine."

Being a gracious, sensitive lady, Deborah knew he was on the verge of overdoing it. When he came by several times and knocked on the door asking, "How's it going?" she replied, "Go away, Vincente, we don't need you now." She winked at me and said: "I think he's somehow competing with Gadge. He doesn't have to—he's a great director. But Kazan's a hard act to follow."

In truth, Minnelli was doing me a favor. Like George Cukor some fifteen years earlier, he went over each transition, each beat, each element of blocking, each change in body language, and the use of each prop, demanding greater specificity, polishing, defining, and re-defining in minute detail the progression of every scene. His directorial guidance would prove to be a refresher course in film acting, and I would be grateful for his pickiness whenever I was in front of a camera in the future. I would do better work because of him. Thank you, Vincente Minnelli, for being such a perfectionist.

And, thank you, John Frankenheimer for introducing me to live television. At twenty-seven, Frankenheimer was already an old-timer. He had cut his directorial teeth in New York in the early days of television. A *wunderkind*, he was part of an adventurous group of young artists who had invented drama designed specifically for TV. Originating in makeshift studios in Manhattan, the prototypical shows Frankenheimer and his fellow directors created were broadcast *live* across the country. East Coast actors, recruited mostly from the theater, comprised the talent pool for *Philco Playhouse*, *You Are There*, *DuPont Show of the Week*, and the other programs where an experimental acting technique would saturate Middle America in the '50's.

New York City was the birthplace and home of live TV until CBS built a state-of-the-art facility at the corner of Beverly and Fairfax in Los Angeles: Television City. Frankenheimer was assigned to direct CBS's flagship program, *Playhouse 90*, a live, ninety-minute show broadcast weekly on the network. Frankenheimer saw a screening of *Tea and Sympathy* before it was released and hired me to play John Cassavettes' college roommate in *Winter Dreams*, an adaptation of an F. Scott Fitzgerald short story. Suddenly, I found myself in a rehearsal hall at Television City surrounded by a group of opinionated actors from the East Coast, all of them—with the exception of Dana Wynter, a movie star—owing an allegiance to Method acting.

I was challenged, curious, and confident, all at once. As was the custom in live TV, I sat around a big table reading through the script with Cassavettes, Mildred Dunnock, Phyllis Love, Joe Sweeny, and four or five other artists whom Frankenheimer had known in New York and flown West for this three-week engagement. In one way, I felt complimented to be part of this prestigious ensemble. In another, it seemed a bit unfair that these New Yorkers had invaded my territory. There were thousands of out-of-work actors in Hollywood; weren't they suitable for live television? Soon it became apparent that Frankenheimer and his chosen band of players had worked together many times, knew each other well, and spoke the same language, a kind of shorthand "Method-speak" which was understood by all. There was no way a Hollywood actor like me could be part of this family without learning this language. Though I was no doubt an outsider from their vantage point, a lowly pledge, I was eager to be accepted as a member of the fraternity.

Shortly after the read-through, I got my first opportunity to apply for a full membership. Frankenheimer took Cassavettes and me aside and said: "I hate the way your relationship is written. The dialogue sounds like it was taken from a grammar book. Go somewhere and improvise the scenes you have together and make it sound like college guys really talk. I'll rehearse around you in the meantime."

Improvise?! In my entire career in films I had never been

asked to improvise. I knew enough about the Method to be aware of the value Strasberg and other teachers placed on improvisation as a means of enriching the text by exploring a scene in the actor's own words during rehearsal. Improv was designed to investigate character, the truth of relationships, and what could be going on in the play that isn't explicitly stated by the playwright. Frankenheimer was using the tool to create dialogue for scenes, asking his actors to substitute their own words for the original text—in effect, writing their own roles so they could play their own dialogue in performance; it was a kind of 20th century update of *commedia dell'arte*.

Cassavettes and I went out on the roof at Television City, the only place where we could be by ourselves. John threw out an idea or two, a discussion followed, then we started to play with some language to flesh them out until we had a scene. We were guided by the script, but not bound to the writer's version of how we related to each other. We were John and Darryl, Darryl and John—we were putting ourselves into the script. In a couple of hours on that roof we got to know each other, trust each other, and give up the tentativeness that afflicts actors who haven't worked together before. It wasn't a personal friendliness, mind you, but a professional intimacy that's hard to describe.

The time I spent with John on that roof was a revelation. Improvisation is not hard to do if you don't make it hard to do. Improv is how we live our lives. We don't have a text to follow when we get up in the morning, we improvise. With or without a text, actors have to trust their creativity, reaching down into their own substance to find the images, feelings, the impulses to do things and say things that bring a living reality to the life of the character, moment to moment. Improvisation, I was discovering, is the basis of modern acting which, in some sense, should always be unplanned and unpremeditated, flowing spontaneously from the inner self.

John Cassavettes was good at improvising; he made it look easy. Little did I know, however, that he would go on to become the most acclaimed improvisational filmmaker in the history of American cinema. I often wonder if he had any inkling of his future pre-eminence in the field when we were standing in the hot sun for several hours fixing F. Scott Fitzgerald's badly adapted characters.

When we went back inside, Frankenheimer stopped his rehearsal and said, "Lay it on me." We showed him the two or three scenes we had worked out. He called the script girl over and told her: "Write it down exactly the way they give it to you. That's what I want to put on the air." I couldn't have been more proud if I had won an Emmy for both writing and acting on this show.

Winter Dreams marked a psychological rite of passage for me. I knew I had been accepted by this cast of New York-based actors, and there was no more reason to feel threatened by their arrival in Hollywood. Quite the contrary, they brought fresh energy to Hollywood via live television. They were shaking up the West Coast acting community by introducing an innovative, vital methodology, and they were raising the artistic bar for every professional in the talent pool.

Most significant to me personally was the hope that this

new wave of actors from the East would somehow bring Stanislavsky's System into the mainstream of American drama. Generally speaking, the actors I was now working with seemed to be probing for a deeper, emotional, subtextual truth. But were they reaching for a level of artistry, or was theirs simply a more sophisticated *craft* than I had learned and depended on in motion pictures? Craft is essential in acting, but the art of acting transcends craft. And my dream was to master the *art* of acting.

I had ventured into uncharted territory. Crossing the border from filmland into TV-land after *Tea and Sympathy*, I was kept busy in live television for the rest of the decade. Accustomed to the process of making movies for so long, I had to adapt to the new medium that the major networks had transported to Los Angeles.

True, it was still acting in front of a camera, but there was a significant difference in how one arrived at a performance in live TV. The demands made on an actor in shows like *Playhouse 90*, *Studio One*, *U.S. Steel Hour*, *Climax!*, and *Matinee Theater* were similar to those an actor faced in the theater. In the movies, a role is strung together like beads over a period of weeks, one scene at a time, and usually not in sequence. In live television, there was a week or two of rehearsal and then came "opening night," ready or not, in front of millions of people. If an actor didn't get it right the first time, it was too late. Unlike the theater, in live TV there was no second night.

As you might imagine, the pressure was enormous to work out all the bugs before we went on the air.

In motion pictures, we'd sometimes rehearse on film, retaking a scene a dozen or more times before the director said "print." And in movies, a director and editor can help an actor's performance in post production, shaping it by carefully editing out the rough spots. In live television, there was no such luxury. An actor had to know how to put together a performance in rehearsal and be ready when the show was broadcast to the country. Actors were more or less on their own, and a sloppy actor didn't last very long in those early days of live TV.

This new medium was essentially living theater with a camera pointed at it. A movie can be shot on a sound stage, a back lot, up in the mountains, on the desert, or at sea. A film director can take a camera on location to the four corners of the world. Live TV could only be recorded in a television studio. Just as in the theater, there could be changes of scenery, but they had to occur in one place. There was no alternative. Cumbersome electronic cameras, laden with a web of thick cables, had to be plugged into a source of electricity. They were huge, close to immobile, and at home only in a TV studio.

Drama created for the small screen by pioneers such as Paddy Chayefsky, Reginald Rose, J.P. Miller, Horton Foote, and Rod Serling were necessarily short on action and other pyrotechnics native to motion pictures and tall on personal stories which emphasized character development. The teleplay (as distinct from a screenplay) was mostly dialogue and less descriptive of the visual action, which was almost nil on the tube. In the earliest dramatic television, there was a demand for emotional depth, forcing both the actor and the director to probe for more dimension in characterization.

The New York, Method-oriented actor was the ideal performer to inhabit the multilayered dramatic world on the small screen. In every show I was surrounded by a cast of players who turned out to be colorful, provocative, high-energy personalities who apparently assumed I was doing what they were doing—making choices that seemed deliberately risky. Brando-esque, the leading men and women were maverick-like and fiercely independent. I could never decide whether it was the characters they played or the characters they were. But the suave, genteel, old-fashioned leading man I thought I wanted to imitate when I grew up was a thing of the past.

A year or so after *Winter Dreams* I did another *Playhouse 90*, this time with Paul Newman and Joanne Woodward. Newly-married media darlings on the way to stardom, they personified the wave of New York actors who would soon be the next generation of nobility in Hollywood. I was relieved to find out that neither Paul nor Joanne were the least bit inaccessible. Paul was no chatterbox, but he was collaborative; Joanne was easygoing, charming, tending to her knitting (literally) during rehearsals. She was social, chatty, and gave little indication that she was sweating arriving at a performance. She must have done most of her work at home.

Paul was just the opposite. I never saw an actor dig harder to mine the script for every shred of meaning, for every possible nuance underneath the dialogue. Director Franklin

Schaffner was his sounding board: "What does it really mean when the character says this? What does it really mean when the character does that?" Paul was like a tiger with a bone, picking every last ounce of flesh off the faded football hero created by Irwin Shaw in his short story, *The Eighty Yard Run*, which had been adapted for television by his brother, David. No question was left unasked, no motivation left unpolished by Paul Newman. He was a nit-picking craftsman who chiseled away at his performance every day in rehearsal, just as he had learned to do in the theater.

One tidbit of information surfaced about the Newmans that intrigued me. She idolized her acting coach, Sandy Meisner, while Paul had sworn undying allegiance to Lee Strasberg. They kidded each other constantly about which of them had studied with the better Method teacher; it was good-natured one-upmanship and most entertaining for the rest of the cast. I tucked this nugget into my memory for future reference.

Some months later, I ran into Paul and Joanne at La Scala, a popular Italian restaurant in Beverly Hills. Stopping by their table to say hello, I told them I was contemplating a move to New York and planned to study acting while I was there. I threw out the question, "Who do you think I ought to go to?" Joanne put down her fork and spent five minutes extolling the virtues of Sandy Meisner, while Paul slurped his spaghetti. Expecting him to disagree and recommend his mentor, Strasberg, I turned to him and repeated the question, "Who do *you* think I ought to go to?"

He looked up, fixed me with those steely blue eyes of his

and, with that famous Newman smile, said, "I think you ought to go to yourself." Paul was always direct and to the point. More than forty years later, his words still reverberate in my head; it may be the most succinct, penetrating, no-nonsense advice anybody has ever given me about acting.

Live television turned into taped television, which then transmuted into television shot on film. There was more than one reason for this evolution. The live, then taped dramas such as *Playhouse 90* and *Studio One* were by nature anthologies; with new actors and original stories, it's hard to capture an audience and keep them coming back every week. A series encouraged audience loyalty, which made reruns more valuable, and being on film made them easier to sell, because the quality of the product was better. All of this, of course, was good for the bottom line.

Since an actor goes where the work is, I segued from live to tape to film without missing a beat. If I wasn't shooting a *GE Theater* with Melvyn Douglas and Myrna Loy, or an *Alfred Hitchcock Presents* with Mildred Dunnock and Nehemiah Persoff, I was trading gunshots with Steve McQueen on *Wanted, Dead or Alive*. I was making a good living, but I was in retard when it came to growth as an artist.

Acting in an episode of a filmed series like *Gunsmoke* or *Perry Mason* was not unlike acting in the B-movies of the '30's and '40's. The common denominators were inferior scripts, limited production time, and absolutely no chance to rehearse. Ever. Since I had long ago gained proficiency as a film actor, I was soon phoning in my performances. What had become of my Stanislavskian fervor, my dream of becoming an artist in that Temple of Dramatic Art?

I had lost my way and needed a new lease on life. At the core, there was a nagging doubt that I would ever be able to find my way to true artistry in front of a camera. For me, film was a dead end: been there, done that. I wanted to feel alive again the way I felt when I gave a performance for the first time, and there was no possibility of a retake. There was danger and risk and immediacy in live TV, and sadly, those days were gone forever.

But wait a minute! There was always the *living* theater. New York and the stage and the theatrical culture Mr. Lewis represented in *Method—or Madness?* beckoned as never before. If I were to salvage my dream, the theater was the place to do it.

I knew then . . . it was Broadway or bust.

FOUR

Beyond Box Office:
Performance as Art

If I had been single, I would have notified my New York
agent, bought a plane ticket, flown East, and started "making
the rounds." As it was, I now had a wife and a baby son, and
being a brand new family man, it was not so easy to pull up
stakes and give up my home in Los Angeles. A strategy was
needed, a way to finance the relocation. My New York agent
told me, "I can't get you a job in the theater unless you're
physically here to audition."

"Audition?" I replied, stifling as best I could the alarm in
my voice. "I haven't auditioned since I was eight years old."

There was silence on the other end of the line. He was trying to find a diplomatic way to break the news that, while my credentials in Hollywood might be impeccable, the Broadway crowd couldn't care less. "Dear boy," he said, patronizingly, "everybody auditions in the theater . . . especially those of you who come from the *other* coast."

Suddenly I realized that, even though I had a head shot and a résumé crammed with film and television credits, those were only the first steps toward getting cast in a show. Being a camera actor, I had to go on stage, naked and alone, and prove that I could act in the theater.

Some honest self-examination was indicated. Why did I want to do this in the first place—pack up my household, leave my home town, and walk away from a successful career that had been twenty-five years in the making? Why was I trying to emigrate to theater when most of the actors who had made any kind of reputation on the stage couldn't wait to come to Hollywood?

In retrospect, I think there were three reasons: my career needed a breath of fresh air; I wanted to pin down what Method acting was all about once and for all; and, most importantly, I was hoping to find Stanislavsky alive and well on the stage. My goal was to turn the idealism generated by reading his autobiography almost a decade earlier into reality. I felt that understanding the System better would help me polish my craft, exploit my talents, and ultimately bring artistic fulfillment.

Method—or Madness? had given me a hint about how to do that. First, Mr. Lewis had published *Chart of the Stanislavski*

System, a succinct distillation of the master's attempt to codify his teachings. Though the *Chart* . . . is concise and furnishes an interested reader with a more coherent presentation of Stanislavsky's teachings than I had found in *An Actor Prepares* and *Building a Character*, a practical application of those teachings was still elusive.

Secondly, the book makes a brave attempt to connect Stanislavsky to his American interpreters, and Lewis balances precariously between two stools, or better yet, between two schools of thought. Being an actor turned teacher/theorist, Lewis made an attempt to reconcile System with Method, both in his thinking and in his work as a theater director. And by doing so, he inadvertently triggered a game plan for getting me where I wanted to go: the Broadway stage.

Surprisingly, it came from an apparent contradiction between Lewis's Method credentials and a partial list of his directorial credits in the introduction to his book: "Saroyan's *My Heart's in the Highlands*, a poetic play, *Brigadoon*, a musical, *The Happy Time*, a comedy of French Canadian manners and *The Teahouse of the August Moon*, which, though somewhat stylized in production, is a traditionally American type of comedy." In the next sentence Lewis is described as "a showman." Could it be? A card-carrying Method-ist who moonlights in show business? Who directs musical comedy? Who stages operas [Marc Blitzstein's *Regina*] and classical theater?

The seventh in his series of lectures is entitled *The Method and "Poetic" Theatre*, wherein he warns "the actor, too, in addition to his present element of emotion, must be able to use all the resources of theatre art—movement, voice, appreciation of music, etc. . . ." In other words, a true theater artist must connect the internal with the external in performance, and must dance, speak the poetry, and sing the lyric with distinction, while at the same time expressing an inner emotional truth.

I knew immediately that this could be my passport to The Great White Way. I would finally have a medium to work in where I could unite the performing I had long ago learned from Bing Crosby in *The Star Maker* with the straight acting I had done in most of my work on camera. There was no dichotomy here, according to Bobby Lewis; Poetic theater employs a performer who acts and an actor who performs. As a first step toward my long-term goal, I would forge a career as a "Stanislavskian song-and-dance man" in musical comedy.

At last I knew what I had to do to get ready for New York. Brushing up on dancing was no problem. I had started taking lessons at the age of three, and at eight years old I could tap dance better than other kids could ride a bicycle. My teacher, Willie Covan, was a friend of Bill Robinson's from their days together at Harlem's famous Cotton Club back in the '20's. The great Bojangles sat in on my lesson one day and later told Willie that I was the best kid dancer he ever saw. Tap dancing has been part of my bag of tricks all my performing life.

Singing was another matter. My first coach, Jack Stern, a former song plugger for Irving Berlin, used to brag about how well I "sold" a song. "Like Al Jolson," he said. Selling a song is a euphemism meaning I didn't really sing very well—I depended on showmanship to make it work. Learning how to sell a song might have gotten me by when I was a cute little kid, but cute wasn't going to work for a grown-up in a Broad-way musical. I had to take serious singing lessons and learn how to belt out a show tune, and there was no time to waste.

I took two lessons a week with Sandy Oliver, a noted vocal coach on the Sunset Strip. She taught me how to think *over* the keys of the piano in a flat line instead of *up and down* the scale. I found myself floating to the high notes rather than reaching for them by pushing the sound out as I had always done before. She taught me how to phrase a line, when and how to breathe, and how to use my interpretive skills as an actor when singing a lyric. For a year or so it was slow going, but when we'd tape a session I could hear steady improve-ment, so I was encouraged.

When I was ready to go to the marketplace, I told my agent that I was willing to fly in, at my own expense, if he could set up an audition or two in New York. He took me at my word. On my first trip to Gotham, I sang for Bob Fosse, who was making his directorial debut with a show called *The Conquering Hero*. The huge, empty Broadway theater was more intimidating than Mr. Fosse, who sensed my nerves and came up on stage to calm me down. He was charming, and considering that this was my maiden voyage, I did okay. But I made one grievous error; I had chosen to sing a pop song in-stead of a show tune. Being an inexperienced auditioner in musical comedy, I didn't know any better. I would never make the same mistake again.

I started to polish my performance skills in stock while I was getting ready for Broadway. I did *Flower Drum Song* at the Sacramento Music Circus, and auditioned for Ernie Martin, co-producer of *How to Succeed in Business Without Really Trying*, to play J. Pierrepont Finch in the London company. He said I was the wrong type. Then I auditioned for the road company, this time for Cy Feuer, Martin's partner. He told me I was the wrong type. In New York for an engagement in *Roberta* on Long Island, I auditioned once more, this time to replace Robert Morse on Broadway. Abe Burrows, the director, and Frank Loesser, the composer, were at this audition.

I got the job.

Feuer and Martin picked up the expense of my relocation; my wife, son and I were set up in a lovely apartment on Third Avenue, and I went into rehearsal to take over for Morse two weeks later. Feuer and Burrows worked on the book with me, Loesser showed me how to sing his songs, and Bob Fosse taught me his Tony Award-winning choreography. In Broadway's terms, I was a beginner, but I was beginning at the top.

The moral of this story is, know what you want. My goal had never been to go to London or on the road; I wanted to live and work in New York, and that's exactly what happened. Maybe the more important lesson was never give up. If I had taken either Ernie Martin or Cy Feuer at his word, I would've given up after auditions one and two. To follow an incredible comic artist like Morse in a role that was tailor-made for him took *chutzpah*. But it never occurred to me that I couldn't fill his shoes. If signing a contract to play *How to Succeed* . . . was the best available opportunity to pay for the Hickman family's trip to the East Coast, and would give me a new lease on life as a real artist, then that's what I would do, without questioning my good fortune.

I was closing in on the summit in my quest for the ultimate performance art. I'm sure it was no accident that base camp for a final assault on the peak was set up in the middle of Manhattan Island. A magnet for ambitious performers of all shapes, sizes, and persuasions, it has been said about the Big Apple, "If you can make it there, you can make it anywhere."

While Washington, D.C., may be the capital of the United States, New York City, in a generic sense, is the performance capital of the world. The first definition of *perform* in my dictionary is "do; the action, effort, or completion of a prescribed or significant deed or task." Synonyms are "execute, accomplish, achieve, effect, fulfill, discharge, render." As you can see, the dramatic artist has no lien on the performance mode, even though, in common usage, performance suggests "the act or style of performing a work or role before an audience."

In the broadest sense, then, New York is a mecca for a wide range of performers in theater, business, politics, athletics, cuisine, painting, architecture, publishing, ballet, opera, finance, religion, journalism—you name the field, the native (or transplanted) New Yorker is in a highly-competitive milieu and must be functioning at the top of his or her form. For these performers, an audience could be a corporate board of directors, a political constituency, spectators at a sporting event, customers in a restaurant, sometimes even a finicky audience of one, if the performer is a salesperson at Cartier or Henri Bendel.

When in performance, the rules are the same for the actor on Broadway, the basketball player at Madison Square Garden, the waiter at 21, or the mayor in City Hall. To perform well in any profession, understanding and knowing how to employ the following basic ingredients is essential:

- A script, step-by-step outline, or game plan which is predetermined and structurally sound, has to be fully absorbed before one enters the arena. The skilled performer does an exhaustive amount of planning and rehearsing before the curtain goes up. Once in performance, success will depend on careful preparation, which unlocks the door to masterful performance. This is a primary rule of performance art.

- The time frame in performance mode is always now. Either the script or game plan has been fully assimilated by the performer, or the preparation has been faulty. It's too late to fix it in performance. The past is over, the future is not yet, and the performer has no recourse but to stay focused and commit to what is happening—right or wrong—in the present tense.

- A great performance is never a controlled, robotic repetition of the script or game plan. The true artist never tries to make it be the way it's supposed to be and never imposes a preconceived result on his or her efforts.

Rather, he or she commits to embracing the surprises that spring up as the events play out.

- A patron, a live audience, or any group of spectators are not secondary aspects of inspired performance but an integral necessity. An essential stimulus for an effective performance of any kind is the spontaneous interaction between performer and audience. Performance is uncontrollably alive and must be nurtured by the living energy exchanged between spectator and performer.

Psychic interaction is not only supremely important between performer and audience, it is equally essential among a cast of characters or the members of any team. Collaboration and unity of purpose are the hallmarks of achievement in the arts, sports, business, government, science, the military—in fact, any joint effort where a team player is the most important contributor to a successful result. We humans are social creatures, capable of forming energy fields which are well-nigh indestructible when imbued with a common purpose. "One for all and all for one" is not just a hokey aphorism; it's a powerful formula for getting things done.

Notwithstanding, a member of a team does not lose one's own identity, and the contribution to the success of a joint venture is his or her solo performance. One must continually perfect his or her own skills, making certain that performances are ego-less and thought-less. Yogi Berra, the Hall of Famer who played for the New York Yankees, was once having trouble with his swing. His inexperienced batting coach advised him to analyze what he was doing wrong while he was at the plate. Berra's reply? "How can I hit and think at the same time?"

Berra was a great hitter. He knew well what I would learn in my years in the theater. Any thinking when you're on your feet in performance is a no-no. Whether you're catching for the Yankees, singing and dancing in musical comedy, or dealing with a gaggle of reporters at a press conference, these rules apply:

- know your game plan;
- stay in the now;
- give up the need for predetermined results;
- interact with your audience;
- be thought-less.

A year on Broadway doing eight shows a week, interacting with a different audience every night and every matinee, was a crash course in the craft and art of performance. Before New York, most of my acting had been in front of a camera. I loved the camera and felt safe when the director said, "Roll 'em." But a camera doesn't react. A camera doesn't get bored, give you rapt attention, or applaud. A camera doesn't cry, and it certainly doesn't laugh at a joke. A camera simply records, freezing the aliveness in your performance on film or tape.

One day it occurred to me that, in the history of the dramatic arts, movies were an afterthought. For almost two and a half millennia there was only the living theater, there was no inanimate device separating performer from audience. Actor and audience were one, in the same space, creating the performance at the same time. During every show, I felt the excitement of that, the riskiness of that, the thrill of that, and I was hooked; ever after I would miss that high whenever I worked in film or television.

I had come East to resurrect the artist in myself by experiencing the Poetic theater first hand, in this case a wonderfully written, Pulitzer Prize-winning musical comedy, *How to Succeed in Business Without Really Trying.* When I left the show, however, after more than 400 performances, I had barely scratched the surface of proficiency on the stage. And I was a long way from realizing the goal I had set for myself, but at least I was out of the starting gate and moving in the right direction.

For the rest of the decade, I would work exclusively in the theater. Stock on the Eastern Seaboard, three or four pre-Broadway tryouts of one-set comedies that were second-rate Neil Simon rip-offs, several tours of *How to Succeed . . .* , a *Where's Charley?* revival at Manhattan's City Center, and the national tour of *George M!* paid the bills. I was living in an expensive apartment, supporting a wife and now two children, and I felt compelled to go where the money was. I made audiences laugh every night and went to mass and communion every morning. I was closer to the pinnacle than ever before, but a complete reconciliation of journeyman actor and spiritual wannabe was still out of reach.

Ironically, I found myself in a time and place of societal

ferment more intense than my own. It was the '60's. The controversial war in Vietnam was raging. New York was teeming with hippies, acid heads, beatniks, and rebels of all ages running around in beads and black tights (what I used to call "anarchy suits"), reeking of stale incense and yesterday's marijuana. It was a topsy-turvy time, revolt was in the air, and what was happening in society was happening big time in the dramatic arts. All over Manhattan, in lofts, warehouses, and garages, actors were grunting, chanting, and parading their naked bodies as an affront to those whom they considered the self-righteous establishment. Uptown, there was *radical chic*, Park Avenue protests, liberal breast-beating that sought atonement for a life of privilege in a revolutionary age. Secretly, I was on the side of the protestors, even though my wife shopped at Saks, my two boys went to expensive private schools, and my fellow parishioners at the Upper East Side parish where I attended mass were dripping in expensive jewelry and mink coats. A bit long in the tooth to be a true flower child, I was, nonetheless, eager to be part of the scene.

In the pages of *My Life in Art*, a revolutionary Stanislavsky not only complained about the lack of true artistry in the acting of his time, but he was appalled by the stale realism which had such a grip on the Russian theater. He railed at lesser artists who were satisfied with the status quo. Rejecting empty commercialism, he was forever questioning, experimenting, seeking fresh, innovative theatrical forms.

In like manner, when I was not on tour, I haunted the tiny theaters off-Broadway and the tinier ones off-off-Broadway, intrigued by the experimentation I saw there and growing increasingly excited about this newfangled dramaturgy. They were nonconformists researching non-traditional dramatic forms, the more unconventional the better. Fascinated by what I saw, I spent every spare moment in a playhouse of some kind—uptown, downtown and everywhere in between—searching for clues to what the new American theater would look and sound like in the latter half of the century.

Crammed into tiny, stuffy rooms in the East Village, soaking up the crude efforts of "performance artists" who were less acting than acting out, I hung in night after night, hoping to mine a nugget of truth I could salt away for future reference. I saw every Broadway production that promised art instead of artifice, once in a while being rewarded with an inspiration or two. More often than not, I was disappointed by what I would call competent craftsmanship. I went to musicals, ballets, mime shows, love-ins, and poetry readings, hopping on and off the subway by myself in an orgy of theatergoing that lasted into the '70's. I was doing nonstop research into the art of drama, the creative use of the actor's body, the unexplored musicality of sound, the demands of an unorthodox language, the necessity of coping with radical performance art where all the familiar ground rules had been thrown out the window. It was exciting. And very risky. For actors who lost their footing, there was nothing to break the fall.

I was intrigued by the writing of Jean Genet, darling of the European avant-garde at the time, and I attended a production of *The Maids* off-Broadway—the play was indeed captivating. But I was underwhelmed by the struggling actors. After visiting several productions of Joe Chaikin's Open Theater, I knew he was on to something, and I sought him out to discuss his theories about theatrical art over a beer in Greenwich Village. I was titillated by the Theater of the Absurd and Eugene Ionesco, a true iconoclast who had obviously never heard of realistic acting. Antonin Artaud, a trendsetter in Europe, traveled his Theater of Cruelty to the United States and found popular success in Peter Brook's landmark production of *Marat/Sade*, wherein Glenda Jackson and her fellow Brits showed us how more expressionistic writing should be played. Edward Albee, an American experimentalist in early plays like *The Zoo Story*, was offbeat and in need of an offbeat actor or two. Jerzy Grotowski's Polish Laboratory Theater came to New York for a very limited run, and it was impossible to get a ticket because there wasn't room for more than a handful of spectators.

Smitten with Samuel Beckett since I first read *Waiting For Godot*, I was nonetheless disappointed in every production of his plays I saw until Irish actor Jack MacGowran, acclaimed as the foremost interpreter of Beckett in the world, came to New York in a one-man show at The Public Theater. What a revelation. A disgruntled Everyman, MacGowran shuffled about the stage doing a weird kind of dance routine, singing—chanting, really—Beckettian rhythms, opening a portal to the Nobel Prize-winning writer for the audience, giving us all an extraordinary example of Poetic theater in action.

Broadway was not immune to the infectious experimentation from across the Atlantic. Walter Kerr, the Times reviewer and dean of New York drama critics in those days, declared the decade of the '60's "the age of Pinter," and after seeing the original production of *The Homecoming*, I understood why. In his best work, Pinter is a dramatic poet of the vast, word-less world of the inner self. "Words are a stratagem we use to cover our nakedness," he once said, in eloquent testament to his distrust of conventional dramatic writing. One observer recalled overhearing Pinter and renowned mime Marcel Marceau at a cocktail party in London absorbed in a discussion about *densities of silence!*

Despite his unique, unorthodox approach to dramatic writing, in late 2005 Harold Pinter won the Nobel Prize in Literature. I'm delighted that the Swedish Academy in Stockholm has recognized Pinter's invaluable contribution to the English-speaking theater for almost fifty years. His writing, which once seemed avant-garde, now officially represents a new standard of excellence for dramatists in the 21st century.

Pinter was always ahead of his time. Even in the '60's the young Englishman was probing beyond the surface of everyday language, dramatizing in his own unique style the mystery of inner consciousness. In so doing, he spoke to many of my countrymen about the need to explore the turmoil below the surface of our national psyche. Young, and not so young, Americans were questioning traditional values, the safety of the status quo; there was an explosion of pent-up creativity across the land.

Was this widespread rebelliousness being reflected in the New York theater scene? Possibly. If it was, it was happening more downtown than uptown. A dramatic revolution was brewing, and my years of theatergoing had proven one thing to me—the modern *literary* theater, whose primary aesthetic was limited to socioeconomic perfectibility, was suffering from hardening of the arteries. Beckett, Pinter, and mavericks like them were leaving conventional ideas and conventional language behind. Formal grammar and syntax is horizontal, linear, one-dimensional; an alternative idiom would be required which did not depend on a literal text. To reach the heights or probe the depths of modern humanity's spiritual odyssey, we have to reach past language, which novelist Ernest Hemingway called "the tip of the iceberg."

My search for a breakthrough theatrical statement seemed endless. Then, serendipitously, I had a glimpse of what was wrong with the "old" theater and found myself pointed in the direction of the "new." In the mid-'60's, The Actors Studio presented a limited run of Anton Chekhov's *The Three Sisters* on Broadway. An all-star cast of Studio graduates filled the major roles under Lee Strasberg's supervision. Kim Stanley, a favorite of mine, was making one of her rare appearances on stage, and I was looking forward to opening night. The reviews were lukewarm, so the project did little to enhance anybody's reputation, including Ms. Stanley's. The most glaring problem I saw in the production was the absence of a clear, stylistic, uniform directorial point of view.

The contrast was startling, at least for this theatergoer, when the following year, The Moscow Art Theatre came to town. I was privileged to see Chekhov played the way he should be played, by a company of actors trained across the Atlantic. Anxious to understand what was going on, I rented a set of earphones so I could listen to a line-by-line translation of the Russian dialogue. Early in the first act I took off the earphones and didn't put them on again. I understood everything perfectly. The ensemble was one. The Chekhovian style was unmistakable. The actor's behavior, vocally and visually, told the story with impeccable skill. Words were not necessary. The truth was in the behavior.

I had an epiphany that night. Having seen *The Three Sisters* performed by a cast of well-trained Method actors and comparing their performances with the splendid Moscow Art Theatre ensemble, I realized how much we still had to learn from our peers from other shores. The Studio actors were emotionally truthful, but they didn't seem to be having any fun. Their voices needed more range and musicality. Their bodies were leaden. They lacked physical dexterity. They lacked humor. They lacked theatricality. Bobby Lewis's Poetic theater was unfamiliar terrain.

On the other hand, the Russian company of artists was poetry in motion—physically extravagant, a feast for eye and ear, a Punch and Judy show in bright colors rather than a monochromatic, dirge-like rendering of a classic play. They invested Chekhov with an energy I had never seen in a cast of actors in this country, and in many ways, they represented the new American theater I was envisioning.

Back to the future, as they say. It was the first—and last—time I would see what purported to be the System in action. If this company represented the training Stanislavsky pioneered in Moscow early in the 20th century, his vision was more futuristic than I had ever imagined. This was an actor's craft of the highest order. But more than that, it was the Poetic theater realized, a performance art that transcended anything I had seen in the contemporary American theater. What had happened? How had we gotten off the track? Without question, when the System migrated to America in the '20's, something had been lost in the translation.

A brief history of events is in order here. In 1923, Stanislavsky had brought The Moscow Art Theatre to this country for the first time. One of his former students, actor Richard Boleslavsky, had emigrated to New York four years before the tour began, and was teaching Stanislavsky's revolutionary ideas about the art of acting at the American Laboratory Theater. It was there in the late 1920's that a young Lee Strasberg was introduced to Boleslavsky's version of the System. Strasberg then evolved his own rendering of Stanislavsky's teachings at the Group Theatre. What would later become known as The Method was, in fact, Strasberg's version of Boleslavsky's version of the experimentation Stanislavsky had begun in Moscow three decades earlier.

Though Strasberg would become the most notable proponent of Method acting over the years, at least a half dozen other teachers were pre-eminent in the drama business by the time I arrived in New York in 1962. American actors on both coasts reflected their teachings, their training, their points of view. Michael Chekhov, with whom I had acted in *Song of Russia* in 1943, would prove to be, for me, the most faithful to

Stanislavskian intent, reflected in his book, *To the Actor*. Originally a member of The Moscow Art Theatre, Chekhov balanced the demands for inner truth with the need for technical virtuosity in the actor's use of the body. Chekhov was famous for his *psychological gesture* exercise and his emphasis on the value of a rich, highly-developed *creative imagination*. Unfortunately, much of Chekhov's teaching was done on the West Coast while he pursued his own acting career in the movies, and his valuable work seemed unfamiliar to many of my East Coast colleagues in the theater.

Stella Adler, who had been a member of the Group Theatre ensemble, was highly regarded by everyone I talked to in the acting community. Having been Strasberg's pupil and briefly a student of Stanislavsky himself, she was the only major American teacher who had personally worked with the master. When Adler returned from her sojourn with Stanislavsky in Paris and told Strasberg he had misinterpreted many of Stanislavsky's ideas, she was summarily rebuffed. Later she went off to teach her own methodology, based on her understanding of the System. Adler stressed the use of the actor's imagination in the acting craft, while Strasberg focused on the actor's personal experience as the primary resource to be used in creating a role. Neither strong-willed theoretician ever reconciled their differences.

Sanford Meisner, ensconced at The Neighborhood Playhouse, also had a distinguished reputation. He had devised the *repetition exercise* to encourage an actor's spontaneity and was, as I mentioned earlier, a guide for some of the finest actors on both coasts. Unlike Bobby Lewis, who also enjoyed a career as a successful director, Meisner's contribution was totally pedagogical, and he was revered as one of the great teachers of his day.

Charles Nelson Reilly's respect for his own mentor, Uta Hagen, was evident in the way he intoned "Miss Hagen" every time he mentioned her name. Thanks to Charlie, I had the privilege of knowing Uta Hagen, another revered teacher, by sitting in on her classes at the HB Studio, and afterwards going back to her townhouse, sipping a glass of wine and discussing the actor's art in America. She was less interested than I was in trying to define the Method, but she taught me a new "respect for acting," which would, years later, be the title of her first book.

While making a living on the Eastern Seaboard, I compared notes on the differences between stage acting and film acting with Maureen Stapleton at Sardi's, exchanged critiques of contemporary drama with James Baldwin and Frank D. Gilroy at the Russian Tea Room, and started work on a libretto for a musical. When I wasn't actually working on the stage or spending every spare evening in the theater, I was continuing my quest to understand the performance art practiced by the best Method actors.

I had almost convinced myself that the hard-core Method actor belonged to some secret society, like Freemasonry, whose members took an oath never to reveal the password or what went on in meetings behind closed doors. I fancied the uninitiated were to be kept in the dark about acting doctrine which only the brotherhood was privileged to know. I decided to break through the imagined code of silence and get the inside info from the man who started it all, the high priest who reigned from his throne at The Actors Studio. I joined either the Director's Unit or the Playwright's Unit, I don't remember which; I do know that as a member I was entitled to observe Lee Strasberg's acting classes, where I would hear the official version of a teaching methodology he had begun developing some thirty years earlier.

I found Strasberg to be a talkative, feisty, overly-opinionated man, but so passionate about his opinions, and so knowledgeable about his subject matter, that he held an audience of actors in the palm of his hand. He was a firebrand who despised shoddy work in his class, and he would take the hide off of a student who tried to get away with it, whether the actor was famous or not. A man of ferocious scrutiny, it was easy to see why he had singlehandedly turned The Studio into a world-famous institute dedicated to Method acting.

His basic teachings were standard procedure for the most informed American actors on either coast, thanks to the crop of talented Studio alumni on stage and screen. There were plenty of *affective memory, sense memory, improv,* and *private moment* exercises, but listening to the guru day in and day out and watching him deal with his students, it dawned on me that his point of view was, surprisingly, much less esoteric than I had imagined.

Obsessed with the actor's inner truth, he probed the deepest psychological implications in the writing. When it came to text, it was the emotional content behind the words he was after. He would complain about a "line reading" (a mechanical, unfelt recitation of the dialogue which is simply bad acting), but he ignored the actor's vocal defects in his urgency to find an emotional truth. During the year or two I sat in on his sessions, I don't recall Strasberg ever giving an actor an exercise to improve the voice or the body. He acknowledged the demands made by Shakespeare or Shaw or Chekhov, but exercises aimed at more extended stylization were not forthcoming. Most of his students chose to investigate realistic writing—Miller, Inge, Williams, Ibsen, Strindberg—and Strasberg focused on psychological depth, ignoring the external part of the actor's instrument. Disappointed, I felt this was inconsistent with all I had learned about the Poetic theater or the theater of the future since coming to New York.

More confusing, it was inconsistent with the Strasberg I met with in the Playwright's Unit one night, when a one-act play I had written was to be presented under my direction. Since it was the first presentation of my work at The Studio, I was a nervous wreck. At the last minute, I was told that the regular moderator of the unit was ill and Strasberg would be taking over for him. I hyperventilated. My short piece, written in the depersonalized style of Genet or Ionesco, was far from the popular theater dominated by Method acting in those days, and I had directed my actors accordingly. Deep emotional life was not an issue; the actor's behavior was choreographed, quirky, and borderline surrealistic. I was afraid The Studio's "Terminator" would rip me and my actors to shreds.

This was not the case. After the presentation, when we sat down meekly to hear Strasberg's critique, he compared the writing favorably to several avant-garde playwrights he admired, enthusing over unconventional work I had rarely heard him refer to in the acting sessions. He praised the actors—non-Studio members—for their skills, and they were as delighted as I was. This was a different Strasberg than I had seen previously—less dogmatic, less doctrinaire, more open to experimentalism and non-naturalistic acting techniques.

When I left The Studio that night, I was able to separate the man from the message he had embodied for more than a generation. Interestingly enough, artistically, the man was larger than the myth he had created. I was glad to find out he was not the mouthpiece for some secret brotherhood I needed to belong to, and it was reassuring to know that he was, after all, an appreciative audience for a variety of forward-looking dramatic styles.

I got busy and spent less and less time at The Studio, but I had learned what I needed to from regular visitations. After hundreds of conversations and sitting in on a dozen or more workshops over the years, including Strasberg's classes, the light bulb went on. Having long been on the trail of a "quintessential" Method actor, I realized I had been chasing a phantom. No quintessential, solitary, identifiable Method actor had ever existed because there never was *one* Method! There was Lee Strasberg's Method, Stella Adler's Method, Bobby

Lewis's Method, Sandy Meisner's Method, Elia Kazan's Method, Marlon Brando's Method, and so on. No wonder the protean fellow had escaped detection; he had assumed so many different identities he was not just lost in the crowd, he was a crowd all by himself.

What was missing at The Studio was not THE Method actor. What was missing was Stanislavsky. But then, Stanislavsky was missing on Broadway, off-Broadway, and in the acting workshops I visited; he was never at Sardi's, Downey's, Joe Allen's, or the other theatrical watering holes I frequented. In fact, he was nowhere to be found anywhere in the New York theater world of the '60's. Lip service was paid by some insiders, and even some of the heavy hitters like Lee Strasberg, but few had any interest in Stanislavsky the man, his teachings, or his lofty vision for a revolutionary dramatic art in the Western theater.

What had happened to the most significant actor/director/teacher in 20th century drama since he brought his theater company and the systematic approach to training actors he had pioneered in Moscow to the United States? I could have avoided years of unanswered questions, unrequited frustration, and disillusionment had I been able to fast-forward to the day I was in Samuel French in Los Angeles and by chance picked up a copy of Sharon M. Carnicke's book *Stanislavsky in focus*. At last, I knew why my hero had disappeared from the scene almost as soon as he arrived.

Ms. Carnicke, an Associate Dean of Theater at the University of Southern California, is a theater director, a Russian scholar, and the foremost expert on Stanislavsky's lifetime of experimentation, writings (both published and unpublished), and the fate of his theories about acting after they were first introduced to the American theatrical community in 1923. Ms. Carnicke knows her stuff. *Stanislavsky in focus* is a *must read* for any serious student of Stanislavsky's System, discussing how it differs from Strasberg's Method and the nature of the actor's craft in the last century.

Her thesis, backed up by impressive scholarship, confirmed many of the conclusions I had come to on my own over the years. Much of what had happened to acting in this country during the last seventy-five years went back to who Lee Strasberg was and the role he played in eclipsing the popularity of Stanislavsky's training methodology when he and his co-conspirator, Harold Clurman, founded the Group Theatre in 1931.

Both Strasberg and Clurman had studied briefly with Boleslavsky at the Laboratory Theatre, but it was Strasberg, as a teacher, who appropriated a seminal Stanislavskian idea, the *affective memory* exercise, and employed it as a basic element of what would become his Method. In *Stanislavsky in focus*, there's a fascinating account of what happened in 1934 when Stella Adler returned from studying with Stanislavsky in Paris and informed her colleagues in the Group that "He [Stanislavsky] was very anxious to get some kind of clarity about his work through me." The Russian master had told Adler that he "felt that his System was somehow at stake."

Ms. Carnicke writes: "this meeting was fateful in the emigration of Stanislavsky's ideas to the United States, and further added to the oral tradition surrounding Stanislavsky's name. When Adler spoke to the Group Theatre that summer about then unfamiliar aspects of the System, she split the Group into camps and challenged Strasberg's sole authority. She particularly opposed his take on affective memory with new information on how the play's given circumstances shape character, the power of the actor's imagination, and what would come to be known as the Method of Physical actions."

The following day, "As Robert Lewis reports, Strasberg reacted by calling a counter meeting . . . to announce that 'he taught the Strasberg Method, not the Stanislavski [sic] System.' He particularly defended his emphasis on emotion, saying 'that we use the practice of affective memory in our own way, for our own results.' On that day Strasberg described both the gulf that had opened between the American and Russian evolutionary branches of Stanislavsky's work, and a rift in the American theatre that exists today."

Unfortunately, especially for the American actor, the chasm has widened and deepened between Method and System since 1934. It would be silly to blame this all on Strasberg's insistence on basing his training methods on *affective memory* alone. There are a number of reasons why Stanislavsky and his American counterpart went their separate ways early on, and why they would each develop their theatrical philosophies in such radically divergent training programs. Their differences far outweighed their mutual distaste for the shallowness of the performance art they were reacting against as idealistic young actors in Russia and the United States.

They were both adamantly devoted to inseminating true

artistry into the craft of acting, but they were so dissimilar in so many other ways that it would have been miraculous had they agreed on much of anything else. Stanislavsky was a patrician, a romanticist, born into the classicism of late 19th century Russian theater, while Strasberg was the child of an immigrant Polish family, indoctrinated in the prevailing trends of political radicalism and Freudianism in the American theater of the late '20's and early '30's.

Stanislavsky was a true pioneer, the first to attempt a systemization for a workable craft in modern acting; Strasberg was a disciple, so impressed with the acting company of the touring Moscow Art Theatre that it would affect the way he trained actors for the rest of his life. Stanislavksy, tending to self-doubt, was addicted to trial and error and ongoing experimentation, revising his original suppositions until he drew his final breath; Strasberg was dogmatic, never questioning himself or his theories about acting. Stanislavsky was more diplomatic, a consensus builder; Strasberg was an autocrat, unwilling to ever compromise his convictions.

Is it any wonder they were so at variance when it came to acting theory, training actors, and the relationship between director and actor in the theater? Harold Clurman, in his history of the Group Theatre, *The Fervent Years*, gave us a vivid account of the performance his partner, Strasberg, was after when training his actors: "He is the director of introverted feeling, of strong emotion curbed by an ascetic control, sentiment of great intensity, muted by delicacy, pride, fear, shame. The effect he produces is a classic hush, tense and tragic, a constant conflict so held in check that a kind of beautiful spareness results. Though plasticly restricted, his work through the balance of its various tensions often becomes aesthetically impressive, despite its crushed low-key and occasional wild transitions to shrill hysteria."

Contrast Stanislavsky's description of the ideal actor's approach to performance in *My Life in Art*: "What was this quality, common to all great talents? It was easier for me to notice this likeness in their physical freedom, in the lack of all strain. Their bodies were at the beck and call of the inner demands of their wills. The creative mood on the stage is exceptionally pleasant. . . . It can be compared to the feelings of a prisoner when the chains that had interfered with all his movements for years had at last been removed. I luxuriated in this condition on the stage, sincerely believing that in it lay the whole secret, the whole soul of creativeness on the stage, that all the rest would come from this state and perception of physical freedom."

Strasberg, "the director of introverted feeling . . . , of strong emotion curbed by ascetic control . . . ," could never countenance Stanislavsky's insistence on training the actor's body as a prime tool in expressing the inner truth; he asked his actors to "make a list of their physical actions." Carnicke tells us that Stanislavsky was convinced that the "line of the life of the human body keeps the actor on track in his creation of the life of the human spirit" because physical actions were, in his eyes, the essential "anatomy of the role and the play." Ms. Carnicke goes on to say that in directing *Tartuffe* Stanislavsky saw the play as "a structure of action."

It would always be a stand-off: Strasberg's near obsession

with controlled inner truth versus Stanislavsky's desire to flow
that truth freely through the actor's body and voice; Strasberg's tightness versus Stanislavsky's expansiveness; Strasberg's tragic pride, fear, and shame versus Stanislavsky's
pleasure of released tension. The stark dissimilarities in these
two men—cultural, psychological, artistic, and spiritual—
were, as I see it, responsible for the gulf between the Studio-
trained actor and the freewheeling, acrobatic ensemble of
The Moscow Art Theatre when they each tackled *The Three
Sisters* on Broadway in 1969.

Most telling of all, their difference was the relevance of
spirituality to the actor's art. Eastern mysticism, which tanta-
lized Stanislavsky, was hocus-pocus to a hardheaded rational-
ist like Lee Strasberg. Having diligently studied both Hatha
Yoga and Raja Yoga, Stanislavsky automatically integrated
Hindu transcendentalism into his teachings. Stressing the
reservoir of creativity in the actor's unconscious, he would
take it a step further, extolling what he called "superconscious" (the greater Self) as the primary field of an artist's creativity. For Stanislavsky, acting as an art was a means of
expressing one's spiritual identity on the stage.

Ms. Carnicke is quite clear about Strasberg's attempts to
explain away or even contradict Stanislavsky's metaphysical
point of view. She tells us: "When Strasberg writes that for
Stanislavsky 'the actor's internal means [. . .] was still called at
that time the 'soul,' we understand that Strasberg wishes to
replace 'soul' with 'subconscious,' reflecting his own assump-
tions about acting as grounded in popular psychology.
Stanislavsky, however, would not equate the two words.

While he uses Ribot's psychology as a jumping-off point, he also incorporates transcendental ideas of emotion in his System. When Stanislavsky asserts that acting should embody 'the life of the human spirit of the role,' he does indeed mean the psyche as 'soul.'"

When Strasberg rather arrogantly disparaged Stanislavsky's "unfortunate Hindooism," he tipped his hand. In *A Dream of Passion*, he went on to write, "I am only concerned with the conscious control of faculties which in other arts can and do work unconsciously or sporadically." Strasberg further dismissed the spiritual dimension in the actors' art when he wrote, "I have found that while individuals who practice Zen, Yoga, meditation, etc., are helped in their personal lives, such disciplines do not help them express themselves in their acting."

Lest it seem as if I'm casting Lee Strasberg in the role of villain as the sole instigator of the decades-old divorce between System and Method, I hasten to add that he was not the only influential teacher, theater professional, or critic who had been exposed to Stanislavsky's visionary thinking in the '20's, '30's, and '40's. During those years, most of his colleagues were immune to the message contained in *My Life in Art*. Where were the Meisners, the Kazans, the Clurmans, and the other artists who were supposedly seeking more artistic expressiveness in mid-century American theater?

The real Stanislavsky, it turns out, was not their cup of tea. The theatrical intelligentsia had no interest in a philosophy of transcendental art. Radicalism was in vogue, and rebellion was far more appealing than some wooly, unrealistic notion of the superconscious. Like Strasberg, intellectuals in the theater prided themselves on being realists who saw no reason to reach beyond the prevailing pragmatism which promised a socioeconomic nirvana. Naturalism in the form of a blue collar work ethic reigned at the Group Theatre and would set the tone, not only for the theatrical style it popularized in the '30's, but the training methodology it spawned at The Actors Studio in the decades that followed.

The fact is neither Stanislavsky's aesthetic nor his systematic strategy for training actors ever took root in the soil that nurtures the American theater. It's as though we rejected a nonresident theatrical philosopher the same way we would refuse to train our actors to speak with a Russian accent. Strasberg, as a teacher, personified the independent Yankee spirit that instinctively rejects anything that isn't "Made in the U.S.A." As I said before, although lip service had always been paid to Stanislavsky, he has remained an alien, misinterpreted and misunderstood by the very people who paid homage to him.

Even the best-informed professionals were confused about this unfortunate turn of events. No less an authority than Harold Clurman would claim in *The Fervent Years* that "the Stanislavsky 'method,' once considered a foreign excrescence in the American theatre, has developed, in one form or another, into the prevalent method for training the young actor in drama schools, 'studios,' and colleges, and that the best young actors (actors between the ages of twenty-five and forty-five) are actors trained *more or less* in the Stanislavsky method—either through former association with the Group

Theatre or through directors and teachers who were fostered by the Group Theatre."

The italics in that long sentence are mine to make the point that the qualifying term "more or less" is misleading. What's in a name? Plenty, if the names are System and Method, used in the context of how one trains an actor in this country. When Strasberg himself published *Introduction to Acting: A Handbook on the Stanislavsky Method* in 1947, no one bothered to question the legitimacy of his title or that what he was teaching at The Actors Studio was less "Stanislavskian" and more "Strasbergian" than anyone, including Strasberg himself, might have realized. But who cared? By that time his teachings had pre-empted Stanislavsky's theories in the minds of his contemporaries, and his Method would end up totally eclipsing the System for the remainder of the 20th century.

That was all well and good for those who were content with the Method as the only way to train an actor. What about those of us who yearned for a fuller understanding of the System, who were seeking guidance from *An Actor Prepares* which, at best, tells only half the story in the sketchiest of terms? To say we were disappointed and frustrated is an understatement. If Bobby Lewis was right and nobody reads *Building a Character* except a few fanatics like myself, I now understand why; in this country, the System was never more than a minor part of the mythology surrounding the Stanislavsky name. He's been a vague presence in the pantheon of celebrated actors and teachers of the actor's art, but almost nobody can tell you why. For most actors, and for those who train them, his System is as mysterious today as it was when The Moscow Art Theatre brought it here in 1924.

This is partly Stanislavsky's own fault. He never stopped reassessing his ideas, questioning his premises, and re-defining his principles; in a way, the System was never finished. And that's the way Stanislavsky wanted it. He never tried to carve his ideas in stone because he knew there would always be more questions, and the answers to those questions would never be definitive. That's why he was a great theorist, a great innovator, and refused to be dogmatic to the end.

I wish I had had this overview in the '60's when I was wandering around New York searching for my hero and trying to figure out why my fellow actors were not equally enthusiastic about learning his approach to the art of acting. I was a stranger in what I had hoped would be the Promised Land, with no fellowship to join, no Stanislavskian sect to belong to, and certainly no one teaching the System I was so eager to learn. My personal odyssey was not over, but I refused to be discouraged.

I would stay alert for clues about what the art of acting would be like in the theater of the future. Still groping for certainty about the nature of that theater, I was seeking the groundbreaking playwright, the original dramatic statement that would fire my imagination as never before. I was driven by forces even I didn't understand, but I was on the path I had chosen and I would follow it until I found out where it led, once and for all.

FIVE

Zen in the Art of Acting

"Perhaps in our art there exists only one correct path—the line of the intuition of feelings! And out of it grow unconsciously the outer and inner images, their form, the idea and technique of the role. The line of intuition at times absorbs into itself all the other lines, and grasps all the spiritual and physical contents of the role and the play."

Constantin Stanislavsky
My Life in Art

Sometime in the late '60's or early '70's, I was sitting in a darkened Broadway theater and had a glimpse of what I have
come to call "the acting of the 21st century." It was only a
peek into the future mind you, but enough of a foreshadow-
ing to remain locked in my memory to this day.

The circumstances were unremarkable. I don't remember
the name of the playhouse I was in (the Martin Beck, I think),
the title of the play escapes me, and I can't recall exactly who
was in the cast, but I can tell you the mature members of the
ensemble were uniformly skilled, reputable Broadway actors,
with long lists of credits on their résumés. The piece was con-
ventionally constructed, and the acting was solid, standard,
and professionally sound.

I stifled a yawn until a young actor entered, taking stage,
causing me to perk up and pay attention. What was he doing?
At first, I couldn't say. His performance was different than
every other cast member—but why? If anything, the others
seemed more polished, and yet there was a mechanicalness
about their acting that was noticeably absent in his work. He
was alive on stage in a way they were not. A kind of odd, electric aura surrounded him. It was as if he had never rehearsed
his role. I couldn't take my eyes off of him. When the lights
came up at the end of the first act, I immediately looked for
his name in the Playbill: Michael Moriarity. For the rest of the
evening, I sat there watching young Mr. Moriarity, studying
his behavior, contrasting his technique to that of his fellow actors, repeatedly asking myself what made him so compelling.

I passed up the subway that night and walked home, sixty
or seventy blocks uptown, analyzing the experience I had just

had, turning one single performance over and over in my mind. It was a clue, certainly, to the kind of acting I aspired to, the kind I felt every actor should aspire to, but how to categorize it, to dissect it, to *teach* it?!

I startled myself. Was I hearing right? Was I really thinking about teaching acting? A working actor, making a decent living but still wrestling with the stage craft as I had since the early '60's, I saw myself as no more than a student of theatrical performance. True, I had enjoyed my brief stint at the HB Studio when I had taken over Charles Nelson Reilly's musical comedy class, but was I prepared to hang out my shingle in a businesslike way, form my own workshop and advertise myself as an acting teacher?

If I did have the audacity to do that, what would I teach? The lessons learned from Fonda, Hepburn, Cukor? The eclectic approach I had osmosed in the '30's, '40's, and '50's would be very difficult to codify. I knew the rules of film acting from A to Z, but it didn't occur to me to condense these rules into a methodology and attempt to teach it. What would I call it—"Hickman's Method?" There were already enough Strasbergian disciples in the phone book, and as I've already indicated, in my mind Method acting belonged to the old theater and was hardly what I wanted to feed into the mainstream.

What was left? Musical comedy? For close to a decade, I had done little more than sing, dance, and make people laugh, thanks to Burrows, Loesser, Neil Simon, and a dozen or so comedy writers whose names I've long since forgotten. I loved jokes, melodies, tap dancing, and performing in front of a live audience; I loved appreciative applause. But there was more to acting than entertaining people, getting a standing ovation or a good table at Sardi's. I wanted to teach something resembling what Michael Moriarity was doing on the stage, but I didn't know precisely what that was. His work serviced the playwright, and he was definitely a contributing member of the ensemble, but there was another dimension to his acting.

I had seen such work from other actors over the years: Fonda did it in *The Grapes of Wrath*; Bergman did it in *Gaslight*; Hanks did it in *Big* and other movies. On stage, Laurette Taylor did it in *The Glass Menagerie*, Olivier did it in *The Entertainer*, and Robert Preston did it in *The Music Man* and *The Lion in Winter*. On occasion, I had even done it myself— by accident. I knew it felt free, effortless, organic, unpredictable. But how does one teach an actor a craft that predicts unpredictability? How does one learn to act in a manner that guarantees spontaneity? Maybe I was getting ahead of myself. Maybe I had to find a way to do it in my own work, not accidentally but by design, before I was ready to help somebody else.

Realistically, I couldn't commit to teaching full-time even if I wanted to. I had a family to support. And, too, I was busy working out the kinks in my personal life which was, as usual, in a state of flux. In 1968, I found myself in a Greenwich Village bookshop standing next to several stacks of paperbacks which suggested that I was in proximity to a best-selling author. Since I have long been addicted to reading books about spirituality, I can never resist the temptation to open one and read a few words to see if it's important to add it to my collection. I picked up *The First and Last Freedom* and glanced at the author's photo underneath the title, a handsome, dark-skinned face with penetrating eyes which beckoned to me. I'm still reeling from that encounter.

J. Krishnamurti's revelations exploded in my head like a neutron bomb. All my pet beliefs about the nature of God and morality and knowledge and the meaning of experience were being questioned, and I was forced to re-examine the whole paradigm with ruthless honesty. In a matter of months, I would shed my history like a skin. Either I had gone through an enormous transformation, or I had completely lost my marbles.

I was on a road without a map, cruising at high speed into the '70's. The country was having cultural indigestion as a result of the unsettling events of the preceding decade, while I was trying to keep my small world from falling apart. I was in therapy for the first time in my life. Incomprehensibly, I stopped going to daily mass, although I have no recollection of making a conscious decision not to, and after being a daily communicant for decades, I was facing a future without the solace of the religion which had sustained me since childhood.

My family and friends tolerated what must have seemed to them bizarre behavior. I was always reading and quoting Krishnamurti; after *The First and Last Freedom*, I read *Commentaries I, Commentaries II, Commentaries III, Life Ahead, Think on These Things, The Flight of the Eagle, Freedom From the Known*, and all the published material I could get my hands on. I bought and listened to Krishnamurti tapes. I got four seats to his appearance at Town Hall and had to give three of them away because I couldn't get anybody to go with me.

"There is no answer, there is only the question." This bold affirmation of a cranky, unyielding Indian avatar became a mantra for me. All my life had been a solitary search for answers, for insights into the meaning of life, and now I was advised to be content with nothing *but* questions. I had always prided myself on being a man of faith, a believer, and Krishnamurti was telling me that believing was a meaningless exercise, a crutch for those who are mired "on a superficial level of consciousness." Give up belief, and the need to know anything, he said, and you will be free to discover, to create. "If you meet a man who knows, flee in terror, you're talking to a fool."

What had begun in my teens when I was introduced to Thomas Merton and Cora Evans, what had started as an attraction to mysticism within the Roman Church, had now catapulted me into a void beyond orthodox Christianity, "a cloud of unknowing." I should have been panicked, but I wasn't; somehow I saw the wisdom in letting go of dogmatic religious beliefs and accepting the mysterious aspect of life on planet Earth. I was getting a glimmer of what the Benedictine monk Hubert Van Zeller meant when he wrote, "The only security in this life is taking insecurity for granted." As it turned out, letting go of the known and learning how to create from the edge of the unknown would become one of the founding principles of my teaching methodology.

In the meantime, I never stopped polishing my craft. My wife, Pamela Lincoln, an actress who had studied with Paul Curtis at the American Academy, insisted that I audit his classes. At that point, Paul was teaching exclusively at his own American Mime Theater downtown on Third Avenue. I didn't see the point of taking a mime class. "I'm an actor," I remember protesting, "What do I need with mime?"

How wrong I was. Paul Curtis was one of the best acting teachers I've ever known. A black Irishman with a fierce commitment to "American" mime, as he called it, Paul tormented my body with physical exercises that would put a man half my age in the hospital. I survived, barely. But, thanks to him, I had a new appreciation for the flexibility, durability, and startling potential for expressiveness of the performing artist's physical equipment.

After swaggering, limping, or prancing around in black tights for several years, I finally got a fix on Paul's unique approach to teaching mime. My muscles were constantly sore, but I had the ability to conceive a specific character internally, instantly allowing that conception to mold my body into a moving sculpture, a feat I have used in my professional life more than once in subsequent years. The creative potency of the actor's physique has been shortchanged in America over the last half century, and spending time in Paul Curtis's classes made that abundantly clear. Paul used to say, "Words lie." He's a mime, after all, but he showed me how to express things with my body so I would never again have to rely on the text to reveal an inner truth.

I don't mean to suggest that the actor's internal mechanisms were neglected at the Mime Theater. In fact, a number of novel exercises were done every class to access the actor's emotional life. One of my favorites was *Conditions*. Deceptively simple, an actor was asked to stand up in front of the group and call out, one word at a time, what he felt at that moment: sad, happy, scared, angry—impulse by impulse—without comment from the teacher. Conditions, as I learned, encourages the student to be aware of the feeling energy that wells up inside and to be willing to express it in a public forum. Later, I told Paul I had borrowed that exercise to use in my own workshop, and he seemed pleased. To paraphrase Martha Graham: All artists steal from each other—the trick is to steal from artists who know what they're doing. I couldn't pay Mr. Curtis a better compliment.

One day, out of the blue, my acting career was interrupted by a serious back injury I sustained while on a pre-Broadway tour of *A Place for Polly*. I avoided surgery by wearing a back brace for six months, but I couldn't walk without excruciating pain, and I knew that acting in the theater, especially in a musical, was out of the question for the moment. A desk job was inevitable.

My writing background in film and television enabled me to land the position of Associate Producer for *Love of Life*, a long-running daytime serial on CBS. But I could barely get up the one flight of steps to my office. I remained ambulatory by swimming at lunch time at The University Club, which I had joined mainly to use the pool. I didn't mourn the end of my performing life as much as I yearned for relief from the chronic pain I felt in my lower back every time I moved. Needless to say, those first months as an associate producer were a time of emotional and professional upheaval as I headed into another phase in my career.

I must admit I liked putting money in the bank every week. Yet while a regular paycheck is good for the bottom line, it's not necessarily sustenance for the soul. I was grateful for the opportunity to prove myself in another area of my profession, but I couldn't ignore a nagging inner dissatisfaction. I knew in my heart that for me, producing a soap opera would never be anything more than a day job. Any artistic ambitions I had were on hold; divorced from the theater by economic necessity, I helped churn out a daily half-hour show and kept my restlessness to myself.

After eight months, CBS asked me to join the network staff as a program executive supervising *Love of Life* and *Where the Heart Is*, two of the four house-produced soaps aired on the daytime schedule. They gave me a fancy new office, my name on the door, a secretary, and an American Express card I was to use when I talked business with writers, producers, packagers, and agents at lunch or dinner. When thanked for my hospitality, I often replied: "Don't thank me. This meal is on Mr. Paley." [William Paley was the founder and Chairman of the Board of CBS.] I was playing the role of an executive and having fun, but I never took myself too seriously.

I was promoted several times during my years as a programmer, ending up as Director of Daytime Programs, New York and Los Angeles, next in line for Vice President when my boss, Bud Grant, was moved upstairs. I was good at being an executive, but before long I began to feel nostalgia for the old days when I could take off my necktie, pick up a script, and get down in the trenches to make some drama.

I guess I was looking for a creative outlet when one day my secretary told me that a friend of mine, Milton Katselas, was on the phone. He had directed *Butterflies Are Free* on Broadway and was on his way to Hollywood to do the film version of the play. Milton asked me if I wanted to take over his acting workshop one night a week while he was away. I jumped at the chance. I saw it as an opportunity to audition myself for the role of an acting teacher. Be careful what you wish for, as the saying goes, because you just might get it.

Being a substitute teacher was nerve-wracking the first class or two, but by the third week I was relaxed and having a good time. Of course, I couldn't really do it my way while I was sitting in Milton's chair, hemmed in as I was by his format. Like everyone else, his students were thoroughly indoctrinated in traditional Method acting and expected their teacher's criticism to reflect that point of view. I adjusted my remarks accordingly.

Like most acting workshops in those days, it was strictly a scene study class. For a brand-new teacher, it was educational watching actors putting up Lady Macbeth, Stanley Kowalski, and Uncle Vanya, while having trouble walking, talking, and bringing themselves on stage. I couldn't wait for Milton to get back from the coast so I could gather a handful of students and put my own theories to the test. I would moonlight at night while working at the network during the day. The time had come for me to put up or shut up, to devise a better methodology and get it on its feet in my own class.

I rented space at the Triangle Theater, housed in a venerable Episcopal church complex on 88th Street on the Upper East Side of Manhattan. I decided to start with the *what* and improvise the *how* as I went along. I would devise a curriculum reflecting my personal biases, opinions, and prejudices about acting, training students in such a way that they would be ready for the theater that was germinating in the 1970's. The new wrinkle in dramatic art, as I envisioned it, would be more than subtextual; it would be *supra*-textual, resonating with the psychic energy that surrounds the words in all directions. This revolutionary theater would be more visual than verbal, more physical than intellectual, and more extended stylistically than naturalistically restrained. This not-so-traditional theater would allow the performer to breathe fresh air, revitalize the training of actors in this country, and would not only incorporate but demand an alternative performance art.

The philosophy behind this curriculum would be decidedly Stanislavskian and would reflect my lifelong conviction that the underlying substratum of all true art is a search for the Holy Grail. I could never teach an art form that ignored or denied its spiritual implications. The monk in me, deprived of oxygen since my abbreviated stay in the monastery, was clamoring to come out of the closet.

The artist and the mystic are bedfellows, not "strange" bedfellows, but companions of the heart. My course of study would start with that essential truth. The pure mystic (the Buddha, St. John of the Cross, Lao Tzu, or J. Krishnamurti) needs no artistic endeavor. Beingness will suffice. The mystical artist, on the other hand (Dante, Michelangelo, Rumi, Da Vinci, Wagner, William Blake, Georgia O'Keeffe, Samuel Beckett, Nijinsky, Martha Graham), creates images, language, forms to communicate with his or her fellowman.

An artist, or anyone outside the arts with a loftier perception of the visible and invisible forces that shape the world we live in, has the right—indeed, the obligation—to share that understanding with the rest of us. Albert Einstein, one of the most revered scientists of the 20th century, was a mystically inclined thinker unafraid to assert the unthinkable. He once said, "The most beautiful experience we can have is the mysterious . . . , the fundamental emotion which stands at the cradle of true art and true science."

Reach past the intellect, he was telling us, and aspire to a truth beyond the known, the mundane, the commonplace. Mystics see what others are unable to see, but they are not otherworldly with their heads in the clouds. He or she may be tuned into higher consciousness, but both feet are still on the ground. He is the renowned quantum physicist, Erwin Schrödinger, who wrote in *My View of the World*, "All of us living beings belong together inasmuch as we are all in reality sides or aspects of one single being, which may perhaps in western terminology be called God while in the Upanishads its name is Brahman."

He is also America's most beloved poet, Walt Whitman, who sang about his mysticism in *Leaves of Grass*, "I hear and behold God in every object, yet understand God / not in the least."

Or he is Joseph Campbell, the illustrious expert on world mythology, to whom George Lucas turned for guidance when putting together his *Star Wars* trilogy. Campbell writes:

> Eternity
> is a dimension
> of here and now.
> The divine lives within you . . .
>
> The goal of the hero trip
> down to the jewel point
> is to find those levels in the psyche
> that open, open, open
> and finally open to the mystery
> of your Self being
> Buddha consciousness
> or the Christ.
> That's the journey.

In her little book, *A Joseph Campbell Companion*, Diane K. Osbon quotes the following words of her mentor describing the link between art and mysticism:

> The artist opens
> the forms of the work
> to transcendence.

Mysticism is a way of perceiving reality with a nonlinear viewfinder, of seeing more than one, two, or three dimensions at the same time, a venture into worlds beyond the senses, unvisited by rational thought. A mystic "knows" without knowing how, but does not question the validity of the information. The mystic who creates depends more on imagination than intellect, which asks too many bothersome questions. The critical, domineering, conscious self tends to get in the way. Einstein summed it up this way, "Imagination is more important than facts."

From day one, more than thirty years ago as I write, I was determined to affirm the role of higher consciousness in the art of acting. Getting a job is nice, being rich and famous is even better, but I have always said I would rather train one true Artist than a thousand second-rate actors with nothing to say. My entire methodology was and is based on that important truth, making it the top priority, the number one principle. The actor is an artist or an imposter, and the most artful creator, whether aware of it or not, employs the most mystical process.

Stanislavsky would demand no less. Referring to the high standards he had set for himself at The Moscow Art Theatre early in the last century, he asked, "Were we successful in finding and creating in ourselves and in the performance . . . the true mysticism which we sought on the stage at that time, the retreat from realism and the entrance into the spheres of the abstract?" Following in his footsteps, I exhorted the members of my first workshop to "stretch their arms . . . to reach beyond the limitations of everyday consciousness and to perform in a more transcendent sphere of reality."

Secondly, I would train the actor's Bodymind as an organic whole, predicated on the assumption that body and mind, matter and spirit, are not separate entities. My years of theatergoing had led me to one conclusion: the stiff, semiparalyzed bodies that so many actors lugged on stage with them had somehow been detached since childhood from the actor's vital energy. The split between the material and the spiritual which permeated American society in the 20th century had seeped into performance art and had done considerable damage to the Bodymind concept in the acting business. The Method actor, focused *inside* the skin—trained emotional resources, imagination, intellect, and will—but ignored the only machinery available to express that valuable inner life, the body. Unaware of the disconnect, the American actor had long been divided in two parts, with emotional life separated from physiology. I was determined to find a way to help the actor re-connect, organically, with both body and voice.

Once more, Stanislavsky was a guide. In *An Actor Prepares*, he charted the artist's inner landscape, while *Building a Character* focused on the outer layers of the Bodymind. Since *Building a Character* didn't come along until almost a generation after *An Actor Prepares*, one may argue that Strasberg's limited interpretation of the System had fully pre-empted Stanislavsky's original thinking. That would explain why the American actor's inner world didn't get hooked up to an external means of expression in the last century.

In Britain, training has tended to go in the opposite direction. Albert Finney and I were cast mates in 1981 in the film, *Looker*. We talked a lot about the way the British trained their actors and how, since Strasberg, the approach has been so different in this country. "You chaps," he said, "train the inside of the actor, while in my country we're devoted to the outside. We should all meet in Bermuda and put the two together."

With a dollop of humor, Mr. Finney was right on the mark. He talked about the six months of strenuous vocal and physical exercises he had recently done to ready himself for a full-length *Hamlet* at the Royal Shakespeare Company. "I had to build the lungs," he said, pounding his chest several times as if he were imitating Tarzan. "I had to fence, then recite the verse, then fence some more . . . it was exhausting." When I told him that the actor's body and voice were of paramount importance in the teaching methodology I had been developing for more than a decade, he was delighted. "Good for you," he said, with that famous grin. "Even if your actors never play Shakespeare, they need to use their voices like a musical instrument and their bodies like athletes in every role they play."

I flashed back to the '70's when I was laying out my first lesson plan, hoping to find a way to perfect the student's whole Bodymind, inside and out, with special emphasis on body and voice. The presumption has always been that movement and sound are the two natural means of expressing what goes on inside of us from the day we are born. We aren't taught to move and make sound, we do it instinctively. We learn how to speak words in a formal way, how to think in a language, but nobody has to train us to wail miserably when we need our diapers changed. As children we cry out because we don't know how not to cry out.

The sad truth is, we modern American actors have been "civilized"—that is, forbidden to express what we feel when we feel it; instead we wait for an appropriate time and place which, for our parents, seldom comes around—if at all. Consequently, as a toddler, the future actor learned to stifle vocal expression, stay mute, and suck the sound back into his or her humanity for self-protection. You probably know the old chestnut, "Children should be seen and not heard." Overcoming a lifetime of prohibition, it's a wonder our actors have the capacity to utter a sound, any sound, when they walk on the stage.

The range of the voice, diction, articulation, vocal power and flexibility would be part of my training procedure, too. Breathing, which so many actors take for granted, is maybe the most important overlooked ingredient of the actor's craft. Having done so much musical theater over the years, where I had to sing, dance and act at the same time, on the same breath, made me appreciate the value of enough air in my lungs. Any work on the actor's voice starts with learning how to take in that air expertly, which is one of the reasons why my classes always began with a breathing exercise.

Last, but not least, I would put an emphasis on an *extended* use of the actor's body and voice: style. I'm talking about the larger-than-life style suitable for Bobby Lewis's Poetic theater. No clumsy, everyday walking, no droning, nasal, monotonous vocal intonations, no sloppy, regional speech patterns would be permitted the actor learning about style in my classes. *Over*-statement was the goal in this phase of the work. And I would insist on every one of my actors investigating non-naturalistic acting whether or not he or she ever intended to play Shakespeare, Sophocles, Oscar Wilde, Kaufman and Hart, or Stephen Sondheim. I would stretch the parameters of the actors' experience and encourage them not to rely on commonplace behavior to play all the characters in their repertoire.

These four "whats" (the spiritual, physical, vocal, and stylistic elements just described) would be the building blocks of my training in those early days. They would not comprise the whole course of study for an actor who is new in the business, but it was a starting point, a jumping-off place for a fledgling teacher developing his own methodology. At the time, I was looking for a word to distinguish my way of teaching acting from the System and the Method. The dictionary was helpful. It defined *system* as "a group of interacting, interrelated, or interdependent elements forming a complex whole," while *method* was defined as "a regular and systematic way of accomplishing something . . . , [an] orderly and systematic arrangement."

In listing synonyms for *method*, my American Heritage Dictionary tells us, "Method emphasizes procedures according to a detailed, logically ordered plan." *System* is "broader in scope," stressing "order and regularity affecting all parts of a relatively complex procedure." In plain words, a *system* puts the nuts and bolts together, a *method* <u>should</u> be a step-by-step plan. The fourth definition of *method* in my dictionary is "a system of acting in which the actor recalls emotions and reactions from his past experience and utilizes them in the role he is playing." How interesting! *Affective memory* is defining Method training, notwithstanding the fact that the notorious exercise had long since been repudiated by several of America's most respected Method teachers, notably Stella Adler and Michael Chekhov. Even the dictionary is confused about what Method acting really is, and the fourth definition ends up being more misleading than helpful to the uninformed student who takes its validity for granted.

For my work, I instinctively chose the word *Process* because it is defined as "a series of actions, changes, or functions that bring about an end or result . . . , [a] course or passage of time . . . , ongoing movement; progression." A process is movement forward, active, ongoing, open-ended, and in my lexicon, a path of discovery. The Process I would teach would borrow from the best of Stanislavsky's System as I understood it, incorporating the workable Method practices I had been using since childhood, adding to the mix a heavy dose of what I had been learning—or unlearning—from Krishnamurti. The original recipe combined three basic ingredients: 1 part professional experience + 1 part System + 1 part mysticism = Process.

Armed with some specific ideas of what I would be teaching in my first class, I was uncertain about *how* I would teach them until the last minute. I had made one firm decision when I laid out the class schedule. I would divide my Process into two parts: exercises and scene study. On Monday night, I would concentrate on exercises; Wednesday night would be devoted to applying the exercise work to staging a text. What I would do on Wednesday would depend on how effectively I had unlocked the actor's body and voice on Monday.

I chose to start with Paul Curtis's Conditions, which gets the actor in touch with the spontaneous energy coming up from the inner self. Hopefully, I would then coax my students into expressing each impulse through voice and body. I had no prototype to point to, since I was making it up as I went along. The first few Monday nights were bumpy. My actors were willing but understandably confused. I recall Marsha Mason, a gifted professional actress at the time she joined my workshop, questioning me when I asked her to give me sound and movement for what she was feeling moment to moment. "What the hell are you talking about?" she asked, incredulously.

I couldn't show her. I could only ask her to do it. Gradually, when it began to happen for Marsha and some of the other actors, I was able to point it out to the class. "That's it. *That's* what I'm talking about." When the sound and movement I envisioned was repeatedly being demonstrated by individual students and the rest of the class could see and hear the exercises done well, it began to happen all the time. One thing led to another, and before long dozens of permutations evolved from Conditions, which, as it turns out, became the cornerstone of all the exercises that have been developed over the years.

I rarely use the word Conditions any more. Labels are arbitrary; words are not what they stand for; concepts about functions of mind and body are not a substitute for real behavior. I would emphasize *doing* rather than defining what we were doing. Students get ideas in their heads about acting, and it's nearly impossible to pry those ideas out later in the program. A good idea can sometimes be a hindrance because a potential artist must be free to experiment, idea-less, in the way an erased blackboard is an invitation to put something unforeseen on it. One has to just do it, and avoid needless theoretical discussion.

For exactly this reason, as I was exploring the *how*, I asked my students to avoid books about theory or acting techniques. When one of them seemed eager to supplement our class work with a text, I recommended *My Life in Art*, mainly to familiarize them with Stanislavsky's vision of a timeless, unsurpassed dramatic art. I wanted them to be as inspired as I was by his message at the beginning of their studies; investigation of craft and technique would follow close behind.

On occasion, I would bring in my dog-eared copy of the "bible" and read a line or two to the class to give them insight into where I was coming from. I quoted Stanislavsky: "But tradition is capricious, it takes on strange forms . . . and becomes a trade, and only one seed of it, the most important one, retains life till the new rejuvenation of the theater, which takes the inherited seed of the great eternal and creates its own and new eternal. In turn, this eternal is carried to the next generation, and most of it is lost on the way, with the exception of a small seed which finds its way into the common treasure cave of the world which houses the material for the great future human Art Religion."

I also wanted my original students to understand the master's views on naturalistic acting: "Those who think we sought for naturalism on the stage are mistaken. We never leaned toward such a principle." Stanislavsky goes on to emphasize his childlike love for outsized theatricality. "The fantastic on the stage is an old passion of mine. If there is fantasy in a play, I confess that I am ready to produce the play for the sake of the fantasy. For fantasy is interesting, beautiful, amazing . . . and, for me, the fantastic is a glass of foaming champagne."

In his own words, or, more accurately, the words of his original translator, Stanislavsky was articulating the stylistic extension I intended to explore in my Process. Stateside, as I saw it, naturalism had dominated commercial theater since the early '40's, and this was the only drama the actors in my workshop had known in their young lives. My goal was to instill in them a love of fantasy, of larger-than-life performance art, of broader imaginative strokes.

And to accept the metaphysical aspect of the work we were doing together. I used Stanislavsky's words to back me up. "Realism ends," he said, "where the superconscious begins . . . THE SUPERCONSCIOUS THROUGH THE CONSCIOUS! That is the meaning of the thing to which I have devoted my life since the year 1906, to which I devote my life at present, and to which I will devote my life while there is life in me." To train an actor claiming Stanislavsky as a forefather without honoring the deep-rooted spirituality in the man and his System is a bogus enterprise.

After about six months we had made significant progress, and the time had come to get down to the nitty-gritty. How was I going to bring the spontaneity of the exercises to the scene work? Little by little, I began to realize that Monday night was all about *not* thinking, while on Wednesday night the students were required to analyze a text and make choices. The problem was they couldn't stop thinking when they were playing a scene. Habitual brain function was the culprit. Neurological researchers tell us that intuitive flow is primarily processed by the right side of the brain, while thinking, analysis, form, language is left brain expression.

Observation suggested that thought shut down intuition when language was introduced in the form of a text. The dialogue was stifling impulses, preventing the student's living energy from ranging freely through the words. Words, after all, are a formal, left brain means of communication, imposing analytical thought, and usually reflect the actor's attempt to control the performance by giving the words a literal meaning. I found that by turning off the conscious mind momentarily, the actor's spontaneity would flow through the scene like a river. I was on the verge of articulating another basic principle of what would become unconscious acting.

As I was pondering this vital information, one of my more tuned-in students, Gloria Carlin, gave me a copy of *The Mystic in the Theatre*, a brief biography of the Italian superstar Eleonora Duse, written by American actor-manager, Eva Le Gallienne. *The Mystic* . . . opened the door wider to an understanding of the union of art and mysticism in the Process I was teaching. Duse's contemporary, Stanislavsky, writes of her influence in his autobiography, citing her as a personification of transcendent artistry in the theater; Duse would become a muse for all of us in the original workshop.

If Stanislavsky is the father of The Unconscious Actor, then Duse is the mother. Stanislavsky was the theoretician, and Duse, the mystical artist, was the embodiment of his teaching on the stage. Born dirt poor into a family of itinerant players and prone to illness most of her life, Duse overcame enormous obstacles to rise to the heights of her profession, a frail actress conquering the cosmopolitan capitals of Europe and the Americas. What was her secret? How did she conquer audiences and critics all over the world?

Studying *The Mystic* . . . for an answer to my questions, childhood memories surfaced about the word *Duse* being a synonym for great acting. On film sets, her name was intoned in awe. My mother had seen Duse on stage and spoke of her with similar reverence. In the '60's, no less an authority than Lee Strasberg had several times said in my presence, "The greatest actor I ever saw, bar none, was Eleonora Duse." Since she never wrote a book about acting and appeared in only one silent film—a fragment of which I viewed at the Museum of Modern Art in New York years ago—we must depend on her contemporaries for insights into her virtuosity.

Luigi Pirandello, the celebrated Italian playwright who

was Duse's contemporary, said of her technique: "Her acting is a quintessential distillation of pure truth, an art that works from a within outward, which shrinks from ingenious artifice and scorns the applause of wonderment that mere brilliancy seeks. With her, to feel a thing is to express it and not parade it. Her art is wholly an art of movement. It is a continuous, restless, momentary flow which has neither time nor power to stop and fix itself in any given attitude."

What, I asked myself, made Duse so unforgettable on the stage? An answer is suggested in William Weaver's *Duse*. Guiseppe Depanis, a critic in Turin, Italy, placed her star in the theatrical firmament as early as 1887: "I can only think of the enormous progress dramatic art would make in a short time if La Duse's artistic criteria . . . were to find many followers. . . . She is a great artist. . . . A glance, a gesture, a silence—and the state of her soul appears to the public in its true light."

During a tour of Russia in 1891, she played St. Petersburg in *La Dame aux Camélias*, and another influential critic wrote: "La Duse is truly a remarkable artist. . . . She does not gesticulate, does not declaim, does not invent scenic effects, but creates characters, *lives* them with a simplicity never before seen on the stage." On another occasion, a young Anton Chekhov was in the audience, and that night he wrote his sister: "I have just seen the Italian actress Duse in Shakespeare's Cleopatra. I do not know Italian, but she acted so well I felt I was understanding every word. What a marvelous actress! As I was watching La Duse, I realized why we are bored in the Russian theatre . . . ."

"One must forget self. . . . Forget self. . . . It's the only way!"

Le Gallienne quotes Duse more than once in *The Mystic. . .*, describing the international star's relentless determination to conquer her ego. Personal aggrandizement meant nothing to her. Duse saw herself as a co-creator, a messenger of the spiritual forces that lie beneath the veneer of physical reality. As her contemporary, Madame Lucia Casale said of her friend, "Her religion was the work of art, and quite legitimately she believed that the artist has in him something of the divine."

As far as I can tell, Duse's craft was mostly instinctive, and her predominant trait as an artist was a drive for self-transcendence. But ironically, her private life was often in shambles. A series of affairs with married men kept tongues wagging in her native Italy during her entire career. Her most notorious lover, the poet-turned-playwright Gabriele d'Annunzio, was a would-be dramatist whose florid, overblown writing she championed and tried to force down her loyal fans' throats. Duse, the darling of the critics, always got raves, while her paramour invariably got panned.

Over the years, I've haunted bookstores for everything available in English about Duse's fascinating personal journey and how it affected her work. Serendipitously, Helen Sheehy's *Eleonora Duse: A Biography* published in 2002, is the most complete, well-researched biographical account of the behind-the-scenes Duse I've ever read. Ms. Sheehy sheds bounteous light on her subject's split personality: "Duse confided to d'Annunzio that her whole life had been a 'sweet, inexhaustible' tormenting search for harmony between life and art—for a moment when the two could touch, 'barely . . . briefly.' With d'Annunzio she felt there were times when she had found that harmony."

Was lifelong torment the secret to Duse's artistry? Or has it always been futile to attempt to analyze what is beyond analysis? Perhaps Ms. Sheehy points the way when she tells us: "To describe Duse's soul was beyond the powers of John Corbin, the *New York Times* critic. He lamented that 'no future generation can know what it is we admire in the art of Eleonora Duse' because 'her art lives wholly within, a thing of the spirit.'" In some inexplicable way she had, as Lee Strasberg said, "achieved a fusion of the inner and the external which we have not arrived at in our theatre. . . . The theatre will require the next hundred years to deal with what Duse represented in this area."

I'm convinced that Duse's acting was indeed a "thing of the spirit," and from the beginning, I have always encouraged my students to follow her and Stanislavsky to the superconscious within. It should be noted that neither Duse nor Stanislavsky were religious in the traditional sense of the word. Spiritual seekers by nature have trouble following orthodox theological practices. Mystics are invariably mavericks, outsiders, and they almost never fit the mold. They are pathfinders, creators, visionaries, malcontents on a mission. Like Stanislavsky and Duse in the drama, they bring their mysticism to a variety of scientific, political, or artistic disciplines. Physicists Neils Bohr and Werner Heisenberg were mystics. Tolstoy, Henry David Thoreau, Emerson, Frank Lloyd Wright, and Isadora Duncan were mystics. Mahatma Ghandi and Martin Luther King, Jr. were mystics. Van Gogh was a mystic. So was John Lennon.

Embrace the mystical path, I was telling my actors in

that first workshop. I exhorted them to be brave, take risks, study their genealogy, and appreciate their heritage. Revisit Stanislavsky and remember that over a hundred years ago the contemporary actor's great-great-great grandmother, Eleonora Duse, was inventing modern acting. My freshman class was asked to blow the dust from their ancestors' historical images and re-imagine them as prophets whose contribution to the dramatic arts bridge the gap of time.

The latent monk and the frustrated artist in me were coming to terms. And I was learning faster than my students. There was no choice. They were smart, asking so many questions that I was forced to work hard to stay ahead of them. My biggest handicap was that I had not yet found a comprehensive pedagogical approach, a workable, continuous lesson plan to sustain me when I wasn't certain what to do next. Fortuitously, a director friend of mine in New York, Don Moreland, gave me a copy of *Zen in the Art of Archery* by Eugen Herrigel. A classic description of a Westerner's confrontation with an ancient oriental culture, the book provided more than a few answers to my students' questions. In *Zen* . . . , Herrigel states, "What is true of archery . . . also applies to all the other arts." At last, I had found my basic *how*.

Herrigel was an academician, a German who had spent years in Japan learning the art of archery. What to the Western world is a sport is a path of enlightenment to a Japanese Master, and Herrigel's description of his personal experiences with his instructor was a revelation for me. I had stumbled on a teaching method that was perfectly adaptable to my needs, an inventive way to train actors founded on a mystical discipline, Zen Buddhism.

The Zen Master whose powerful presence inhabits *Zen in the Art of Archery* was (and still is) a guide, a frame of reference for teaching my Process. For three decades, he has provided a practical artistic philosophy, immense wisdom, information, and encouragement. Kenzo Awa. Let's add his name to make it a triumvirate: Stanislavsky, Duse, Awa.

I told my students then, and I tell them now: Don't try to understand the Process. Just do it. Zen acting originates in the deeper Self, as did Herrigel's manner of releasing a shaft from a bow. Performing the Zen way "is not speculation at all but immediate experience of what, as the bottomless ground of Being, cannot be apprehended by intellectual means, and cannot be conceived or interpreted even after the most unequivocal and incontestable experiences: one knows it by not knowing it." Most of the original members of my class were dumbfounded when I laid out these ground rules for them.

Herrigel warns that "the way of the 'Artless Art' is not easy to follow." That's an understatement if I ever heard one. Using a paradoxical approach to performance art is a stumbling block for so many of us in the West. A paradox is an anathema to the Western mindset. How could our society value "artless" anything when all it hears is a contradiction in terms? Logic is all. Linear thought pervades all. To a thought-dominated American actor, spending time deciphering a Zen *koan* is about as idiotic as putting hieroglyphics on a résumé.

The average actor isn't interested in a higher wisdom that's impossible to digest intellectually; the average actor craves a pre-digested method that will guarantee a successful career. That's why he or she is the "average" actor.

The Zen Master's counsel is to never lose patience. I tell my actors, as he told his students: "Don't think of what you have to do, don't consider how to carry it out! . . . The shot will only go smoothly when it takes the archer himself by surprise." Naturally, this surprise can only occur after years of breathing, drawing the string, and releasing the arrow, a contradiction for any archer (read, performance artist) who doesn't have a taste for the discipline demanded of the aspirant who has not yet persevered in this practice.

Master Awa told Herrigel that he "must learn to disregard himself . . . and to become, in a radical sense, self-regardless, purposeless. Much practice is needed. . . . But once this practice has led to the goal that last trace of self-regard vanishes in sheer purposelessness. . . . The right art is purposeless, aimless! . . . What stands in your way is that you have too much willful will. You think what you do not do yourself does not happen."

In other words, too much conscious mind mucks up the artist's natural creativity. In Zen, the student soon learns to stop controlling, to quiet the left brain, and to come to terms with the greater Self. Intellect and intuition must accommodate each other's differing functions, embracing a partnership in which they work together as a creative team. An artist cannot perform at his or her best with a flabby thinking mind or suppressed, suffocated instincts; a healthy Process depends on both a union of these two forces and renouncing the managing ego.

The stumbling block for the uninitiated Zen artist becomes obvious when asking the question, "Okay, when I give up my ego, who plays the role—who gives the performance if *I* don't?" Herrigel's response is based on his own years of training in Japan: "'It' takes the place of the ego, availing itself of a facility and a dexterity which the ego only acquires by conscious effort. And here, too, 'It' is only a name for something which can neither be understood nor laid hold of, and which only reveals itself to those who have experienced it."

The ego chooses, narrows, specifies limitation; the greater Self is all encompassing, expansive, undefined. Thought knows; the greater Self observes the knowing. Balancing the outer and the inner mind brings about the superlative performances of actors *and* everybody else. Not because one is a proponent of a radical, revolutionary teaching methodology—this is just the way human creativity works.

A reminder. Bringing Zen consciousness to the art of acting doesn't result from our going to a mountain top, chanting and reciting a mantra all day long. As that fine British actress, Glenda Jackson, once observed, "Acting is a sweaty business." Reaching a level of transcendent performance in any field is labor intensive; the harder we work, the more enlightened our performance. That's why I followed Master

Awa's instructions: "Far from wishing to waken the artist in the pupil prematurely, the teacher considers it his first task to make him a skilled artisan with sovereign control of his craft." Craft, craft, and more craft is the bedrock of Zen training and, as it has been from the beginning, the foundation for unconscious acting.

When it all began in the '70's, we were taking baby steps in finding a way to train Zen actors. After about a year, the *what* had been clearly defined, the *how*, thanks to Master Awa, was in place, and all that was left for my students to make this new Process their own was to integrate the exercises we did every Monday into the Wednesday night scene work.

Easier said than done. My task was to convince the freshman class that my unorthodox ideas about performance art were workable and would lead them to a successful career in show business. My point of view was unproven and, maybe even worse, unconventional. They had to see the Process come to life on its feet, and students had to do it themselves before they would become converts to unconscious acting. That's always the case when you ask an actor, or anyone else, to go where they've never been before.

I was patient for several reasons, not the least of which was that I myself was putting it all together as I went along. And, too, I knew that my first students were less resistant than skeptical. The Unconscious Actor, figuratively speaking, was still in diapers; barely twelve months old, he was busy investigating himself and becoming comfortable in his skin. Art, or solid craftsmanship, for that matter, was out of the question.

Before anything else, the novice had to stop trying to act and simply be present, a real person in a truthful moment in time. That wasn't easy for anybody, and it isn't easy for most students some thirty years later. I remember one newcomer to New York, a likeable young Texan named Gary, who was desperate to be a working actor in the theater. Brand new in the big city, he had decided to be so ingratiating while he was "acting" that he would seduce every audience—the class, casting directors, producers, theatergoers—on his way to the top. Unfortunately, the reaction he got from the only audience he had ever known, his classmates, was the exact opposite of what he intended.

One night he stood up to do a solo exercise. He cracked a few stale jokes and instead of laughter, there were groans from his peers. He looked confused, so I tried to help him.

"Why are you smiling all the time and trying to be funny?"

"Am I?" he replied, still confused.

"You're working so hard to be charming, and you're already charming. Why don't you just be here, and be who you really are?"

"That's not enough," he said, almost defiantly.

"You're not enough?" I countered. "Why not?"

"I want to be a success, a successful actor on Broadway. I have to charm the pants off those folks out there or they won't hire me, and they won't buy tickets."

I turned to the class. "Is the strategy working?" The answer was a chorus of "no."

If he was shaken, he didn't show it. "That's you guys. This isn't the real world. I'm learning how to act here, that's all. Out there is what counts."

And that was that. For months he tried to make the strategy work, both in the exercises and in scene study. Every time I tried to dissuade him, my words fell on deaf ears. If anything, he was more unctuously engaging each week until he had alienated most of the class.

Then one Monday night, something extraordinary happened. He got on his feet to do an exercise, and he was simply Gary—somewhat shy, uncertain, vulnerable, but very winning, and very witty. The class could hardly keep from cheering. Before he sat down, I asked him, "What happened?"

"I was watching a talk show," he said, "and Dustin Hoffman came on. He's a great actor. And I watched him real careful. And I realized Dustin Hoffman just shows up. He doesn't do anything else, he just *shows up*."

Gary had learned a major lesson, and he was on his way. No more fake charm, no more playing an idea of himself, no more being anyone but who he was. It was becoming more obvious every week that an aspiring unconscious actor must begin the journey by just "showing up." Mastering the craft would come slowly week to week, and performance art would follow over time.

Little by little, Marsha, and then her classmates, began living the Process moment to moment during the exercises and feeding those spontaneous impulses through their scene work. It was all coming together, and for the first time, I could point to a scene or two that were true illustrations of the kind of acting I had been searching for all those years. It was happening right there in front of my eyes.

Meanwhile, back at the network I was moving closer to an active role in producing television shows. With colleague Tony Converse, I had developed and produced several original ninety-minute dramas for daytime. And one of them, *Tiger on a Chain*, was nominated for an Emmy. My stock at CBS was definitely on the uptick. I was given an assignment to develop a serialized situation comedy, *Side By Side*, for the nighttime schedule. When it was one of two pilots given a green light for taping in New York, I lobbied for, and got, the job of producer. Leaving the program staff and going back to my first love—making drama—would change my life in a totally unforeseen way.

Though *Side By Side* didn't get on the schedule that season, the show was good enough to give me credibility as a producer of prime time television. I wanted to go in that direction, but there was very little opportunity to write, produce, or direct drama for television on the East Coast, so I accepted a job as Executive Producer of *Love of Life*, which meant I could pick up a paycheck every week while I planned my next move. There was no doubt in my mind that if I wanted to get into nighttime, I would have to pull up stakes and return to Los Angeles at some point.

Norman Lear gave me the chance to make the move sooner rather than later. On one of my trips West for a story meeting with the head writer of my show, I had a brief meeting with Mr. Lear and told him I had a knack for situation comedy, and that I'd love to write and produce one for prime time. Before Lear could respond, his secretary called him out of the meeting, and I returned to New York wondering if I would ever talk to him again.

A month or so later, he called and asked me if I wanted to help him produce a pilot for a project he had created. "Think about it," he said. "It would mean leaving New York and moving back to L.A."

"I don't have to think about it," I replied. "When do you need me?"

"In two weeks," he said.

I didn't hesitate. "Norman, I'll be there. And thank you."

I gave my notice to CBS and started packing my bags. My kids were in school, and Pamela had nearly a year left on her contract to appear on *One Life to Live* at ABC. They wouldn't be able to join me for some time, and I hated leaving my family behind, even for a few months. But I bit the bullet, bought a plane ticket, and said farewell to friends and colleagues in a city where I had lived and worked for fourteen years.

When I said goodbye to my students I had a lump in my throat. We had been together for nearly five years; most of them were veterans of the very first class. They had been open enough, dedicated enough, and hard-working enough to prove that the kind of performance art I had envisioned for years might someday become a reality. Each of them had made a significant contribution to the development of the Process, and I couldn't have been more grateful.

Marsha Mason was now a movie star with several Oscar nominations to her credit; and many of her original class-mates were busily engaged on stage, in film, and in television, and I was proud of each and every one of them. I knew their training was sound because I had gotten on the stage while I was at CBS, and I was thrilled to discover that what I had been teaching my students to do, I could do myself—*by design!*

During the years that I made a living as an actor I had often done superlative work, but when problems arose I was not always able to solve them. When I produced and directed Jules Tasca's zany comedy, *A Chip Off Olympus*, at the Triangle Theater, I cast myself in the lead role to check out my own technique—and it was a revelation. I still had problems, but now there were ready solutions to every one of them. The Process I was developing had made me a better actor, too.

But I had another job now, three thousand miles away, and I had to give it my full attention. Would I ever act on stage again? Or teach? I couldn't know for sure. Teaching acting had been a sideline, the best way to explore the ground-breaking theatrical art I had long pictured in my mind while making a living as a professional actor, writer, and producer. The dream was still intact but unrealized, unfulfilled. On some level, I knew that. I also suspected that someday, somehow, the dream would come to fruition.

SIX

Out of Control, In Full Command®: The Process

"Living is a form of not being sure, not knowing what next or how. The moment you know how, you begin to die a little. The artist never entirely knows. We guess. We may be wrong, but we take leap after leap in the dark."

Agnes De Mille

Sitcom City

There's a wonderful show business story that has been going around the industry for years. Some say it's apocryphal, the invention of a wag, but no matter, it's a great story. It seems that the venerable character actor Edmund Gwenn was terminally ill and comatose in his room at the Motion Picture Home in Woodland Hills, CA. An old friend, George Seaton, who had directed Mr. Gwenn when he played Santa Claus in *Miracle on 34th Street*, was sitting at the dying man's bedside silently sharing a final moment. The director was startled when Gwenn opened his eyes and uttered his last words: "Dying is easy. Comedy is hard."

I think Mr. Gwenn was right about comedy. Nonetheless, I have always had a yen to make audiences laugh. Maybe this can be traced back to my childhood working in movies where my father was going off to die in the war, my dog was getting run over by a truck, or my pet duck was being eaten by a rampaging predator. A movie moppet had to suffer and cry easily, because when a child cried on the screen it wrung the hearts of the audience. Whether I liked it or not, I had been typecast as a tragedian, and I yearned to grow up someday and play comedic roles.

Returning to Los Angeles, I had come full circle from being a "serious" actor in the movies to producing situation comedy for Norman Lear. My education in the art of making audiences laugh had begun when I spent a year on Broadway in *How to Succeed . . .* ; Abe Burrows, Frank Loesser, Bob Fosse, and producer Cy Feuer taught me more in those twelve months than I would have learned in decades had I been trained by lesser artists. Afterwards, I was typecast once again and acted in nothing but comedies, practicing what Burrows and the others had preached, and made a living for close to ten years on the stage.

Abe, as he was affectionately called by those who knew him, was sitting in my dressing room before curtain one night, chatting about the problems that arise when one is dedicated to making people laugh. I seized the opportunity to pick the brain of this wily play doctor whose comedic skills were unparalleled in the theatrical community.

"When you're writing a show like *Succeed*..., how do you know if a joke is funny?"

Burrows shrugged. "If the audience laughs."

I was stunned. "You're the best there is. That's the only way you know?"

"What other way is there?" he said, as though the answer should be self-evident.

"What do you do if they don't laugh?"

"I write another joke."

When one toils in the vineyards that produce hearty laughter, one is always at the mercy of the audience. Hundreds of audiences later, I know that for a fact. What I was asking Abe to give me that night at the 46th Street Theater was some rule of thumb that would help me predict, *before* I got in front of the audience, whether or not my choices would play funny. Why? To avoid public embarrassment, for one thing; there is nothing more demoralizing than expecting to get a laugh and ending up with egg on your face. For another, an artist who wants to play comedy successfully either gets laughs or gets another job. There is no alternative.

If dying is easier than comedy, why in hell would any professional actor want to risk being a comedian-for-hire? For me, the answer was simple; there was no greater high than hearing an audience laugh at my performance. Getting a laugh is addictive, and once I was hooked, I was hooked for good. That's why, ever since I left the world of soap operas in the '70's, most of my writing, producing and acting has been dedicated to comedy and polishing the tools of that trade.

It should be obvious—but it isn't—that tool *numero uno* is a sense of humor. My take is that some people have one, some people don't. I'm not talking about acting foolish, being silly, and breaking up your friends at a party when everybody is feeling no pain. I'm talking about *thinking* funny. In recent years, I've had the privilege of associating with three of the funniest men alive: Jonathan Winters, Mel Brooks, and Jerry Seinfeld. They can all be hilarious much of the time, spontaneously and under all kinds of circumstances. But their humor is individual, unique, and always an expression of each one's personal slant on life.

There is no Humor 101 or One Size Fits All approach to comedy. Aspiring comic actors must trust their instincts about what's amusing, and go with what makes them "feel" funny in a role. What won't work is trying to do it somebody else's way. And never forget, if you get a laugh in rehearsal and nobody laughs the second, third and fourth time you do it, don't give up before you get on stage. If what you're doing feels funny to you, commit. Laughter often comes from surprise. The opening night audience hasn't heard you deliver the joke and will probably laugh the same way your cast mates originally did during rehearsal.

And then there's "timing." Having good timing is not something separate from but an ingredient of a good sense of humor. And it always comes from gut instinct, sensing how to use silence, when to pause or when to use a look to get your laugh. The pros know that a punch line often depends on the reaction of a fellow actor to make the joke work. Action/ reaction is an integral part of all good performance art, and comedy is no exception.

I don't want to give the impression that having a funny bone and good instincts is enough when you want to be successful at comedy. Mel Brooks, with whom I spent many hours on a tennis court as a doubles partner, can be hilarious just playing tennis. He can adlib and improvise with the best of them, on the court and off. So it came as a bit of a surprise when he told me once: "I never leave anything to chance when I'm making a movie. It's all been worked out in the office months in advance."

Making audiences laugh as a producer, writer, director, or actor is hard work, and enormous skill is involved. A lot of comedy is technical, mechanical. Good set-ups and good jokes are often found after countless rewrites, hours of rehearsal, and the discipline to go back to the drawing board over and over, until the mechanics are just right. Creating comedy is labor intensive; unless you're ready to roll up your sleeves and work hard, you should find another way to make a living.

Thank God I knew this by the time I went to work for Mr. Lear. He had nine—count 'em, nine—hit shows on the air when I was associated with his Tandem/T.A.T. company, and he had producing, writing, directing, and casting input on every one of them. He was a dervish, a perfectionist who drove himself harder than any of his employees. As a result, he was the most successful producer in the history of the sitcom business.

Just being around Lear for several years was the equivalent of attending a graduate school for comic artists. The years I had spent in the theater—working in shows like *How to Succeed* . . . , *Barefoot in the Park*, *Where's Charley?*, and *The Apple Tree*—was time well spent preparing me for the formidable task of writing and producing a half-hour comedy to meet the boss' high standards.

During one of our first story meetings, Lear informed me that in the first three pages of a script for any of his shows, the writer must tell the audience who the major character in that episode would be, what the story would be about, and yes, by the way, there must be 2½ jokes a page! The kicker was that if the writer couldn't do it, he'd do it for you. Anyone hired by Norman Lear who didn't have the know-how already had better learn fast how to get to the point right away, be clear about the story being told in that episode, and make sure that the exposition was funny. A daunting task for any writer/producer, to say the least.

But what a training ground it is, creating a half hour of comedy every week. Every seven days, you have to come up with a comic idea, a slant that is slightly cockeyed, a truthful premise that you will twist and stretch like a rubber band until there is enough tension in the absurdity that it squeezes relief or laughter out of the extended truthfulness of the characters' lives.

As a craftsman, I came to love the science of comedy and its exactitude. Comedy must be precise. An extra word (even an extra syllable) in the straight line or the joke can kill the laugh. A pause in the wrong place or a pause that's too long distorts the rhythm of the scene and can be fatal. And comedy is so fragile that the tiniest wrong nuance can bring the whole thing down like a house of cards.

Making a sitcom is a strenuous, 24/7, stressful way to make a living. And the payoff isn't the weekly check, it's hearing the studio audience laugh when they're watching the show being taped. While I was at Tandem/T.A.T., I had the good fortune to be cast in episodes of *Maude* and *All in the Family*, which turned out to be two of the most creative experiences of my life. I was reminded how enchanting it is to act with superlative comedic artists like Bea Arthur, Carroll O'Connor, and Jean Stapleton.

On the downside, when I was casting my own shows, it soon became apparent how few such artists there are around Tinseltown. Watching actors from the Los Angeles talent pool audition, I found myself wishing more of them had read Stanislavsky's *Building a Character*, especially Chapter Five, "Plasticity in Motion," where he discusses the movement of energy, the inner dynamic which is responsible for changing rhythms, pace, and tempo. Most of the Method-trained actors I auditioned in the '70's were ill-equipped to deal with the stylistic demands of comic acting, and their readings indicated that most of them had never wrestled with the musicality of Neil Simon or Noel Coward on stage in front of a live audience. Had I not had that opportunity myself, I would never have been able to function as an actor or a writer in the sitcom business.

In a way, when I look back I'm surprised I was able to pull it off. Not only was Norman a hard taskmaster, but I was under severe pressure in my personal life. I was living alone—my wife and kids were still in New York—and as soon as I got back to Los Angeles, the doctors told my mother she had liver cancer. In the daytime, I was at the studio figuring out how to make audiences laugh; at night, I did my best to comfort my mother who was terminally ill with an awful disease. I was learning that if there's an art to creating comedy, there's an art to dying, too.

Once, when Lear asked me how my mother was doing, I told him that she had always been terrified of death, but she was coming to terms with her fear and gaining an acceptance and tranquility I had never seen in her before. We talked about a particular groundbreaking episode of *All in the Family* where he confronted the network's taboo about dealing with death on a situation comedy. "There's humor in everything," he said, "and the death of a loved one is no exception."

I agreed, quoting a favorite author of mine, Gilbert Keith Chesterton, who once wrote, "If you can't laugh at a dying man, you can't laugh at any man, because we're all dying, whether fast or slow." Norman smiled, wrote that sentence down on a card, got up from the conference table and pinned it up on the bulletin board in his office. "I wish I'd had that quote when I was battling with CBS about what I wanted to do on *All in the Family*. It might've made my life easier."

This was not an unfamiliar subject for story meetings with Norman Lear. We had often discussed the need to find comedy in the tragedy in our shows and vice versa. It had become clear to me that drama couldn't be separated into tragedy or comedy because, by the nature of the human condition it reflected, it is always tragic-comic. And the heavier the piece, the lighter the touch it demands.

The days following my mother's death were challenging, an opportunity to see if I could find humor in our family crisis, including the day we picked out her casket. My dad, brother, sister and I were greeted at the funeral parlor by a caricature of an undertaker wearing a mournful expression and a bad toupee, who tried to sell us an overpriced item with a placard on it reading "Celestial Chariot." When we all started to giggle, the solemn sales rep for marked-up caskets was confused. Apparently he had been trained to give solace while gouging grief-stricken customers who wouldn't notice they were being taken to the cleaners. My family was the exception, I'm sure. Instead of buying into his sales pitch, we were finding the whole thing ludicrous. I was proud of us, and I think my mother would have been, too.

After the funeral I went back to work with a heavy heart, but I knew, as I had never known before, that laughter and tears are two sides of the same coin. When we deny the pain, we choke off the humor; when we refuse to laugh at those traumatic events in our lives, we prevent the healing that comes from the honest expression of our sorrow. As a dramatic artist, whether you see yourself as a tragedian or a comedian, always flip the coin over repeatedly or your work will suffer. That's one of the best lessons I learned while I was living in "sitcom city."

I also learned how nearly impossible it was to come up with a good show every week of the season. Writing a well-constructed, half-hour script takes time, many drafts, numerous fixes. In TV, everything is fast; the script has to be ready yesterday, and there is never enough time. The pressure is so great that it's a miracle anything ever gets on the air that's even a notch above mediocre. After a season or two of non-stop running twenty-four hours a day, I was exhausted. I had come West full of enthusiasm for being a situation comedy producer, and two years later, I was out of gas. Besides being physically worn out—I'll never know how Norman Lear survived—I was discouraged to find that most of my colleagues at Tandem/T.A.T. did not watch television. They didn't even watch other sitcoms; they simply cranked out the product with expertise, episode after episode, to please the audience but never themselves.

This disturbed me. One day I asked myself, "If you weren't making a living writing and producing it, would you be interested in watching what you were producing on the air?" When the answer was no, I knew it was time to get out of the sitcom business. CBS offered me the job of Executive Producer for *Alice*, but after much soul searching, I turned it down. Instead, I made a deal at Paramount to develop a miniseries, a movie-of-the-week and a nighttime hour show based on the award-winning documentary, *Police Tapes*.

Having started my career at this studio so long ago, it felt like I was coming home professionally. For a while it was very comfortable; they gave me a fancy office, a brand new typewriter, and plenty of time to develop my shows. The pace was slow, I was writing every day on my own schedule, and I thought I had found my niche. For about six months. I soon learned what a "development deal" really is; I thought it meant being creative and writing a show I believed in. Not so. I was less a creator than a huckster pedaling my wares under Paramount's aegis to one of the networks.

It was like *déjà vu* all over again. Except during my stint at CBS in New York, I was the *buyer* and the studio rep was the *seller*. Having been on the other side of the desk, I knew that most of the network program execs I was "pitching" were more interested in job security than buying good shows. Why? Because if they committed to one too many projects that didn't work, they'd be out of a job.

In those days, when you created television shows you spent an enormous amount of time and energy on ideas you deeply cared about with only three possibilities [CBS, NBC, or ABC] to see your project get to the pilot stage. With many buyers trying to find a way to say "no," being a sales rep for a studio was mostly a lose-lose proposition. I decided to get out of development hell and make a living some other way.

The truth is I didn't like playing the game: making pitches, "taking" meetings, schmoozing over drinks, discussing Nielsen ratings, demographics and counter-programming, which seemed to fascinate both low-level and high-level network suits. I was definitely on the wrong track. But where to now? I had rented a house in L.A., brought my family, furniture, and professional life back to the West Coast, and I had to pay the bills doing something that would provide more creative satisfaction. As I pondered the future, I received a call from an old buddy that put me back on the path I thought I had left behind in New York.

Debbie Reynolds Has Her Own Studio?

The caller was Charles Nelson Reilly. After coming to Los Angeles to do a television series, he had turned himself into a successful talk show and game show personality. But he was still a teacher at heart, and he had decided to start a school for actors, singers, and dancers: The Faculty. He would teach a course in musical comedy, his forte, and he was asking me to become one of the instructors and teach my approach to acting.

"I'm busy, Charlie. I have to finish writing the treatment for a miniseries I'm taking to CBS."

"Just ten weeks. Ten weeks. Help me get my school off the ground."

"Okay," I agreed. "Ten weeks, and I'm out."

"It's a deal. Come on over and see the space I've rented. You'll love it."

"Where is it?" I asked, pencil in hand.

"It's at Lankershim and Victory. Debbie Reynolds' studio."

I dropped the pencil. "Debbie Reynolds has her own studio? Since when?"

"Since she bought an old post office and turned it into five or six sensational rehearsal studios. Wait'll you see 'em."

I did like the space, and I kept my word. I taught for ten weeks, then another ten, and by the end of the next year, when The Faculty went out of business, I was still teaching and loving every minute of it.

That's how The Unconscious Actor migrated West and

took up residence at Debbie's [I've known her since we were kids at MGM] professional rehearsal facility in North Hollywood. At the D.R. Studio, there are individual spaces which can be rented by the hour; dance teachers, choreographers, auditioners, and musical producers keep the place busy all the time. I like working in a rehearsal hall because it gives my actors a chance to stretch themselves and do the demanding physical part of the Process.

I would rather the actors I'm training see their classroom as a place to *rehearse* instead of a substitute playhouse where they are expected to *perform*. Quite a few acting classes take place in a theater, real or simulated, with a stage, wings, and a section where students who are not working in a scene are a perceived audience. New actors are suggestible. The moment they find themselves on what seems like a stage, enshrined in the lights and in front of a class, they start to act. They can't help themselves. Notwithstanding the awful truth that they don't know a thing about acting, they are budding artists so eager to flex their muscles and prove themselves that they will start posturing before they have a clue about what they are doing. In their terms, they are acting, but what they are really doing is skipping the thing they need to do most—learn the craft.

Being a diehard football fan, I am constantly drawing analogies to the sport, referencing great performance art as exemplified by players like Joe Montana and Jerry Rice, Super Bowl champs from the San Francisco 49ers' glory years and two of the best who ever played the game. When they were at the top of their forms, Montana, the quarterback, and Rice, his intended receiver, stayed long hours after team workouts perfecting pass patterns that would put them both in the record books.

Unflappable, Montana rarely changed expression whether he threw a touchdown or an interception. His longtime mentor and coach, Bill Walsh, was once asked to assess Joe Montana's most significant quality as a champion. Walsh's answer was a surprise, "Serenity." I find it ironic that for years the NFL was dominated by a Zen quarterback.

Jerry Rice's superhuman work ethic astonished teammates, sports writers, and fans. He ran up and down hills to stay in condition between seasons while less motivated players ate hamburgers, drank beer and got fat. Rice knew, as did Montana, that conditioning is the key to becoming a Hall-of-Famer. Performance artists of the first rank understand that to play well on Sunday, they have to practice well during the week—every week. Championships are not won by talented athletes but by athletes who know how to prepare. You've heard the adage, "Practice makes perfect." Well, it's an adage—okay, a cliché—because it's true. I like the old joke where the tourist asks the pedestrian, "How do I get to Carnegie Hall?" And the pedestrian replies, "Practice, practice, practice."

Vladimir Horowitz, one of the most celebrated concert pianists of the 20th century, once said: "If I don't practice one day, I know it. If I don't practice two days, my wife knows it. If I don't practice three days, everybody knows it." Practice does make perfect, or near perfect. In the acting business, practicing one's craft is called rehearsal, so if an actor doesn't know how to rehearse, he or she will be covered with flop sweat on opening night. It's that simple. Learn how to rehearse or pay the price: failure.

No one entered the workshop without first coming to the D.R. Studio, meeting with me, and auditing a class. Many teachers who run professional workshops don't allow auditors, and I have never understood why. In any learning experience, the most important relationship is that of student and teacher. A prospective student has to have a sense of who I am and where I'm coming from; conversely, I have no interest in having a relationship with anyone who doesn't seem to be a good candidate for unconscious acting.

An auditor is usually nervous, sometimes shy and diffident, once in a while cocky, and almost always having trouble being who they really are in the pre-class meeting. When they are young they're often apologetic about their lack of training or professional experience. I reassure them that inexperience is of no consequence to me. Veteran professionals with dense résumés are sometimes set in their ways, judgmental, closed to investigating an alternative technique, and worst of all, incapable of letting go of preconceptions to—as Agnes De Mille recommends—"take leap after leap in the dark."

The most common question an auditor asks is, "What kind of acting do you teach?" Fifteen years ago, this meant they were asking, "Do you teach Method or Meisner?"—the two most recognizable methodologies to an inexperienced drama student. I rarely hear the word Method these days, though the Meisner technique still crops up now and then. In present tense Los Angeles, "What kind of acting do you teach?" is conditioned by the glut of advertising in the trade papers for cold reading workshops, on-camera classes, acting in commercials, acting for film, sitcom acting, soap opera acting, musical theater acting, you name it; someone has hung out a shingle and is teaching it. Understandably, kids from out of town who want to become professionals are confused by the bombardment of alternative training programs being offered. To me, acting is acting, and it's a mistake to compartmentalize it into film acting or stage acting as if there were differing techniques for different dramatic mediums. I teach a comprehensive approach which will apply to any acting, whether in front of a camera or a live audience.

If the auditor appears to be interested, I explain my debt to Stanislavsky, his importance as a teacher and theorist in the history of modern acting, and how I see my Process as a 21st-century extension of the work he began a hundred years ago. But I try to make it clear that most of what they are about to see is my invention: exercises I have developed, a rehearsal plan that is uniquely my creation, and a point of view about acting that reflects my personal values.

In the workshop, I'm the team leader, but I'm not the team. A drama class is a complex set of relationships—teacher/student, student/teacher, student/student—and each of these relationships depends on openness, honest communication, trust, mutual respect, and unfailing support for the common good, as well as each individual's develop-ment as an artist. I see my classes as a microcosm of the drama business; our text is the creative game plan, the stu-dents are the ensemble, and I am their director. A good direc-tor is one part commanding general, one part motivator, one part psychiatrist, one part social worker, one part team player, and one part actor with enough expertise to bring all these el-ements together and translate them into dramatic art.

I encourage students to comment on each other's work if they have constructive criticism. Praise, of course, is welcome as long as it's accurate, but I hold a tight rein on these ex-changes. A performer's ego is easily bruised, and I monitor what he or she hears, not just from fellow students, but also from the teacher. Actors always want to hear how wonderful their acting is, and I have to tactfully break the news that they aren't Tom Hanks or Meryl Streep yet, without destroying their self-confidence. Diplomacy is almost synonymous with healthy collaboration, as essential as mutual respect. All stu-dents learn better and grow faster when they are respected as members of the team.

The emphasis, however, has to be on each student's progress in learning the Process. Ultimately, an ideal team is composed of experts at what they do individually. The goal is to go into one's deepest personal truth and to express that uniqueness in performance. Our way of working not only en-courages self-expression, but demands it.

The Process is valuable mainly because it's a guidance sys-tem meant to teach the fundamentals of performance art. It is designed not to confine performers, but to free their natural instincts. Nothing in the training received imposes a theoretical straitjacket after graduation from the workshop. I tell my students that I cannot teach them how to be creative; I can only help them remove the barriers that are in the way and show them how to do what, on some level, they already know how to do. That is, CREATE. Which means anything they want to create—a performance, a career, an Oscar, you name it—they *can* create. My biggest problem, I must tell you, is to get them to believe it themselves.

Nobody, including the teacher, can travel with a student into the zone. A teacher guides, encourages, and supports while students learn their craft—then releases them to find transcendent art on their own. The training gives Zen artists the tools of the trade. How they employ those tools as professionals in the creation of a performance is up to them. If the Process being learned becomes their own, it will serve them well throughout their entire careers.

The Mechanics of Creativity®

The Unconscious Actor is, for better or worse, my alter-ego. All the bits and pieces of energy, the ideas, prejudices, talents, interests, passions, strengths and weaknesses—in fact, all the myriad influences which I've listed throughout the book—are in his genes. The Process is a compendium of all the useful information acquired over the decades I've spent in show business.

Though I made a living in the drama, I have always had three other abiding interests: metaphysics, how we humans turn mind into matter, and gardening. Unconscious acting incorporates the lessons learned from all three pursuits. The more I studied metaphysics, the more I understood the creative process; the more I investigated the relationship between the invisible and visible worlds, the better I grew things in the garden. I came to the realization that forces are at work, forces we cannot see or even fully understand which we can harness to create a better life, a more artistic performance, a greener garden. There are laws of creativity, and students in my workshop learn about these laws at the same time they learn how to act.

If we break down the Process into its constituent parts, we are talking about defining what I like to call *the mechanics of creativity*. Not a vague set of ideas about acting nor some mumbo-jumbo about becoming artists, but a down-to-earth, practical, scientific naming of parts—a study of how to create a role, a performance, a career. We wouldn't entrust our cars to a mechanic who didn't know how to take apart an internal combustion engine and put it back together again, because we know full well we'll end up walking to work.

The same rules apply in the acting profession. We must know how to take our actor's engine apart and put it back together with accuracy and efficiency, not some of the time but all of the time. To do that we have to know the laws, absorb the principles, and master the mechanics of creativity.

I'm fully aware that dissecting human consciousness and assigning name tags to different mental functions is a challenging enterprise. Unfortunately, there is no owner's manual available to the vast creative machinery in the greater Self. Creativity cannot be disassembled piece by piece like a Leggo set nor can the ability to turn mind-stuff (or formless psychic energy) into matter be reduced to a simple formula. Still, to teach my Process there is no alternative but to take the risk and attempt to distinguish the indistinguishable.

The First Principle: *Unconscious acting is a mystical discipline.* Students enrolled in my workshop are, whether they realize it or not, Zen artists in training. I don't keep this a secret. The two textbooks I recommend are *The Mystic in the Theatre* and *Zen in the Art of Archery.* Sometimes a new student buys both books and reads them avidly, and sometimes the assignment is ignored, which is a pretty good indication of how much interest there is in becoming an unconscious actor.

Mystic. Most Westerners, including new students, are

leery of that word. Our Yankee ambivalence about mystics and mysticism is documented by my American Heritage Dictionary: *Mysticism* is "A spiritual discipline aiming at direct union or communion with ultimate reality or God through deep meditation or trancelike contemplation"; or "Vague and groundless speculation." Thus, a mystic is either on speaking terms with God or full of hot air. The vast majority of acting teachers I've known over the years would be skeptics; seeing acting as a spiritual discipline would be too high-minded, not practical enough, not based in factual reality.

My answer is, "Reality is in the eye of the beholder." What is real to an investment banker is hardly real to a Zen Master. If one chooses to rely on one's senses as the only source of data, if one's deity is logic and deductive reasoning, then the external world is a product of the conscious mind, nothing more.

My experience dictates a totally different set of facts. As I see it, we humans are tuned into a universal consciousness, and to accept this assumption is a prerequisite for optimal creativity. We are each individual expressions of Mind on the superconscious level; Infinite Intelligence, Source, Nature, First Principle, the Force, It, or Tinkerbell—it makes no difference what we name this limitless Mind, it is at the spiritual core of our identity as human beings.

Since we're also earthbound creatures, we exist in more than two dimensions simultaneously, though how many more none of us knows for sure. Maybe Jesus knew, the Buddha, Chuang Tzu—I can't say. But I do know that all of this supra-physical experience is beyond the realm of analytical thought. As Stanislavsky said, "Ninety percent of our being is un-conscious." Ninety percent! To relegate our creativity to the ten percent that is the conscious mind would deprive us of the most richly endowed source of our being.

It's axiomatic that mystical artists must be willing to give up the familiarity of the known and, like Columbus, sail off towards the Indies without a clue as to whether or not they will fall off the earth or find the riches of the East. To create is to discover, and that means we have to leave the safe harbor and venture out onto an expansive ocean that is unfamiliar territory, to venture where we've never been before.

Be brave, I tell my students. You are all part of a universal dynamic, pungent flavors in a cosmic soup so rich, spiritually nutritious, and creatively satisfying that to push yourselves away from the table before you taste it is self-deprivation. Dig your spoon in, cool it with a breath or two, then take a mouthful and swallow. You'll never regret it.

The Second Principle: *Universal Mind and individual mind are partners in creativity.* Individual or conscious mind is the ego-self that distinguishes this from that, life from death, good from bad, yin from yang, past from future, and so on. It is this ego-self that is focused in the world outside of ourselves; it is this ego-self that thinks, that conceives limitation, distinctness. Thought parses and separates universal Mind into multiple forms that we use to communicate with each other in the time/space continuum. The essence of inspired creativity, if you will, is combining our higher and lower selves, chopping up formlessness into matter, and actualizing the material world.

Conscious thought concretizes the intangible and imprints itself on energy as form: sentences, molecules, babies, mathematical equations, rocks, symphonies, clouds, the Lincoln Memorial, you and me. Instead of mind-stuff, form is architectural stuff; it has a kind of stable continuity in time and space that is *in*formed by pure energy. Consequently, the structure, pattern, or design of any work of art is its form.

As I've said previously, the hermit has little use for forms, but mystical artists must create them to communicate with their fellow humans. Using structural patterns, the creative mystic bridges the abyss of separateness and shares deepest fancies and feelings with the audience. At the highest level, the mystical artist's universal Mind is having a transcendent conversation with the audience, a transaction that lifts them both into another sphere. Thus, an unconscious actor is communicating on two levels, expressing universal Mind and individual truth at the same moment. Glenn Close describes it this way: "I think that acting is basically setting up energy fields. I always think of characters as kind of disturbing molecules in a certain way. And that's what, for some strange reason, projects. It carries through the air to the audience, and it's all mental energy. It's no different in theater than in films. The luxury of theater is that you have a live audience and you feel the exchange."

The Third Principle: *The foundation of unconscious acting is awareness.* The fact is, all creativity begins and ends with awareness. Everything. I define *awareness* as "the nonjudgmental, choiceless observation of what is." No judgment or choice, no conscious mind. No conscious mind, no thought. No thought, no control. Awareness is another term for the greater Self, an expression of our beingness. Not ours really, this beingness, but a shared connection with all creation. Committing to total awareness suggests that we are ready to surrender completely to "what is," giving up any need to have "what is" any other way. Being aware is the jumping-off place for unconscious acting, and, without awareness, budding Zen artists are lost in a maze of predetermined ideas, thoughts, controls, limits, and boundaries. They can never be free.

Ultimately, choice, a function of the actor's conscious thinking mind, presumes awareness. No awareness of an alternative line of thinking, an alternative course of action, means no choice is possible; there would be no alternatives to choose between. As we shall see, one who has mastered the mechanics of creativity must make a series of choices from the moment he or she begins to construct a form. Informed choice-making depends on peripheral awareness extending in all directions to infinity. Awareness presents an unconscious actor with a canvas containing numberless possibilities, an inexhaustible source of information that never runs dry. This quantum field, however, is completely useless if we refuse to acknowledge its existence and deprive ourselves of the data it contains. The most sophisticated computer cannot compete with an aware human being, but we have to learn how to program the software, to perfect the mechanics, or we're always wondering why the psychic equipment that is so impeccably designed fails when we need it the most.

The Fourth Principle: *The Unconscious Actor lives and creates in the now.* To the mystic the present moment is all there is. The past is over, the future is not yet. The merely conscious actor, addicted to thought, is trapped in memory, which means imprisonment in the known; the Zen artist embraces the unknown, realizing that the known is always old, a lifeless form devoid of living substance. The known is a reminder of a previous reality that has no vitality here and now. And, worse than that, the known is forever boring and redundant.

The Unconscious Actor functions in the present moment, preferring a state of discovery in the unknown to a meaningless repetition of the past. He or she resides comfortably, effortlessly, in a limitless sphere where *anything* is creatable. Without the limitations imposed by thought, universal Mind is unbounded, ever-expanding, realizing a variety of forms in a cascading rush of energy. That's why enlightened performance begins in the actor's unconscious.

I like to say that the actors I want to train are out of their minds. They have an appetite for being out of control, in full command. They understand that the knowing, thinking, judging ego-mind is forever imposing "shoulds" on the spontaneous expression of the greater Self. "Should" is one of the most dangerous words in the language because it is so subtly, deceptively tyrannical. Conscious control is to be resisted in whatever guise it appears. My students soon learn that when the creative flow accelerates, the thinker or controller instantly hits the brakes. Unless the actor is able to assume command from a higher vantage point, he or she will chug-chug along the highway of creativity, one foot on the gas pedal and one foot on the brakes, making little progress and always yearning for a smoother ride.

In the command center, awareness is eternally in charge. I'm convinced that the primary struggle facing every performance artist results from an inability to function from this command center in harmony with the thinking mind; from this vantage point, performance is now or never. The conscious mind, on the other hand, continually hangs on to the past or projects into the future, compulsively attached to another time and place. On a conscious level, everything "takes time," an obedient concession to the demands of the time/space continuum, but true unconscious performance is only possible in the now. We don't need a rocket scientist or a parapsychologist to tell us why there is often a glitch in our performance art.

In *A Dream of Passion*, Strasberg says of the actor: "Proper control of his energy is a primary requirement. . . . I am only concerned with the conscious control of faculties which in other arts can and do work unconsciously or sporadically." And again, "The whole point of the emotional-memory exercise is to establish control over emotional expression." These words reflect a concern that is at the core of all old-fashioned methodologies. I believe this compulsion to "control" is a result of Strasberg's distrust of any form of superconscious input in acting; he relied on two-dimensional training stressing control, control, and more control. Denying a higher universal Mind left him no recourse; unlike Stanislavsky, Strasberg could never conceive of a command center wherein the actor easily supervises the creative process from a place of higher consciousness.

The Fifth Principle: *The primary source of all creativity is imagination.* Located deep in the unconscious, the imagination is the cornucopia of artistic expression. A fountain of images, spontaneous ideas and story lines, it is the source of every artist's greatest achievements. Imagination is the mechanism we use to dream (asleep or awake), to fantasize, to fictionalize, to mythologize, to dramatize and most assuredly, to create a performance. We are all born with an active imagination, and we use it fully and spontaneously when we're children, but something happens on the way to adulthood that robs us of this God-given faculty. Our thinking minds take control of our lives.

As kids, we see fairies, ghosts, goblins, and boogiemen, but the adults who raise us tell us that all those fantasies we love are only figments of our imaginations. We are taught to judge our spontaneous creativity negatively; it's not realistic to live in a fairyland, it's not healthy to have a relationship with a pretend creature; we have to grow up and live in a so-called real world. (How could actors ever play scenes with each other if they're not comfortable with pretending?)

As we grow up we're taught to be reasonable, rational, to think logically, and to absorb the "facts" the educational system has decided we must learn, or we fail. The bottom line is that our society trains its children *not* to be spontaneous, *not* to fantasize, *not* to trust their most precious gift—their imaginations. Instead, they're taught to function within a thought box, to distrust their unconscious, to shut down their spontaneity—in effect, to stop being creative.

Having taught hundreds of our citizens young and old, I

can tell you the biggest hurdle I have to overcome is the inability of student actors to use their imaginations. Notwithstanding all the heartaches and problems of growing up as a child actor, I was never discouraged when it came to using my own. Every director I worked with praised my natural ability to fantasize, and that's the main reason they advised my mother to never sign me up for acting lessons. If I could, I would teach all the students in my workshop to use their imaginations the way I did when I was a kid. But that's impossible. All I can do is remind them that somewhere inside each of them is their childlike gift for fantasizing and encourage them to bring it back into their lives as they learn to become unconscious actors.

The Sixth Principle: *Emotion is the language of the heart.* Emotion supplies the fuel which drives our creativity—the more high octane the better. How we *feel* about what we're creating in our lives is infinitely more important than what we *think* about it. Feelings are hot, dynamic, uncontrollable; thinking is cold, calculating, always measuring and judging emotion like a stern parent. The conscious, analytical mind can't help but distrust an open heart.

Sharing heartfelt energy with one another comes naturally to *Homo sapiens*. Observing small children at play, it becomes obvious that we are born expressing our feelings as highly-charged, emotional beings. A two-year-old child doesn't need training to learn how to access his or her emotional life, he or she does so constantly, so strenuously that adults have trouble keeping pace. Children haven't yet learned to censor themselves, to stop and think before they express an impulse, to deny their feelings, to decide whether or not instinctive behavior is acceptable to the adults that tower over them. They are free to be who they are and to explore their world joyfully, playfully, spontaneously. They're having a good time and don't care who know it.

Unfortunately, for most children the romp doesn't last very long. For some repressive parents, socialization begins in the cradle. If baby cries and makes mommy and daddy frown, baby soon learns to adjust its behavior accordingly. Crying is bad, cooing is good. Cooing makes mommy and daddy smile. This means that the two most important authority figures in baby's environment are pleased and will take care of baby, which equates with survival.

This is good data for staying alive in an aberrant society. But cooing when one wants to cry, at any age, isn't conducive to employing the language of the heart as a performance artist. If one has been trained since childhood to feel one thing and express another to avoid unwanted feedback, emotional energy has been suppressed, stuffed back inside, or worst of all, its joyful expression has dried up altogether. Once we learn to stop and think, to judge the acceptability or unacceptability of our impulses, emotional spontaneity is well-nigh impossible. Get the barriers out of the way and feelings will flow. It's as simple as that.

The Seventh Principle: *The voice of our creativity is intuition.* *Intuition* is defined as "the act or faculty of knowing without the use of rational processes; immediate cognition." If our creativity had a voice, it would sound like intuition. The more aware we are, the louder this voice which speaks to us with a vocabulary all its own: images, feelings, ideas, impulses to do things, to say things, guidance from the greater Self that generates everything we do as people and as artists.

Ralph Waldo Emerson saw intuitive urges as resembling "those little birds alighting on the window sill that must be noticed immediately or they fly away forever." Intuition is always immediate. Impulses are always now. If we have an impulse and we're not aware of it, it "flies away," never to return. We act on an impulse when we hear it and feel it or we don't act on it at all; we can honor the next impulse, but the one we ignore is gone forever.

I exhort my students: trust your intuition. That's a tall order for the hardcore thinkers and analyzers among them who are often frightened of the unexamined, unwanted information coming up from their inner selves. But trust intuition they must, and when they do so they are endowed with a bold, inventive tool that enhances their capacity to create performance art a hundred fold.

These seven principles are the cornerstone of the curriculum I teach in the workshop. To reiterate:

1. *Unconscious acting is a mystical discipline.*
2. *Universal Mind and individual mind are partners in creativity.*
3. *The foundation of unconscious acting is awareness.*
4. *The Unconscious Actor lives and creates in the now.*
5. *The primary source of all creativity is imagination.*

6. *Emotion is the language of the heart.*
7. *The voice of our creativity is intuition.*

Unquestionably they result from the metaphysical bias underpinning all my work in the drama business, a bias that infuses everything I do as a teacher. The value of unconscious acting rests on the validity of these premises, and I make no apology for "spiritualizing" performance art or for my attempts to convince each of my students to get on board.

Understand, though, that I never suggest an aspiring unconscious actor become part of a cult, join a sect, or adopt any theological position. A student doesn't have to believe in anything. There's no requirement to accept a Heavenly Father, seek nirvana, or follow a particular philosophy of life. Zen artistry does not require the novice to meditate, pray, chant, fast, sleep on a straw mattress, or bathe in the Ganges. There's no morality involved, no code of ethics to follow, nor any promise of spiritual redemption.

Students don't even have to believe in the Process; they are only asked to do it. All that's required is a commitment to being the best performing artist that he or she can by doing the work and finding out where the training leads. It's not to become someone you're "supposed" to be, but to be who you really are every time you're on your feet in performance. I like William Hurt's slant on the subject: "Acting is about telling the truth. And it's an adventure. It isn't about what I know before I do it. It's about what I can discover while it's happening."

I'm disconcerted by my dependence on words to describe the mechanics of creativity in action. Each of us experiences the mechanics I'm writing about, but most often we don't know *how* we do what we do because the machinery is invisibly tucked away inside the Bodymind. So I've invented a visual aid to help us understand what's going on in the inner self when we're creating a performance.

Keep in mind we're not machines like a PC, a Rolls Royce, or a vacuum cleaner. We humans are *gestalts*, a physical and psychological "configuration or pattern so unified as a whole that its properties cannot be derived from its parts." A gestalt is a kind of living organism, a field of energy which defies disassembly. I am undeterred. The mechanics of creativity subdivides the human creative act into its essential components; in the diagram on page 187, I isolate each one while we study its function before re-merging them in the safety of the gestalt. In my view, this one-page snapshot illustrates the gestation of all performance art.

I advise the interested reader to study the illustration carefully then refer to it when it's helpful as I describe in more detail each unit of the mechanics, how they are interrelated, and how they each contribute to the progressive nature of all creativity:

A.   The actor's higher consciousness (alias his or her awareness, command center, or field of pure potentiality) makes Zen artists who they are, living and creating in the now. Let's reduce this field of spiritual energy to one four-letter word: *soul*.

B. Inspiration originates in the soul. To inspire means "to arouse by divine influence . . . , to breathe life into. . . ." This breath of life I call a *creative impulse*; it is the origin of a brand new reality in time and space. Like a seed, this will sprout in the rich, invisible soil of *unconsciousness*, nurtured by the creator in much the same way an unborn child is sustained in a mother's womb. Inspiration is a gift from the soul and arrives at the doorstep of conscious awareness uninvited. The performance artist can send an invitation by making all the preparations (practicing one's craft). He or she can unlock the front door and put down a welcome mat but then must be a patient host while waiting for the guests to arrive. Inspirational impulses cannot be forced to show up under pressure; they come when they're good and ready. A creative impulse carries an electromagnetic charge which engages the *imagination*, instantly producing *images* that in turn stimulate a response from the emotional reservoir: the *heart*. *Emotion* and images, interacting, generate the dreamlike scenarios which are the foundation of performance art. It's as though imagination is the picture-maker of the soul, while feelings supply the vital energy necessary for bringing the pictures to life. All of this happens, of course, below the threshold of the *conscious mind*.

C. *Intuition* is the driving force which spontaneously brings these emotionally enriched images into conscious awareness. When the artist imagines boldly and feels deeply, a combustible dynamic occurs that condenses this flow of intuitive energy into a thought form, a conception, a new thing.

D. I term this new thing, this new psychological event, an *idea*. An idea is like a visible seedling which is continuously being nourished by vivid imagery and fervent feelings flowing from the unconscious, representing the creative impulse as it begins to take shape in material form.

E. An idea stimulates thought for the first time in the conscious mind. Thought introduces analysis to the process, as well as logic, experimentation (trial and error), and deductive reasoning. Analytical thought, interacting with intuition, moves the idea further away from abstraction and closer to the solidity of matter.

F. The more the idea takes shape mentally, the more the imagination and the heart kick in to produce an increasingly energetic force which brings the idea to fruition. Thus, a potent combination of image, emotion, and thought moves the idea forward towards complete manifestation.

G. The final stage in this evolution depends on the magic of *belief* and the relentless power of the human *will*. Belief erases all doubt, as repeated *affirmation* reinforces the desired outcome; will, on the other hand, is the apparatus by which the creator makes a *decision*. There must be an unwavering finality about this decision. No matter how long it takes or what obstacles

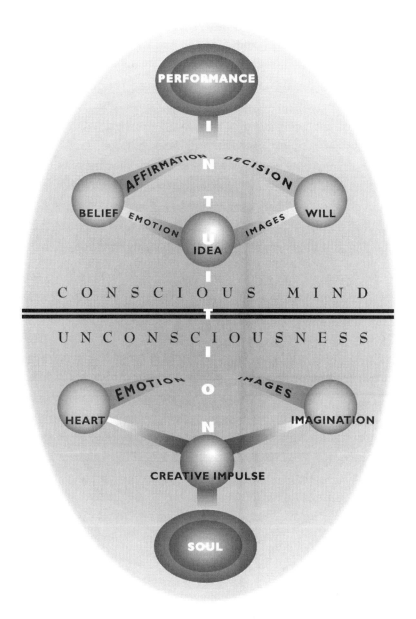

have to be overcome, decisiveness reigns in the mechanics of creativity.

H. *Performance* excellence is not a once-in-a-while accident for those who have mastered the mechanics of creativity, it is a foregone conclusion. Of course, all of this information is useless if the performer simply learns how the mechanics work but does not employ them on a regular basis. There are no short cuts. Even though this creative machinery is inherent in one's humanity, the various functions described above should be isolated, worked on individually, and re-integrated into the mosaic of performance art.

When the Zen artist has harnessed his or her life force and perfected the mechanics of creativity, an enhanced current of electromagnetism is available for creating any new reality: an actor's performance, a playwright's script, a director's film, a composer's symphony, a choreographer's ballet, a painter's canvas, a sculptor's statue, an architect's museum. As psychic energy is transformed into matter and original ideas are actualized, an artist transcends the commonplace and demonstrates the awesome creative power of the human spirit.

Since this book focuses on acting, a performance art that is too little respected in the drama business, the rest of this chapter offers the interested reader a condensation of the course of study I teach in my workshop. Please remember, my passion is teaching the actor's *ART*. As I think I've already made clear, in my view, artistry is an unrealistic expectation if the student actor is not well grounded in craftsmanship.

One doesn't learn the craft by reading about it, theorizing about it, or talking about it, but by doing it; the doing is what counts. Nonetheless, the words on the following pages are an earnest attempt to put the Process I teach on paper for the interested reader. Be alert and read between the lines. As I repeat, ad infinitum, what's really going on is in the white part of the paper.

Exercises: Flow

After decades of acting with more actors than I could ever count—some good, some not so good—I've come to the conclusion that there is "head" acting and there is "heart" acting, and they are rarely part of the same package. The head actor is usually a technician, a skilled craftsman, but there's always something missing in the work. The heart actor feels more than thinks, relies on instincts, is hit or miss in performance, and when it doesn't happen the way he or she would like it to happen, always wonders why.

This is the result of the training actors have received in this country for almost a hundred years. It's all so ingrained that by now we've come to accept this dichotomy as a fact of life, or worse, a problem without a solution. And possibly that's been true . . . until now. The Process I've been developing all these years is an antidote to either/or acting: unconscious actors think with their heads, feel with their hearts, and are *whole* Zen artists in performance.

Starting with the most basic exercises we do in the workshop, the student learns how to plumb the depths of unconsciousness and acknowledge the inner Self as the source of creativity. All the exercises are, as they have always been, my way of putting Stanislavsky's eloquent words into action. For him, acting was "movement from the soul to the body, from the centre to the periphery, from the internal to the external, from emotional experience to physical embodiment." Connecting the "internal to the external," an integrated actor's body and voice is the goal of the more than one hundred exercises I've experimented with over the last thirty years.

In his marvelous little handbook, *Stanislavski for Beginners*, David Allen once more quotes the master: "Alas for the actor if there is a split between body and soul, between feelings and words, between internal and external action and movements. Alas, if the actor's physical instruments falsify and distort the expression of feelings. It is like a melody played on an instrument which is out of tune."

The great Duse herself spent years "tuning the instrument." A tuned actor, in my Process, has activated the unconscious and embraced "the line of intuition of feelings," as Stanislavsky termed it, which "absorbs into itself all the other lines, and grasps all the spiritual and physical contents of the role and the play." Unprompted images from the imagination coupled with the emotional colors that enhance them, flowing intuitively through the student's body and voice, become the building blocks which will someday be used to construct a performance.

A concert pianist who doesn't have his piano tuned would never dare play a concerto in public. Likewise, a student who isn't diligently tuning his or her instrument is not ready to tackle a role in scene study. A teacher who ignores this requirement and allows an unprepared neophyte to plunge into Ophelia, Forrest Gump, or Uncle Vanya has failed the student and is responsible for potentially disastrous results.

The dozens of exercises I employ to tune each student's instrument may be based on Stanislavskian principles, but they are essentially my creation, representing my point of view about Zen artistry in the 21st century. What I have understood of the System, I have applied in my teaching, reflecting the challenges I encountered as a professional actor. What I teach my students is a result of the problem-solving I did on my own over the years.

In creating the exercises, I have pirated ideas from fellow actors, picked up a new slant here and there from a favorite director, and borrowed from the methodologies I respected, such as the training at the American Mime Theater, improv techniques I learned from Viola Spolin's *Improvisation for the Theatre*, and lessons in the value of physical imagery contributed by Michael Chekhov in *To the Actor*. Once in a while an exercise has been spontaneously generated while I'm working with students as I help them understand some aspect of the Process.

We do solo exercises, two actor exercises, multiple actor exercises, character exercises, improvs of all kinds—mostly nonverbal or sometimes using gibberish—even exercises that help students penetrate the psychological barriers unwittingly erected between themselves and their classmates. But each exercise reinforces the same theme, designed to help a student connect the intuitive flow of energy to body and voice as he or she begins to translate the mechanics of creativity into performance art.

Since, according to the seven principles at the heart of those mechanics, all creativity originates as a spiritual impulse from the soul, in my exercises we're all adventurers in the mystical world of Stanislavsky's superconscious. I try never to confuse my students with theoretical discussions about metaphysics. I make it clear that actors don't have to become metaphysicians; they only have to be who they really are and leave the theorizing to me.

Now and then I allude to Principles One and Two, but mainly we focus on the last five principles as I talk each exercise class through the *Prep*. Let me set the scene. We're in Studio D where there's plenty of space to move around. All the students are on their feet, breathing evenly and deeply, centering themselves. I ask them to stretch and become more mentally alert; while they are stretching they should be able to locate the life energies that are stuck in their bodies. "Don't analyze what's there," I advise them, "or why it's locked up in that area of your body. Just be aware of it."

By so doing, I have introduced the third principle and the foundation for all the exercise work: *awareness*. I often remind them awareness is "the nonjudgmental, choiceless observation of what is." Amazingly, even some of my longtime students start to do the exercises in their heads, somewhere in the past or the future where they've spent most of the day before they came to class. It's virtually impossible for an actor—any actor, skilled or unskilled—to live everyday life in a hazy state of consciousness and suddenly turn on awareness as though flipping on a light switch.

Because teachers in this country have been doing concentration exercises for so long, I think it's important for me to distinguish the significant difference between my concept of awareness, which is inclusive and embraces all data from the inner and outer environment, and what most students are doing when they "concentrate," which excludes unwanted information that they assume doesn't belong inside the focal point of their attention. Concentration is a mind game; it excludes. Awareness is 360 degrees—all encompassing, reaching out to and embracing every atom in the field. Concentration constructs fences around consciousness; awareness is expansive, has no boundaries, permeates all experience. The aware performing artist always allows and includes what is, moment to moment, in his or her art.

Being aware is being in full command. Years ago I acted with that wonderfully zany comedienne, Vivian Vance [Lucille Ball's sidekick in *I Love Lucy*], in Neil Simon's *Barefoot in the Park*. After a performance one night I said, "Did you notice that guy asleep in the second row during the last scene?"

She seemed surprised, "You mean you see what's going on in the audience?"

"How can I help it, they're sitting right there in front of me. Don't you?"

"Oh, no," she replied, "I'd be distracted if I acknowledged them. When I'm concentrating, I pretend they're not there."

This somehow worked for Vivian in her long, successful career. But I would never recommend that a student actor pretend that the audience isn't there. I believe the first thing performers should do when they walk on stage is go into the auditorium psychically and invite everyone out there to come to them. Form a psychic bond, as Glenn Close does, and let the audience become the other character in the scene, extending one's awareness to the back wall of the theater.

I actually learned about the difference between awareness

and concentration in the movies. There's an unwritten law that an actor never looks directly into the lens; it's a big no-no. On the other hand, awareness of the camera is a staple of good film acting. I came to view the camera as an all-seeing eye, remarkably uncritical, lovingly and faithfully recording every nuance of my performance. Never would I ignore the camera, which would be tantamount to pretending my best friend wasn't there. As a kid actor the camera seemed to love me, and I had no trouble loving it back.

Self-awareness, then, is of paramount importance in all the exercises, but students also learn never to isolate themselves from their classmates in the Prep. The class is a replica of every professional actors' workplace—a field of energy where the actor is a cog in a larger whole, the *ensemble*. Acting is a communal art. Gymnasts, stand-up comics and public speakers are solitary performers, but for an actor, inevitably a member of a cast, awareness of self must be extended to awareness of all the other selves in the group, wherein everyone is creating a common dynamic. This communal awareness breeds mutual togetherness, trust, and support.

In a cast one narcissistic actor with an inflated ego can spoil the entire project. A case in point: when I was working for Norman Lear, I picked up a copy of the *Los Angeles Times* one morning and saw a front page story about a star of one of his company's top ten shows having unexpectedly left the program. When I got to the studio, I had an early meeting with Lear and asked him what had happened.

"I fired him," he said.

"But, Norman, his character is like a rudder on that show."

He smiled. "Not any more. He got the big head, couldn't get along with anybody. We're writing him out."

"Won't that hurt the show?"

"Not as much as his continued presence would hurt it week to week. When a cast is together for a season, it's a family. One dysfunctional member of the family makes the whole family dysfunctional. I can't afford to have that happen on one of my shows."

And that was that. One of the biggest stars on television was not as indispensable as he thought he was. I emphasize this when we start the Prep. "Be aware," I tell them, "not only of what's going on in you but in each of your classmates, too. Be sure you're working in harmony with each other. If you're out of sync, it's a problem." As in a cast of professional actors, the kinetic energy of the students is fluid, ever changing, intensely interactive, which makes it a microcosm of the real world out there in the acting business.

Having established the primacy of awareness in the Prep, we move on to activate the next principle, which asserts *awareness only exists in the now.* I ask my students to stop thinking about what's happening now, analyzing why it's happening, or deciding how it should go in the next moment. Let the moment be what it is, and never try to make it what they think it ought to be.

Obviously, this means letting go of conscious control. And thought. In this culture, accustomed as we are to thinking our way through life, we don't know what it's like *not* to think. Joseph Chilton Pearce calls the plague that pervades so much of our waking consciousness "roof brain chatter." The *ya-da-ya-da-ya-da* inside our skulls never shuts up, but if we're going to do the exercises well, we have to find a way to turn the chatter off. This takes practice, and before anything else, we have to become aware of when we're thinking and when we're not thinking—not just while in class, but every day.

In order to learn how to be fully aware in the present moment, I advise my students (as well as the interested reader) to spend as much time as possible in conscious breathing:

> *Sit by yourself . . . clear your mind as best you can . . . breathe in deeply to a slow count of four or five . . . give your full attention to the brief pause after inhalation before you let the breath out . . . exhale . . . then pause again to rest in the brief space that occurs automatically before you inhale again . . . this is the best opportunity you will have to visit your deeply spiritual Self which is always in the now.*

Yogis have been breathing to expand their consciousness for centuries. We in the West tend to take breathing for granted. We ignore the potential for personal growth that automatically occurs every two or three seconds, with every inhalation and exhalation. We breathe to live, we breathe to strengthen our Bodyminds, but if we can breathe with a more enlightened, heightened awareness, a marvelous, more intense oxygenation of our creative mechanics can result.

At this point in the Prep, the students have left the superficial level of consciousness where they live most of their
everyday lives and have reached down into deeper regions of
themselves, making contact with the source of their creativity. They become more fully aware and appreciative of the
living energy that continually vitalizes their entire beings; I
call this energy *life force*.

Scientists are suggesting that all energy vibrates on certain
identifiable frequencies, and this animating flow is no exception. I've found that under guidance, my students are able to
distinguish three components of this flowing energy when we
start to work with it at the beginning of each Prep—light,
sound and emotion:

> *First, close your eyes, bringing your awareness to the cen-
> ter of yourself and imagize a bright, white light that
> slowly, gradually spreads throughout your being, allow-
> ing a distinct, personal vibrating frequency to cause your
> body to pulsate with movement.*
>
> *Second, return your focus to the solar plexus while
> moving your body, and then add the sound of your unique
> personal frequency, opening up the voice with the vowel
> "AAAHHHH" as you continue to pulsate with movement.*
>
> *Third, add another vibration by allowing the feel-
> ings that spontaneously accompany your flowing energy
> to pulsate with the frequencies of light and sound
> through the voice and the body in full, free-flowing
> sound and movement.*

My students' ability to sustain each frequency—distinct, yet blended in one continuing expression of individual and communal life force—is truly amazing. The dedicated ones confirm that they are able to distinguish the frequencies of light, sound, and feelings as they are flowing intuitively through their voices and bodies. They have taught me how much actors are capable of expanding their awareness by doing the exercises on a regular basis.

Once the student's life force is connected to voice and body, we add to the mix a specific, on-the-feet investigation of the last three of the principles concerning imagination, emotion, and intuition. Often I'll start the work on imagination by asking the students to stretch as a character they've been working on, always extending it as far as they can into their bodies. Once in a while, we'll practice creating a spontaneous character in the moment:

> Go deep into yourself and show me a picture of who you are right now. Next, allow your life energy to flow fully through this picture of yourself as a character, holding the form in your face and body while you move with flexibility. Then, walk with your character while keeping the energy flowing through it.

This exercise effectively circumvents the conscious mind and engages the actor's imagination. Doing this well, the students learn how to sustain a fixed, concrete image in their bodies. I'll often have them drop the character, allow their own energy to move the body as themselves, and then go back to the character, not once, not twice, but three or four times, back and forth, until there's as much ease and speed in the transformation as possible.

There are several reasons why this is part of the lesson plan when a student is being introduced to unconscious acting. First and foremost, acting is not about becoming someone else in front of an audience or a camera. Uninformed actors talk about "the character" as if there were some objective reality outside of themselves that they were planning to fit into. There is no "the character," I remind them, there is only you, skillfully using yourself in such a way that you *suggest* you are another person or "the character" based on the blueprint the author has given you in the script.

I can't stress enough that, on stage or in front of a camera, an unconscious actor doesn't play scenes with other characters—a writer's abstractions—but with a vital, ever-changing human being with whom he or she has to stay in contact; there must be an organic, real exchange of energy between actors in performance. This truth is axiomatic in our Process: actors don't play scenes between an *idea* of who they are supposed to be and an *idea* of who their scene partner is supposed to be, but with each other's living, breathing reality. I'll describe how one learns to do this when we get to scene study. For now, we're setting the stage for the technique of characterization in the exercises.

Someone quoted Uta Hagen as saying, "You go up there and talk about yourself, but what the hell, use his words." I love that quote, and I use it all the time in the workshop. A student actor is usually trying to become somebody else in a role, so I nip that tendency in the bud in the exercises. "It's *your* body and voice I want to access in the Prep, *your* imagination, *your* deepest truth, not some idea of yourself, or some idea of a character that doesn't originate in *your* soul. Acting is all about being you in a more intensely personal way, and I want that you surfacing at the beginning of class."

The fact is, most inexperienced actors start *thinking* about a role before they elicit an imaginative response to the author's words. My advice is connect your life force to your own body and voice, re-awaken your imagination, and let the character come alive in your body before you do any other work on characterization. Perhaps start with something physical; I read that Dustin Hoffman spent months trying out different limps before he found just the right one for his peerless performance of Ratzo Rizzo in *Midnight Cowboy*; for *Tootsie*, he spent weeks walking around New York City in high heels and a dress, finding the soap opera actress that would transform him into an hysterically funny female character in front of the camera.

Ultimately, I'm aiming at improving every student's ability to fantasize and invent images, inhaling the fumes of fancy until they become intoxicated with the invaluable contribution their imaginations will make to artistic creation. If one's picture-maker in the unconscious is asleep or slovenly inactive, it needs a shot of adrenalin to wake it up. When a slumbering imagination hasn't been awakened, it's impossible to create a performance that anyone wants to watch or listen to; the acting will always be stale, stiff, and robotic.

Moreover, once the imagination is functioning, so much

depends on the performing artist's ability to tangibilize the images being created. A student burdened with a sluggish, unexpressive body has work to do. From my standpoint, helping an actor embody the stream of reveries and dreamlike imaginings that arise from the unconscious is one of the main objectives in all the exercises that are done each week.

Painters use a brush and a canvas to convey images, sculptors use a block of marble and a chisel, writers use a pen or a computer, but performing artists have no other creative instrument than the Bodymind. They don't need another one if they are physically connected to, and trust, their imaginations. Deprived of what the dictionary defines as "the power of the mind to form a mental image or concept of something that is not real or present" and the skills necessary to materialize mental images, Zen artistry is out of the question.

As in every other form of communication, "a picture is worth a thousand words." If this is true, and I think it is, acting is directed more at the eye than the ear. Unhappily, while attesting to the need for training the actor's imagination, acting teachers in this country have, in the main, failed to find a workable means of uniting imagery with bodily expression. Michael Chekhov's *psychological gesture* is a valuable way to translate a set of ideas about character into a physicalization, but that's transcribing words or concepts into an image rather than turning spontaneous images into physical forms. Spontaneity being a primary characteristic of the Process, a student must learn to flow images moment to moment through the Bodymind in an ongoing creation of his or her role. Images that can't be pictorialized without prior reflection are of no value to an unconscious actor.

Ideally there should be no lag between a spontaneous image and its expression in physical form. A little boy playing cops 'n robbers doesn't have to rehearse; he just physically acts it out. As we discussed earlier, while growing up we were not only discouraged but often punished for entertaining our imaginings, and as adults we suffer the consequences of this negative programming. With the exercises, I try to help my students become conscious of the problem and find a way to liberate them from the damage done in childhood.

One of my actors, a jazz musician and a literate, intellectual man, was having trouble finding the internal source of his images, and his wooden, unresponsive body was more a liability than an asset when he tried to physicalize them. He asked me how he could get out of his head and stop thinking all the time.

"Do you ever daydream?" I asked him. He gave me a look which implied, "What kind of foolish idea is that?" He said: "You mean, like when I was a little kid? I haven't daydreamed in thirty years."

"Then it's time you did," I told him. "A half hour every day. It won't solve the problem, but it's a start."

I am constantly coaxing my students to go to the place deep inside where their dreams come from and show me what's happening in there, show me what it *looks* like. Deprived of words and sound, actors are forced to use the body to express themselves. They have no choice. Actors really want to use their bodies more imaginatively, and the exercises, starting with the Prep, are the best way I've found to show them how.

Simultaneously, as students revitalize their imaginations, the source of their emotional lives is stimulated, and they learn how to do the Prep with an open heart. The linkage between images and feelings is automatic. We have already gone into the importance of a powerful scenario as a stimulant to emotional response, and vice versa. Nonetheless, images originate in the imagination, while emotions flow from the heart, and though they often work together, hand in glove, they flow through the Bodymind on separate wavelengths. I call attention to that fact in every Prep.

To get my students' emotional lives flowing spontaneously, early on I ask each of them to put into sound and movement what they are feeling:

> *Send whatever emotional colors are coming up right now through your voice and your body, and allow each emotion full expression as it happens. It doesn't matter why you're feeling it or what might have caused these emotional impulses . . . just feel them and express them.*

This sound and movement must be organic, which means connected to something happening inside that reflects the activity of the non-conscious, inner self. The content of this activity is often reflected in emotion. Feelings which flow spontaneously—joy, anger, fear, sadness, calmness, anxiety, frustration, and so forth—are instantly tangible, instantly recognizable, and give students a chance to identify specific changes in their consciousness. Expressing joy, anger, or fear in sound and movement is automatically trusting one's life force and is a device to access the actor's unconscious self. As a by-product, the student is able to release pent-up feelings and bring a greater emotional range to his or her creative process, a plus for any performing artist.

The implicit message is, when you trust your feelings you're telling the truth. Feelings that flow spontaneously are always authentic; if they're of the moment, honest, real— such feelings are never wrong. They can be judged badly by those who enjoy dictating what we're supposed to feel during a social or dramatic event, but the heart is unaffected. If we're coming from the right place, we feel what we feel, and that's the end of that.

Once students get past some of the conditioning they've endured since childhood, they begin to feel the first flush of liberation and can't wait to do the rest of the exercises. Being aware of the ever-changing energy available, they are astonished by the richness, depth, and variety of their emotional lives. Feelings are meant to flow freely, and once the gates of control, locked for so long, are flung open, there's an emotional stampede to get out of the corral.

"Whoa! Slow down!" the startled student's conscious mind cautions the inner self. "I don't mind feeling the upbeat stuff, but all that anger and fear is unappealing. Unacceptable. Besides, I'm revealing too much of who I am to the world out there, and they can use this information against me." This is when I step in with encouragement: "First of all, there's no such thing as positive emotion and negative emotion. Feelings, to paraphrase Shakespeare, are neither good nor bad but thinking makes it so."

It's amazing how afraid we are of our fear, how judgmental we are of our anger, how anxious we are about crying our tears. We've accepted society's rules and blindly obeyed them all our lives. Some emotions are good, and we're encouraged to express them. Some emotions are bad, and even if we feel them, they should never be unveiled in polite society. We are taught that happiness, joy, love, good humor are positive, while anger, fear, sadness, grief are negative and should be swept under the carpet and left there, where they belong, below the surface of respectability.

Suppressing emotional energy is unhealthy for any human being and is a root cause for untold psychological and physical malaise. There are many professions, however, where a placid exterior is encouraged; a CPA's performance may be enhanced by suppressing emotion. In fact, if he or she bursts into tears while doing your income tax, you'd find another accountant. But a performer who can't cry, or get angry, or feel afraid in a dramatic situation is in deep trouble. An actor playing one of the great characters in theatrical literature has to be prepared to feel and express the full range of human emotion. Irrespective of how abnormal, frightening, repugnant, sexually disturbing, ugly or debased, a performing artist must be willing to squeeze any truthful feeling, any emotional color, onto the artistic palette.

My students are encouraged to put all the colors and characteristics they hide from the rest of the world into their exercise work, especially any feelings or personal qualities they're ashamed of. I remind them that anything they can feel, each member of the audience is feeling or has felt before entering the theater. Revealing disowned human energy in a performance resonates like nothing else because the audience instinctively recognizes it, knows the truth of it, and is touched by its revelation. Feel everything you're capable of feeling, I exhort them, and find out how you might want to use your personal emotional truth as an actor. All the unpleasant humanness the average performer refuses to own is what a great performing artist employs to make art universal.

Some students are upset with themselves when unacceptable emotions surface in the exercises. "Why are you concerned," I ask, "What's bothering you?" "I'm so nervous, so scared," they reply. "How can I act when I'm feeling all these terrible feelings?" My answer: welcome them. Embrace the nerves, the fear, the anxiety. When they look at me with a confused stare, I remind them that nobody ever wrote an important piece of drama about people who were happy, relaxed, and mellowed out. Dramatic art is about nervous, frightened, anxious, on-edge people. Good characters are forever in trouble. This goes for comedy as well as tragedy. Alan Arkin says: "In drama, if the toilet doesn't work, you call a plumber. In comedy, it's a matter of life and death!"

That's one of the reasons why, unlike so many American teachers, I never do a relaxation exercise. If I had to wait to be relaxed, I would never have acted in my life. Relaxation to me is lying in bed on Sunday morning reading the *New York Times*. Performing, which demands a huge infusion of life force, bringing up all the richness of one's psychic energy, would be impossible if one were truly relaxed. Forget relaxation. Release. Let go of control and feel what you feel, releasing all of those feelings into your performance. That's a major tenet of unconscious acting.

Of course, it's not always easy to persuade new students that whatever they're feeling at the moment is fine and should flow easily and effortlessly through an exercise. Students with suppressed emotions—usually anger, sadness, or fear—find it difficult to release what they've been holding onto for years. Whatever the feeling, it has been sitting on top of their instruments, building up a head of steam, to the point that when it does come out, there's an explosion of feeling which shocks them, and they immediately shut down again.

I patiently explain that whatever emotion they've been suppressing has acted like a cork in a bottle, and the rest of their emotional life is all backed up behind it. To access all of their feelings, without exception, they have to pull the cork and let them all pour out. I can usually discern what students are most afraid of expressing because it is the first thing to come out when they let go.

Like a genie, emotion that has been bottled up has magical powers once it is released into the exercises. Allowing one's feelings to flow is not the only goal of the exercises, but any technique that isn't being fed by spontaneous feelings is arid, mechanical, predictable. I reject any predetermined emotional content in performance art. Whenever actors are on their feet, doing the exercises or later working with a text, they must be surprised by what they're feeling moment to moment, or they aren't doing what I teach.

The arch enemy of The Unconscious Actor, as should be apparent by now, is anything that hinders, obstructs, or restricts the natural flow of life force through the voice and the body. Liberated energy, which includes images, feelings, ideas, impulses to do things and to say things—flowing first in the exercises and finally through a performance—is the hallmark of unconscious acting.

The "line of intuition of feelings" is the performance artist's most precious source of information. Intuitive impulses from the inner self form the basic building blocks of this art. Flow, intuitive flow, is what the Prep—indeed all of the exercise work—is about. In order to access this flow, the ever-changing energy that is coursing through one's instrument, the actor must respond instantaneously to each impulse as it happens, expressing a series of these impulses with total abandon, first through the body, then the voice. Any physical rigidity strangles an impulse before it is born in movement; fortunately, just learning to flow intuitively releases bodily tension and helps an actor move with greater flexibility. He or she is then ready to bring a well-oiled instrument to the individual exercises.

The work I do with individual actors is an extension of the Prep. I call on one, two, three (or more) actors and explore with them, in a variety of ways, an expansion of the skilled use of flow. The first solo exercise is *Name and Bow*. To the uninitiated, it looks deceptively simple:

> *The student pretends to be all alone on a stage. He or she enters, stands center in front of the class, and introduces him/herself: "My name is (states name)." He/she waits for a long five count, being fully aware of what's going on inside, while at the same time being fully aware of what's happening between him/herself and the class. He/she bows, waits for another five count, remaining fully aware of what's happening, then exits.*

When I call the student back to center stage, I often ask: "What do you think you just did?" New students are almost always confused. They don't think they did much of anything except introduce themselves to their classmates. They are surprised when I tell them they did the most important thing they will ever do in the workshop, that is be fully present in front of an audience, doing nothing more than being in the now.

Moreover, when I add that this is also the most important thing they will ever do as performing artists, they look more puzzled than relieved. It can't be that simple; what about all the skills they have to learn? All the stuff they don't know how to do? I have already cautioned them with as much diplomacy as I can muster during the Name and Bow that they were already "doing" more than enough: pretending not to be scared, covering their nerves with bravado, talking too much, hiding behind a false persona, selling themselves with fake charm, shutting down their life force, and so on. More being and much less doing is the point of the first individual exercise.

Success in the individual exercises depends on students letting go of who they think they are, the person they have always presented to the world, and to be who they really are. I'm encouraging students to first, get in touch with themselves and then, share those selves with each other. That's why, after one or two solo exercises, I add another actor to the mix, and we begin to deal with the art of communication.

The drama is a medium of communication before anything else. Let's face it, most of us don't communicate very well with family and friends. How in the world are we going to communicate effectively with a fellow actor, a director, or an audience unless we have somehow worked out the kinks before we are on a set with Tom Hanks, or on a Broadway stage opening night?

My three rules for optimal communication are:

1. Students must be aware of what's going on inside themselves, moment to moment;
2. Students must be aware of what's going on inside their fellow actor(s), moment to moment;
3. Students must be aware of what's happening because of their interaction with their fellow actor(s) and how that dynamic is changing, moment to moment.

Look at it this way: if I'm aware of my own inner life, but I haven't got a clue about what's happening inside you, how are we going to communicate well? If I'm reading you great, but I don't know where I'm at, what am I going to communicate? And suppose you and I are in touch, on the same vibration, but I'm not aware of the changing dynamic caused by our interaction. If that's the case, ongoing communication is impossible because somewhere along the way I lost contact with the flow.

It matters little how many actors are involved in an exercise since the objective is always the same, students learning to communicate with each other by exchanging living energy in the most effective way. Sometimes the exchange is silent. When two or more actors pick up vibratory alterations in each other's energy fields, they are communicating through means other than the senses:

> *I ask a pair of students to close their eyes and simply feel each other's flow so they can identify what's happening between them without eye contact. At times, they turn their backs to each other, moving only when they become aware that the transmission of their partner's energy is causing the movement.*

There are exercises featuring communication through movement only, then adding sound through the open vowel, "AAAHHHH." Next I'll add a wrinkle that introduces informal verbiage to the exercise:

> *Tell each other in gibberish what's happening between the two of you and how your relationship is affected as you communicate your innermost thoughts and feelings to each other.*

Since gibberish has no identifiable meaning or content, this spontaneous language allows the actor to open up and safely communicate the most intimate, personal truth—thus beginning the transition from pure sound to formal English. From gibberish we go to communication through ultra-simple, predetermined language with each actor speaking in turn: "Rosencrantz/Guildenstern," or "Help me/Help yourself." The goal is to keep the flow of deeply personal energy moving through words that will soon, in scene study, become a dramatist's text.

There's quite a bit of improvisation in the exercises, focused more on the imaginative use of the body than on dialogue; text of any kind is an infrequent guest in the exercise work. I try hard to separate organic sound and a cultivated use of the actor's voice from the interpretive demands made by a script. Most actors, indeed most performers who depend on verbalization to communicate with an audience, are so intent on saying the words a certain way, making the words mean what they're supposed to mean, they forget that the transmission of psychic, feeling energy is what elicits response from a group of spectators. I'll take it a step further; in my view all human interchange is essentially telepathic, mind-to-mind, while formal language can often interfere with direct, nonverbal communication.

Years ago, a colleague quoted Robert De Niro as saying: "In acting it isn't what you say, it's what you don't say that counts." My exercises are about everything you don't say, everything *but* the words. The Process I teach isn't so much about the writer's contribution on the surface of the page;

words are not the essence of a Zen artist's performance. In any valuable piece of dramatic writing, underneath the text is where the drama is. Great dramatists know that. And great actors know it, too. That's why accentuating what the student doesn't say is an ideal bridge to scene study.

Many actors are addicted to the text because, unwittingly, they've been trained that way. Silence—wordlessness—scares them to death. Deprived of the safe, potentially preordained meaning of the words, they are forced to hang out in the mystery of the unknown and discover a performance without depending on premeditation. The fact is, when we stand on a stage, or walk in front of a camera, we feel naked, vulnerable. That's the way we're supposed to feel if we're dedicated to unconscious acting, but to the inexperienced, nakedness and vulnerability are not ideal qualities to reveal when spectators are present. Grasping at straws, we will reach for the only crutch available under the circumstances: the text.

Our exercises strip away the playwright's words and any other protective device the student depends on to feel safe in front of an audience (or a camera). I tell my students that if you're looking for a profession where you can feel safe and protected, get out of the acting business. Acting is about self-revelation, not self-protection. Reveal your greater Self in the exercises and see what happens. If a performer can't abide the openness demanded by the exercises, regardless of any technical skills acquired, he or she will never become a performance artist of any stature.

One footnote: I've done my best to give the reader a sense of what we do in the segment of class dedicated to flowing energy, but the brief description of a few exercises is little more than an appetizer before the main course. On paper, it's extremely difficult to demonstrate the effectiveness of liberated life force moving freely through an actor's instrument. The only possible way to fully appreciate what these exercises offer the aspiring actor is to get on your feet and do them. When students have done them over a period of time, their significant value is obvious, and they can't wait to get to the workshop to do them one more time with their classmates.

The Unconscious Actor never stops practicing flowing energy through the voice and the body.

Scene Study: Form

Now we're ready to enter Phase Two of the Process. Having practiced the exercises on a regular basis, the students have learned how to be fully present in the moment, connect the intuitive flow of impulses to the body and voice and, most of all, to simply be themselves when in front of the class. This means the instrument has been tuned, and they are ready to learn how to play a scene, and then a series of scenes, which will someday add up to performance art.

In scene study, for students to simply be themselves is no longer enough. They must re-invent themselves through every role in their repertoire. From their own heart, and nerve, and sinew, they re-imagine themselves, using the texts of plays and film scripts to learn how to characterize. They never try to *become* the character, only to suggest a human being other than themselves. In effect, every character created as an unconscious actor is, in some way, a reincarnation.

Up to now, in the exercises, we have been arousing the incredible creative potential in each student's unconsciousness. In scene study, we add the essential contribution of the conscious mind to the Process. We now have to confront the most crucial problem in acting, the marriage of spontaneous impulses with a predetermined *Form*. The issue is balance: intuitive flow and conscious thought; instinctive urges and intellectual analysis; impulsive energy and choice.

Simply put: Flow *and* Form.

Do you recall the either/or mentality I mentioned earlier?

As acting teachers in this country have tended to focus on head or heart acting, there has either been a heavy dependence on text and how to interpret it in a traditional, literary approach to acting, or a strong emphasis on theater games, improv, and exercises. My own experience as a performer made it abundantly clear that spontaneity without a tangible formation to hang it on was a river of energy with nowhere to go. Conversely, too much thinking that didn't accommodate the life blood of impulsiveness was a straightjacket from which there was no escape. All unguided, right brain flow led to directionless motion, while overemphasis on left brain intellectualizing resulted in a well-made construct that was lifeless and unappetizing.

As far as I'm concerned, there is no alternative. To do a student justice, somewhere along the way he or she has to learn that dominant flow or overwhelming form—either one—will cause a destructive imbalance in the Process. And unless they find this out early on in their training, the chances are they will be just that, out of balance, for the rest of their performing lives.

In scene study, then, the student builds form by utilizing flow in a new and different fashion. In the dictionary, *form* is defined as "the shape and structure of something as distinguished from its substance." In my view, form is frozen flow. Form imposes boundaries on free-flowing life force. Form is limitation, "this" not "that," an organizational imprint on the promptings of inspiration.

If flow is changeability, form never changes; it is always the same. Form is images, feelings, ideas, concretized for continuity moment to moment. Flow springs extemporaneously from the unconscious, while form represents the deliberateness of conscious, analytical thought. Form is the direct result of an act of will, a decision which supplies stability to the creative act, a framing which holds a performance—any performance—together.

Referring once more to the mechanics of creativity described earlier, the Process taught in the workshop reminds us that an actor's performance begins in the unconscious and rises to the level where the intellect is engaged to actuate the original creative impulse. The soulful energy accessed in the exercises (images and heartfelt feelings) begin to take shape as ideas in the conscious mind during scene study. In partnership, intuitive flow constantly furnishes formal thought with a stream of fresh information, while the student learns to make choices about what to do with it.

The strength of any acting choice, a willful activity, is conditioned by how an unconscious actor believes the character would behave in the given circumstances of the script. He or she then finds the motivation for that behavior as they explore the scene material. If actors can't believe in what they choose to play in a scene with all their heart and soul, the choice will never work in performance. Should the writing suggest a motivation the actor can't believe in and make his or her own, I recommend substituting one that will fulfill the author's intent without doing violence to the actor's point of view. Affirm your choices passionately, keep them to yourselves, but be prepared to reconcile them with the choices your fellow actors (and the director) are bringing to the table.

Unconscious actors must be strong-willed yet open to compromise, willing to collaborate and to alter the interpretation of a role if a better way to go is indicated. Openness and a willingness to be convinced are not signs of weakness; they are sure signs that actors have confidence in themselves without the need to be right all the time. Scene partners have to structure dramatic material in a spirit of togetherness. Students are able to do this—create a form, make choices, be collaborative—by learning how to rehearse.

How to Rehearse

After teaching for so many years, I now realize the most significant contribution I can make to the success of young actors as performing artists is to show them how to *Rehearse*.
I'm talking about a model that is foolproof and works every
time. Even the great Stanislavsky failed the student actor in
one very important way: he didn't delineate a progressive,
step-by-step, methodical procedure for arriving at a performance. The System doesn't provide such a procedure, neither
does the Method, and this oversight has negatively affected
the training of American actors for most of the 20th century.

I'm not suggesting that Stanislavsky or Strasberg or the
others who promulgated their ideas haven't furnished students with wonderfully helpful guidance for learning the
craft of acting. On the contrary, as in my own case, the
teachers I've mentioned in this book have inspired legions of
dramatic artists with their vast knowledge, their acute per-
ceptions, and their wise understanding of what acting is all
about. As I said earlier, Lee Strasberg was a captivating
speaker and a passionate man of the theater with a shrewd
sense of how to introduce the actor's art to several generations of drama students.

But if you've studied his methodology as I have, I think
you'll find that, like so many of his disciples, he never laid out
a cohesive blueprint for rehearsing scene material, one that
would show an inexperienced actor how to start *here* (the beginning) and go *there* (a fine performance) with some degree

of certainty. Many contemporary teachers say great things about the actor's craft and can teach the tricks of the trade, but they don't always supply their pupils with a comprehensive plan for creating a performance.

I suppose I'm more sensitive than some to this problem, since I had no formal training in the early days of my career. When I grew up, I often felt lost, hungry for guidance I could depend on. With all I had learned from the unrivaled dramatic artists I had worked with and the nuggets of information I had tucked away in the back of my mind, I still had trouble rehearsing an author's text. Like many actors, I would try a little bit of this and a little bit of that, and most of the time it worked. But I was never sure I could go where I wanted to go, or exactly *how* I would get there. One of my major goals as a teacher was to help other actors solve that problem for themselves.

That's what scene study in my classes is all about—how to rehearse. Over the years, I've worked out the bugs in the Process and simplified the guidelines I now teach new students about a specific way to prepare. In the beginning I would ask a student to choose a scene, memorize it, and bring it in so we could work on it together. That's the standard approach in most scene study classes. However, I've found that many actors, experienced or otherwise, interpret a scene analytically, deciding how to "act" it before beginning rehearsal. This is bad news for any artist and a fatal mistake for future unconscious actors.

As an antidote, I came up with a better method for initiating students into scene study. We create their inaugural scene (a monologue) from scratch:

> *We sit in a circle, breathing in sync, and do a simple im-*
> *aging exercise to stimulate everyone's imagination. Then*
> *each student chooses a real-life relationship where there is*
> *mutual affection despite some conflict which has never*
> *been resolved. Any relationship like this is fertile ground*
> *where the seeds of drama are easily planted.*
>
> *Then, the student closes his or her eyes, imagines a*
> *confrontation with that friend or spouse or boss, ex-*
> *pressing the grievance in gibberish while being aware of*
> *the emotional charge that energizes the Bodymind. As*
> *the energy flow builds in intensity, we all get on our feet,*
> *open our eyes and play the scene in gibberish with each*
> *other. After we discuss what we've done together, each*
> *student's assignment is to go home and translate what*
> *has just been expressed in gibberish into formal English.*

The following week, each student reads that two- or three-minute monologue which will launch him or her into the rehearsal mode. There are several advantages to approaching scene study this way: fledgling actors find out they don't have to depend on a writer to create a role to play, they can do it all by themselves; they inaugurate scene study by telling a personal truth through a dramatic text, a prototype for every scene played in class; and, most importantly, they have circumvented the thinking self and, by engaging the imagination, have already begun to create a performance from the unconscious mind.

I caution actors who begin rehearsing that first monologue to take off their "writer" hats, forget that they have created the text from their own life experience, and put on their "actor" hats. This gives them the freedom to interpret the script from the performer's point of view, as if it had been given to them as a professional assignment. A student should never bring a preordained attitude about characters and relationships to the rehearsal process, and whether or not he or she has written the scene, the rule still applies.

The rehearsal approach I teach is a well-ordered, one-step-at-a-time process of trial and error. Trial and error is really the only way to create a performance that will have a solid structure. In the theater, this is essential if a performance is going to be repeatable night after night, reflecting the consistency demanded of a professional actor. In film acting, where a director may print Take 3 or Take 33 and snippets of a performance are later edited and pieced together in post production, a structure is equally important. An actor in the theater might spend weeks constructing a performance in a rehearsal hall, whereas a film actor is usually restricted to solitary preparation, mostly at home the night before a shoot.

The culprit is lack of time. When creating drama for the stage, adequate days for rehearsal are in the budget; in movies and television, a half hour on a sound stage with the director and another actor or two might be the only chance one has to rehearse collaboratively. After *Sophie's Choice*, Meryl Streep said, "I bring in a finished performance and hope the director knows what to do with it." Obviously, her days on the screen had taught her to rehearse on her own, expertly, and later make whatever adjustments are necessary on the set. That's what film acting is all about.

How effectively actors prepare on their own will depend on how much time they have spent in a class or a rehearsal hall on their feet. The homework a film actor does is a distillation of countless hours trying out a little bit of this idea, a little bit of that choice, making note of the ones that feel good and eliminating the ones that fail to give a sustainable interpretation of the role. When you have to do this at home in a few hours there can be no guesswork; an actor has to have a solid grasp of a rehearsal plan and be able to trust it completely when preparing the following day's shooting schedule.

The student must come to understand that rehearsing is a lot like building a house. It happens in stages. First you lay a foundation, and then you begin building a framework. If you're foolish and try to erect the framing before you have laid the concrete, the whole formation will collapse and you'll have to start all over again. If you're going to rehearse well, you cannot skip steps; you have to raise the edifice, one building block at a time. Your survival will depend on how much you know about the art of preparation—whether you have weeks, perhaps months, with other cast members, or a solitary few hours at home by yourself.

After finishing the initial monologue, students choose material for their first scene. To do that intelligently, aspiring actors should acquire a library of dramatic writing (plays, screenplays, television scripts), anything they can get their hands on that will familiarize them with what dramatists have done, and are doing, on the page. A text is a blueprint similar to the renderings an architect gives to a contractor. A contractor who doesn't know how to read blueprints expertly is not much of a contractor.

The same can be said of an actor who doesn't read scripts. Surprisingly, many would-be actors don't read drama. They haven't read Shakespeare or Arthur Miller or the Roberts (Towne and Benton), two of the best screenwriters of their generation. Oscar Wilde's name has a familiar ring to it, as does Noel Coward's, but they have no idea how influential both men have been in the universe of contemporary comedy. Oh sure, young actors may have paged through *Barefoot in the Park*, but even then they are ignorant of the considerable body of Neil Simon's work.

That is why I am constantly reminding my students to get on a reading program. To read drama, any kind of drama, half an hour a day. Learn to appreciate dramatic writing, to x-ray and diagnose it, and to evaluate it before attempting to interpret it in rehearsal. An illiterate actor is incapable of choosing the best script material for scene study, so even before taking step number one starts off on the wrong foot.

To assist inexperienced students, I will often suggest a scene that, in my judgment, is right for them; but thereafter, I encourage them to choose the characters they want to play and the writing they want to bring to life on their own. Someday as professionals they will have the opportunity to choose texts that reflect their deepest personal and artistic values. An actor who doesn't take a strong stand about expressing those values is just another journeyman for hire, content to get a job, no matter what kind of dramatic statement he or she is asked to make. We already have more than enough of those actors in the profession.

After they decide to work on a specific scene, I ask them to answer three questions:

A. Why is it a good vehicle for you?
B. What challenge does it offer to help you grow as an actor?
C. What do you want to communicate to the audience through the material?

The choices an actor explores during rehearsal should stem from a desire to evoke a certain response from an audience. If the students are not learning to communicate something specific through their performances, rehearsal will be aimless, disorganized, and pointless; unless the actor has a point to make, why is his or her acting worth the audience's time—and money—in the first place?

While pondering these three questions, students are advised to read the scene as many times as possible, absorbing the author's words and ideas without analysis, "metabolizing" the text as I call it, until the writing is an organic part of their consciousness. No choices yet, no thought yet, no breaking it down yet, just a simple absorption of the content of the scene. And certainly no premature decisions about interpreting the material prior to rehearsal.

Reading the text incorrectly is a trap for most students because they come to rehearsal with preconceptions about the scene: how it should be played, and what they should look and sound like in performance. Without realizing it, they have lifted the words off the page and assigned them definitions from the dictionary. They think they "know" what the words mean— and what the characters intend them to mean—before investigating the inner life of the scene. They have attached themselves to a superficial, word-oriented presentation of the text, and worst of all, they're not aware they're doing it.

Anthony Hopkins has a great way to start work on a script: "I just take the text and I absorb it. I eat the text. I go through it over and over. . . . I read it 150 times. . . . I take whole pages of it and I figuratively devour it. Then I sleep on it, go do something else, I go to the movies and I come back to it the next day. . . . That's how I work. . . . Learn it, absorb it. Don't have any ideas about it. Don't judge it. *Digest it.*" I recommend all my students follow Sir Anthony's example. In case you missed it, he's describing his version of unconscious acting, staying out of his head at all costs, depending on his intuition to guide him when he's starting to develop a role.

Having read the text correctly—so often that it's been properly digested—the student's imagination is engaged, intuitive impulses surface, and it's time to add conscious, analytical thought to the mix. Then and only then do I suggest that the actor asks the key questions that are guidelines for breaking down a character:

1. Who am I?
2. Where am I?

3. What do I want?
4. Why do I want it?
5. Who do I want it from?
6. What's in the way of my getting it?
7. How do I get it?

The student actor writes these seven questions in a journal or the script. We actors need a map when we're in unfamiliar territory, and using these questions as a compass can help us when we lose our way in rehearsal. Regardless of how experienced or skilled one is, rehearsing is always a path of discovery through a no-man's land unmarked by actor-friendly signposts to keep us on track. Jo Anthony, a prominent actor/director I knew in the theater, told me once, "No matter how many times I've rehearsed, it's always the first time."

Never expect to have definitive answers to any of these questions when you first ask them; hopefully, after having rehearsed the answers will be obvious in your performance. And take the pressure off of your power of analysis to give you the right data. Go about living your life while the questions are simmering inside you. The best, most original images and ideas will spring freely from your unconscious if you let them. As Sir Anthony says, "sleep on it, go do something else. . . . Go to the movies. . . ." In other words, distract your thinking mind and allow your imagination to do its job.

The last pre-rehearsal assignment for students in the workshop is to talk with their scene partners, decide what their set

is going to look like, and draw as detailed a floor plan as possible, making sure everyone has a copy—which will come in
handy when they set up their scene in class. They then rehearse for at least ten hours on their own before the scene is
presented in the workshop.

Character/Place/Relationship

The moment is at hand when students meet with their fellow
actors and formal rehearsal begins. Their assignment is as follows: use the agreed-upon floor plan to put up your set; read
through the scene non-interpretively to hear the words out
loud for the first time; follow with some well-chosen communication exercises starting with sound and movement to
warm up on your feet. By this time, everyone should be ready
to go.

As I see it, there are three major phases in rehearsing a
scene:

- *Character/Place/Relationship;*
- *Secrets (subtext);*
- *Beats & Blocking.*

Within these phases are a sequence of steps that provide a
game plan which will always serve the actor when he or she is
creating a role.

The primary phase, *Character/Place/Relationship*, is foun-
dational. My students like the acronym CPR, which is apt
when one realizes that this is when an actor begins breathing

life into a text. Asking the question, *Who am I?*, the Zen artist listens intently for intuitive responses to the writer's description of the *Character* he or she is about to play. In allegiance to Stanislavsky, artists do not view the character as someone outside of themselves but as already residing in their own being.

Again quoting from *Stanislavski for Beginners*, we see how the Russian master implemented his ideas about acting while rehearsing Anton Chekhov's *The Seagull*: "In Chekhov's plays it is wrong to try to act, to perform. You must be—that is, you must live, exist, following the deep, inner, spiritual line of development." This insistence on *being* the character would later become a cornerstone of the System for training actors that Stanislavsky would instigate at The Moscow Art Theatre in the early 1900's.

The author goes on to discuss how Stanislavsky "discovered ways to help the actors to define this inner life, and to 'live' on stage. In his production notebooks Stanislavski [sic] set down a whole range of activities for the characters. So, for example, someone 'unhurriedly takes out a small comb and during the whole next scene he combs his beard, then takes off his hat, combs his hair, straightens and does up his tie.'"

This helped create a sense of continuous life on the stage. Speaking of his cast, Stanislavsky said: "They felt external truth, and intimate memories of their own lives arose in their souls, enticing from them the feelings which Chekhov was talking about. In such moments the actor stopped playing, and began to live the role, became the character. . . . It was a creative miracle."

The insights Stanislavsky gained from staging *The Seagull*

might well mark the advent of a new theory behind modern acting, the expectation that in the 20th century actors would *live* rather than *act* the character. To reference that, the contemporary Zen artist begins to work unconsciously, avoiding intellectual analysis which would automatically create a separateness between him or herself and the character in the script. To begin with an idea or set of ideas objectifies the character at the moment the actor wants to depend exclusively on soulful identification with the person being lifted off the page.

I advise students to assume they are the character and the character is them. "When you're impersonating an identity other than your own," I remind them, "the only equipment you have to do it with is you. What you think, the character thinks; what you feel, the character feels; what you imagine, the character imagines." This is what I believe Stanislavsky was saying when he coined the phrase "living through" the role. The *animus* that invigorates a character in unconscious acting is the actor's own soul.

As a rule of thumb, brand-new students should choose roles that are close to who they are so there is no temptation to "act" like somebody else. As they progress in the craft, I encourage them to flex their muscles as character actors by choosing roles that seem to be further from themselves, but I think that's a mistake early on in the training. "Let's get all of *you* on the stage first," is my exhortation, "and leave the perils of extended characterization for another time."

While the character is in the early stages of gestation and some possible data about *Who am I?* is percolating inside the actor, the question *Where am I?* follows in tandem. In order for the character to live in the scene, there must be a *where* in which to live. Much of the pre-rehearsal homework is mental, but an actor has to physicalize rehearsing from the first moment on the set. The physical life of the character and the environment in which the scene will be played is what I call *Place*.

Character and place are so closely allied they have to be spoken in the same breath. Place is the magnifying glass with which the character reads fine print, the couch napped on, the bedroom slippers worn around the house, the cool breeze that ruffles the curtains on the open window in the study, the tick of the clock on the shelf, the daguerreotypes on the walls that specify the year, and so on. The student cannot do too much work on place and cannot be too specific about every physical detail. Why? Because acting is more visual than verbal; writing is about words. Acting is about behavior— internal and external behavior—and the actor must know how to physicalize the inner life of the character in order to communicate that truth to an audience. Mindful of this, Stanislavsky "set down a whole range of activities for the characters" in *The Seagull*. Activities translate into behavior, and finding the most interesting, meaningful activities becomes a major goal for an actor in rehearsal.

"An ounce of behavior is worth a pound of words," according to Sandy Meisner. What astonishes me is how many trained actors don't know that. In rehearsal they stand around saying their lines, waiting for the director to tell them what to do. Once in a while a director will accommodate them, but I tell my students not to count on it. Many directors don't understand the actor's problems and don't know how to help. I learned that by the time I was nine years old.

Most of the good film directors I worked for in those early years were a fountain of interesting behavioral ideas. I came to depend on them and their keen suggestions that kept me alive in front of the camera. I was lazy by the time I got to the theater, and I found that I was one of those standing around waiting for direction. And while I was waiting, I felt like a disembodied spirit. I was talking, but I wasn't doing anything. I was more than a little uncomfortable. Once I got smart I brought in plenty of activities, and I was never again at a loss for something to do on the stage.

Place, then, is all about what the actor is doing while exploring *Relationship* with a fellow actor in the context of the play. In the first stage of rehearsal, students are living through their characters with each other, ignoring any temptation to perform the text prematurely. I ask them to connect with each other in the place they've chosen to make real for themselves; to bring at least five props or personal objects to rehearsal that are relevant to the relationship and will help them physicalize it; and to always work from their personal truth, never forgetting they're rehearsing not with a "character" but a real, live actor who has likes and dislikes, strengths and weaknesses, hidden fears and anxieties similar to their own.

Some actors energetically make drinks, cook dinner, or change their clothes, busy for the sake of being busy. I point out that the tasks they are looking for are not general in nature but specific behavior that expresses their relationship with the other actor. Does Character A have a favorite chair that Character B shouldn't sit in? Is Character B constantly cleaning his glasses to avoid eye contact with Character A? Is Character A reading a book and Character B watching television because they are incapable of opening up to each other? Student actors have difficulty finding what I call a *logic of behavior* in their relationships. In the absence of a director who will tell them how to enter, where to stand, or how to use the props, they wander around trying to find something to do while they recite their dialogue. I teach my students to first, recognize the need for a logic of behavior and then, to start their investigation by using their own lives as a way to find it.

To illustrate, let us say the scene is an argument between a girlfriend and a boyfriend at their apartment before dinner. She's already home, and he comes in from work. If I'm playing the boyfriend, I don't just enter and start talking. I plan his behavior based on my own habit patterns when I come home from a hard day of teaching: I open the door with my keys, put them, my cell phone, wallet, and briefcase on the bench in the entranceway, kiss my wife, sit down in a chair—always the same chair—take off my shoes and socks, and put on my slippers. I turn on the television in the kitchen, check the mail (which she has put on the dining table), open whatever is of interest, read it, sometimes showing it to her, and so on.

Naturally, as I continue to rehearse CPR, I modify these behavior patterns based on what the other actor and I are learning from each other, how we're exploring our relationship, and the new and different objects we're each bringing to rehearsal. Gradually my original ideas are replaced with new physical life as the work progresses. But starting with my own habits is a valuable way to begin rehearsal, and more often than not, some of that behavior ends up in the performance.

In addition, I suggest students bring their most cherished foibles, idiosyncrasies and hang-ups with them to rehearsal, regardless of how vulnerable this might make them feel with their fellow actors. Mutual trust and acceptance is a necessity for unconscious acting. If they're going to really live through their roles and put themselves—all of themselves—into their work, they can't hold anything back. Much of the time we're too polite and socially correct in the acting business, and we have to learn how to take chances and be more aggressively incorrect.

To this end, an actor should never recoil from conflict when investigating the relationship with a scene partner. Conflict is the motor which drives the drama and is inherent in all good dramatic writing, from Sophocles to Tennessee Williams to the best sketches on *Saturday Night Live*. I ask my students to accept each other, warts and all, and find a way to put whatever conflictual energy that emerges between them into the scene. If what they have chosen is well-written, there will be plenty of conflict on which to build the drama. Nonetheless, I want them to find an individual passageway into their characters, to bring a unique interpretation to each role while justifying the author's blueprint by investing it with uncensored personal truth.

Secrets (subtext)

When enough rehearsal hours have been spent on CPR, students are ready to move on to Phase Two: *Secrets (subtext)*. It is then and only then that they tackle the entire text of the scene. During Phase One, they have been relating through physical activities, gibberish, improvised language, and finally a fragment of the writer's dialogue. Living energy has continued to flow moment to moment through each one of these steps, and now that spontaneity is assured, it's time to make specific choices that ultimately furnish firm underpinnings for the scene.

As I've said, the text is a given, a gift from the author; if the writing is sound, the arc of the drama has already been established on paper. A scene should have a clear beginning, middle and end; this is the "spine" of the scene, as Elia Kazan used to call it. The spine, or what I call a *rising arc of intensity*, exists primarily in the subtext. The black marks (the words) on the page of a script are not what the scene is about. The scene is always in the white part of the paper. The black marks often have deep meaning; they are beguiling, seductive, and suggestive of what's inside the package, like the wrapping on an expensive gift. Good dialogue is a reflection of the subtext, but an actor who is only acting the words is performing on the most superficial level. One has to dig deeper into oneself, into one's character and the scripted relationships to create a subtextual reality which breathes vitality into a dramatist's literary creation.

The author's words give clues to what the scene is about,

and hopefully the actor has a sound dramatic structure to work from; but the choices made subtextually will form the actor's own interpretation of the role. Only the actor can supply the inner life of the drama, the motivating influences behind the character's intentions, the *What do I want?*, the *Why do I want it?*, the *Who do I want it from?*, and so forth.

During rehearsal, the skilled actor essentially creates a complex psychological profile of the character, filling in the blanks with the images and feelings from the unconscious. At the same time, he or she begins to make conscious choices about the exact nature of the "actions" (Stanislavsky's word) that will invigorate his or her performance. This doesn't occur in a vacuum, however, since actors must react honestly to what other actors are doing and the input received from the director.

Disclosing one's Secrets can reduce the pent-up energy generated by a powerful choice and squander a valuable surprise element when you're mixing it up with other actors. Make a choice, play it, and find out how it works. If you like the behavior it gives you, make a note of it. If not, discard the choice and go on to something else.

Theorists and teachers who write books about acting love to stamp favorite nomenclature on the subtextual choices a skilled actor can play, causing confusion for those who lack experience in the trade. To clarify, I've reduced the variety of labels I've heard over the years to three basic categories: *prior event; event;* and *action*. These three kinds of Secrets will give the actor specifically different behavior, subtly but clearly distinct, if properly executed. They are all the tools an actor needs for a comprehensive exploration of the subtext.

Prior event: Sometimes called "prior circumstance," this is any situation or event which has occurred in the previous life of the character having special meaning for, or influence on, the scene in rehearsal. It can have happened twenty years before or two minutes prior to the beginning of the scene. The choice is the actor's. Sometimes the play will specify or dictate the prior event, but more often actors will need to create one so the characters will be clear about where they're coming from motivationally when they enter the scene.

There are several good ways to investigate prior event:

- write it out in narrative form as if it were a short story;
- create a series of images with your imagination as though you were making a movie in your head;
- improvise it, by yourself or with other actors.

It is important to investigate a prior event so it will give your character clear, specific, detailed behavior in rehearsal. Students should try all three ways several times to find out which of these techniques best suits their individual approach to creating a subtext.

Event: Simply put, this is what's really going on between the characters in the scene that they're *not* talking about. Usually it's a noun: "a first argument;" "a final goodbye;" "I'm pregnant." If it's well chosen, it can give an actor behavior that reverberates far beyond the meaning of the text. In a *New York Times* interview, Jack Nicholson, discussing his Oscar-winning performance in *One Flew Over the Cuckoo's Nest*, revealed that his subtextual design for the role was "that this guy's a scamp who knows he's irresistible to women and in reality he expects Nurse Ratched to be seduced by him. This is his tragic flaw. This is why he ultimately fails.... That's what I felt was actually happening with that character—it was one long, unsuccessful seduction which the guy was so pathologically sure of."

Nicholson goes on to explain that this "unsuccessful seduction" was neither suggested by the script nor the book it was adapted from. It was a choice Nicholson made himself, and he discussed it with no one except his co-star, Louise Fletcher. Every actor of Nicholson's caliber knows that the greatest power the actor has is the ability to make interesting, exciting subtextual choices that will resonate through the performance.

In the case of *One Flew Over the Cuckoo's Nest*, his choice turned out to be a workable event for the entire film, but sometimes a chosen event will not support a scene, or even part of the scene. That's why a student is encouraged to try alternate choices in rehearsal to find the special Secret that will illuminate the text. An actor is never content to play what the text *seems* to mean on the page, but what it is *intended* to mean in performance.

Action: This is defined as the character's overall objective in the scene, directly related to how an actor decides to affect the other actor. An action, invariably a verb, is an active intention distinguished from an event, which is a more passive reaction to a situation such as the choice Nicholson made in . . . *Cuckoo's Nest*. Please note that actions like "to seduce him," "to charm her," or "to intimidate them" are not destinations that must be reached by the end of the scene. Rather, they are directions to go subtextually and, if properly chosen, will provide a thrust of emotional and physical behavior that will sustain the actor throughout the scene.

Choosing the right action is the best device an actor has for defining and exploiting the central conflict in a scene. If a solid conflict is lacking in the writing, it can be supplied by a skilled actor; this can be a significant contribution, since it is conflict that moves any dramatic situation into a higher gear. In a two-character scene, it's easy to identify the primary conflict in the writing, but when there are several other characters on stage at the same time, an actor must decide which of them is the object of his or her intent or apply that action to all of the other characters at the same time.

During rehearsal, pay close attention to what the other actor appears to be playing in your relationship. If there is a pattern in his or her point of view and there is no conflict emerging to engage your characters, alter your action and try different choices until you find one that maximizes the conflict in the scene. *Never* suggest a different point of view for your fellow actor that you think will help you play your intention. Let your partners play their actions, and you play yours, keeping in mind that whatever you choose to play should ultimately feed the intensity of the dramatic arc in the scene.

An unconscious actor makes subtextual choices but never tries to predict how they will play in rehearsal. He or she finds out how they will play feeding off the spontaneous reactions evoked by the other actor(s). In my training methodology, an action or any other choice plays a little bit differently both in rehearsal and in performance, because it is always being played for the *first* time. My students are told, "You should never know how you're going to play a choice until the other actor's reaction *tells* you how." At first, they have a hard time hanging out with their scene partners and letting go of a pre-determined result. But when they've learned to trust the Process, they realize how good it feels to become less result-oriented and discover how their subtext will play, unpredictably, moment to moment.

I insist the students link action and every other aspect of subtext, to specific, vivid, visually interesting activities that will tell the story of the scene without undue reliance on the text. Professional actors should be skilled enough to give expression to prior events, events and actions, and to paint pictures that will hold an audience's attention without depending on the writer's words to do the job for them. When the actor's Secrets come to the surface and the subtext is revealed through behavior, it is then and only then that an actor is truly a performance artist.

Beats & Blocking

Once a student has thoroughly investigated Character/ Place/Relationship and has spent sufficient time exploring the white part of the paper in Secrets (subtext), he or she is now prepared to build a comprehensive form in *Beats & Blocking*. Using the data accumulated earlier, it is in this,

Phase Three of my rehearsal procedure, that well-trained unconscious actors organize their ideas and stitch them together into an original, personal dramatic statement. It's now or never. After Beats & Blocking, the period of preparation is over, and an actor's performance should be essentially intact. If not, he or she leaves the rehearsal hall with an ill-defined, muddled point of view.

That's why a truly skilled performing artist must grasp the craftsmanship entailed in building Beats & Blocking. No matter how inspired, without a meticulously designed direction for a scene to go an actor is attempting to steer a ship without a compass and disaster looms in uncharted waters.

I define a Beat as "a unit of intention based on a change in relationship between the characters." These changes, or *transitions*, resulting from the ongoing conflict between the characters, should be indicated in a good script. What a skilled actor supplies is the subtextual logic supporting these shifts in relationships in collaboration with a director and fellow actors. Explicitly ordered Beats are the only way to clarify the beginning, middle, and end of a dramatic story, the progression of a scene, or any other fragment of drama, from start to finish.

Beats & Blocking go hand in hand. I have deliberately used an ampersand to join them in matrimony to make that point. Beats & Blocking are like railroad tracks that run parallel to each other. Beats are the subtextual track, Blocking is the physical extension of that subtext, and without both tracks in place, side by side, the scene is automatically derailed. In my metaphor, Beats are the inner structure of the scene while

Blocking is the outer structure, and the text, like railroad ties, holds the two together.

Blocking, the outer track, is defined as "the planned, diagrammed movement of the actor in a scene." In my workshop I distinguish Blocking from *activities*—specific behavior involving the actor's body, objects, furniture, and so forth, employed during execution of the diagrammed movement. Physical behavior, especially Blocking, is more effective in motivating transitions than anything found in the text because it more easily manifests the internal relationships of the characters as they play out their conflict. Conversely, arbitrary movement without specific subtextual motivation is nothing more than an actor aimlessly walking around a set. Ideally, Blocking (and activities) reveal, by external expression, an actor's internal logic of behavior.

Remember Stanislavsky's exhortation that the "line of the life of the human body keeps the actor on track in his creation of the life of the human spirit." If you're an unconscious actor in training, you learn to see physical actions the way Stanislavsky did, as the essential "anatomy of the role and the play." A piece of Blocking then, such as entering a room and taking off your coat, either reveals the intent of the character you're playing or is meaningless movement, nothing more. Entering a room and taking off your coat is organically connected to the Beat you're playing or you're not physicalizing the inner life of the character in the scene.

If there are no Beats, there are no vertebrae in the spine of a scene, and consequently there is no skeletal frame on which to hang the emotional lives of the characters. A text without

specific bone structure is just a stream of words with no mus-
cular or nervous energy to animate them. A performance
without Beats tends to fall apart because it hasn't been fully
thought out and organized. If there are no Beats, there is no
understandable progression in the inner workings of a character, and the audience has to fill in the blanks about who that
person is and why he or she is behaving in a particular way.

Blocking is a visual aid, like a skin that holds the images,
feelings, and motivations of the character together. It is the
physical representation of the unspoken, psychological content of the drama. What goes on in the white part of the
paper tends to be abstract, which is why a skilled actor never
depends on words to tell the story but instead pictorializes
meaningful subtext every step of the way.

That's the reason an actor, like an athlete, needs to practice
the formal use of the body in rehearsal. It's analogous to golf,
for instance, where a new player learns to create a swing by
consciously building specific behavior into large muscle memory while repeatedly swinging the club on the range. Neither
good Blocking nor a good golf swing happens spontaneously;
each is a result of good repetition. The process for both the
actor and the athlete is the same, to assimilate this movement
as soon as possible and repeat it as many times as necessary so
the unconscious can take over. Then the wise performer forgets about it. An actor cannot try to remember how he or she
is supposed to move in performance any more than a golfer can
be thinking about how to swing the club during a tournament.

This is all so important because the same technique a student employs laying out Beats & Blocking for a scene will

some day apply to structuring an entire performance. I want actors to see themselves as storytellers. Remember, a performance, like any good story, has a beginning, a middle, and an end. There should always be a rising arc of intensity in the story instigated by the central conflict between the principal characters, where the antagonist ("bad guy") is working hard to keep the protagonist ("good guy") from reaching his or her objective. The mounting tension that results from this collision of energetic forces propels the story forward to a climax, at which point the protagonist usually prevails.

An actor should always tell the story from the character's point of view and see himself as the hero of the piece. Actors are cautioned not to judge how their characters behave on the page but to find good and valid reasons to justify that behavior. The more unlikable the character, the greater the danger there is in playing him or her as a heavy. If actors search for the evil in the "good guy" and the virtue in the "bad guy," they will avoid a mortal sin in acting, transforming a dramatist's characters into one-note stereotypes or boring clichés.

A reverence for good storytelling is a trait shared by all successful actors. When Russell Crowe accepted the Best Actor award from the Screen Actors Guild in 2002 for his performance in *A Beautiful Mind*, he revealed his personal commitment to this idea in his brief remarks. "This is a great job, and I want to encourage every one of you in this room to give everything you've got to the story. God bless narrative. God bless originality. Good night."

I have created a brief, two-character dramatic incident to demonstrate how I teach students to break down a scene in rehearsal and lay out Beats & Blocking. They are instructed to follow the structural curve of the *narrative* by creating a subtext to support the storyline suggested by the author. Having developed psychological profiles for their characters during Phases One and Two of the rehearsal process—Character/Place/Relationship (CPR) and Secrets (subtext)—students should have a clear sense of what their objectives are and what should happen in their relationships by the end of the scene. They should have a strong idea about the central conflict which propels the story to a satisfactory conclusion. And the actors should have a tentative plan for how they want their characters to arrive at a resolution before they come to rehearsal.

Starting at the beginning of the scene, students carefully work out Beats & Blocking until they are able to incorporate their respective choices and intentions in a mutually agreed-on scenario. A word of caution to students everywhere: never try to impose your point of view on a scene when you're laying out Beats & Blocking with your fellow actors. You'll get the best out of your collaboration if freedom of expression is encouraged by everyone in the scene. Remain flexible at all times or you will shut out infinite possibilities. Embrace whatever reactions your scene partners have to your choices, and be willing to rework those choices accordingly.

In a professional engagement, a good director is indispensable as a guide, but actors should know how to create a workable set of Beats & Blocking for themselves so they'll never have to depend on a director who may not know how to help. To that end, in my workshop I insist that Beats be precisely labeled and Blocking be definitively regimented so a student's intentions are neither fuzzy nor hard to follow for any of the participants in the scene. I've given two fictitious actors the assignment of laying out Beats & Blocking in the following text:

> *Jack, a handsome, charming man in his twenties, has spent an evening with Jill, an attractive woman about his age. They are on their way home after a candlelight dinner at a local restaurant. This is their first date.*

JILL   It was a great evening! I haven't had so much fun in a long time . . .
> *(As they cross an intersection, she reacts)*

        That's my street . . .

JACK   I thought we'd go to my place . . . I've got some champagne on ice.

JILL   It's getting late.

JACK   It's only 10:30. What's the rush?

JILL   I have an early breakfast meeting.
> *(He pulls the car over to the curb, turns off the ignition, reaches over and kisses her)*

        You'd better take me home.
> *(He tries to kiss her again)*

        Take me home.
> *(He starts the car and turns around)*

JACK   Okay. Fine . . . *(Pause)* I thought you were
having a good time.
JILL   I was . . . until . . .
JACK   . . . you remembered you had an early
breakfast meeting. *(Pause)* Maybe we'll do
it again sometime.
JILL   Call me.
JACK   Let's do it when you'll be able to sleep in.

Typically, this is the kind of scene film actors are given to play, where the words are sparse but where there are rich possibilities for subtext. What's going on between Jack and Jill in the verbal exchange seems obvious, and the scene overall seems to be pretty much a cliché. They apparently had a good time on their first date. They talk about going home early. He tries to kiss her. She pulls away. Where's the compelling drama in that?

The task for the performing artist is to take what seems commonplace and turn it into an interesting dramatic event. The inexperienced actor will probably play the superficial meaning of the words. And that's all. In the hands of untrained actors this two or three minutes of screen time could end up being monumentally boring.

The clues are there, however, that a skilled actor will pick up on to give the text greater dimension. I have the advantage over the reader because I had a strong sense of what was really going on in this relationship when I wrote the scene. Any stage directions that represented an author's attempt to fill in the blanks or restrict a performer's freedom of interpretation were deliberately omitted. Thus, it's a virgin canvas for the actor's vital contribution: Beats & Blocking.

In the first two phases of rehearsal, Actor A (Jack) worked on his character as a man-about-town, accustomed to "scoring," as he terms it, on a first date. For him, the successful Secret he explored was an action—"to seduce"— which seemed to elicit a positive response from his scene partner. He is working from that base as he begins laying out his Beats.

On the other hand, Actor B (Jill) decided early in rehearsal that if she were too open to his sexual overtures there would be no conflict. So she enters Phase Three having chosen to play her character as a dedicated professional woman, attracted to Jack but unwilling to become one more easy conquest for a man she hardly knows. She has chosen a prior event—"getting slightly tipsy on Dom Perignon"—as a good way to support an upbeat Secret for the beginning of the scene and her first line of dialogue: "It was a great evening! I haven't had so much fun in a long time." During his first Beat, Jack hums along with the music on his car radio and feels confident that *I've softened her up for the moment of truth.* Jill, grateful that he hasn't made a move on her all through dinner, is playing, *Thanks for being a gentleman.* However, surprised when he passes by the street to her apartment, she makes a transition to her second Beat, *Now what?* She says: "That's my street."

Jack, a bit overconfident, continues to play his first Beat when he replies: "I thought we'd go to my place . . . I've got some champagne on ice." Jill knows exactly what he's suggesting and stalls momentarily: "It's getting late." He presses her for a positive sign that she will play ball: "It's only 10:30. What's the rush?" Jill's line is: "I have an early breakfast meeting." But her tone is emphatic; she's now playing her second Beat, *No way am I going to your place tonight.*

Deciding he may need a change in strategy, Jack turns onto a darkened side street, cuts the engine, takes her in his arms and kisses her. This Blocking aggressively manifests his second Beat, *We're going to make it tonight, or you'll never see me again.* Jill pulls away, having made a transition to her third Beat, *You've gone too far.* Her line is: "You'd better take me home." He ignores her reaction and tries to kiss her again. She pushes him away this time and says, more emphatically: "Take me home."

Stung by her rejection, he turns the engine over, puts the car in gear, makes a U-turn, and says: "Okay. Fine. . . ." But it's far from fine. He's hurt, and he's covering this hurt with bravado. He isn't accustomed to this kind of rejection, but he doesn't want her to see that she's gotten through to him. He cranks the music up higher and hums along with it, playing his third Beat, *I'm a popular guy. I don't need you.* They ride in awkward silence as Jill repairs her make-up.

Suddenly, Jack, feeling insecure, needs reassurance. His line is: "I thought you were having a good time." His fourth Beat is, *Tell me I haven't lost my touch.* Sensing his vulnerability, her attitude softens, and she makes a transition to her fourth Beat, *I didn't mean to hurt you.* She says: "I was . . . until. . . ." He knows where she's heading with that statement, so he gets himself off the hook by finishing her sentence: "you remembered you had an early breakfast meeting."

When she smiles, acknowledging his cleverness, he realizes he's attracted to her in a new way. He makes a transition to his fifth Beat, *You're different. I like you.* He expresses this verbally with the line: "Maybe we can do it again sometime." She encourages him by responding: "Call me." She's playing her fifth Beat, *I think I like you, too.*

At the end of the scene, Jack and Jill have reached a tentative accommodation. He says: "Let's do it when you'll be able to sleep in." His subtext is, *Next time, I won't try to force the issue. We'll do it if it's right for both of us.* When Jack is moved to touch her hand, a warm feeling passes between them. They might be able to have a mutually satisfying relationship after all.

I hope it's obvious that the real drama in this short, simple scene and the psychological content of the relationship between Jack and Jill is everywhere but in the words. Much more revealing is the physical action, the tone of voice, the pregnant silences—telltale signs that reflect our human tendency to communicate obliquely, indirectly. In good dramatic writing, the characters use language to hide from each other, to avoid telling each other the truth. That's why skilled actors rely on Beats & Blocking to get the message across.

At the end of this encounter, the relationship between Jack and Jill has changed four or five times, causing transitions from Beat to Beat with increased conflict between them and a rising arc of intensity until the scene is resolved. If the actors have played their choices well, the audience has followed a carefully defined negotiation between a man and woman based not on what they said to each other, but on the underlying tension arising from their individual human idiosyncrasies and their emotional responses to the situation.

Moreover, Beats are like chapters in a novel, headlining the upward momentum of a dramatic story as it unfolds. Students learn to depend on the writing of course, because the guidelines for effective storytelling are built into a good script. And the better the writer, the denser the subtext; the more complex the people are on the page, the more options a skilled interpretive artist has when bringing them to life on the stage or in front of the camera.

Hopefully, three of the most important qualities of effective storytelling are also in the script: urgency, surprise, and suspense. The alert student who has been sharpening the ability to evaluate dramatic writing through a daily reading program has no trouble identifying the life and death urgency in a good script. He or she knows how to make the most of the writer's well-timed surprises and suspenseful stratagems and, as a consequence, will make choices that enhance those factors in performance.

Also, the actor will be able to spot inferior writing which lacks urgency and look for some way to supply dramatic intensity when putting the story together in Beats & Blocking. Surprises can sometimes be imposed on material *within a scene* by choosing unexpected intentions, activities, or Blocking; on the other hand, it's practically impossible to generate suspense *from scene to scene* when a dramatist hasn't supplied it in the first place. Through their reading program, students should have learned to find the fault lines in a script so they are aware of problem areas before they start to rehearse.

Veteran actors know how to diagnose a script, what can be done to exploit the strong points in the text, and how to help the weaknesses in the writing as they create their roles in rehearsal. In a professional situation, they don't have to do this on their own because they will put Beats & Blocking together under the guidance of a director. An experienced, knowledge-able director, an actor's best friend, handles the cast with a light touch, never imposing his or her will on them, but at the same time, never shirking responsibility to provide supervision for the entire company. The best directors are either former actors or artists who have taken special pains to learn the actor's craft. They know better than to move actors around a set like toy soldiers to make a nice "stage picture." They, too, direct from the subtext, helping their cast create diagrammed movement that tells the story organically.

Should an actor have to deal with an unskilled director, my advice is block each scene as you're asked to, then go home and find out *why* you make each move, motivating it by and con-necting it to your subtext. Let's assume you've been asked to enter, take off your coat, cross to the window and open it, not because it's the physicalization of your first Beat but because it's a contrivance the director is using to bring light into the set from offstage. Do your homework. Choose to enter, take off your coat, and cross to the window as directed because the other character in the scene *closes up the house on a hot day to ir-ritate you*. Open the window as an act of defiance, thereby kick-ing off the conflict in the scene. The beauty of it is neither the director nor the other actor needs to know you're justifying your Blocking subtextually. And it's better that they don't. As Jack Nicholson says, "Keep your secrets to yourself."

When the student finishes laying out Beats and sets the commensurate Blocking, rehearsals are coming to an end. Only after all the subtextual work is done and the physical mechanics firmly established is the actor ready to do run-throughs of the whole scene from beginning to end. It should be obvious that this procedure can only happen in a workshop or a rehearsal hall for a period of days or weeks, where there is sufficient time to go back to the drawing board and fix the problems that need fixing. In film acting, the presumption is you have done this so often that you are capable of doing your homework on your own when necessary and are ready to make last minute adjustments with your fellow actors on the set.

When it's time to do run-throughs in the workshop, it's assumed that all the players are comfortable with the outcome of the work they've done by themselves. When they bring their run-throughs to class, I act as a director and help them polish their rehearsal work and find an appropriate *tempo* for the scene. It's difficult, if not impossible, for a company of actors to add finishing touches to a scene without directorial supervision.

Tempo, sometimes called pace, is the rate of speed at which the scene is played in performance. Tempo will depend on the style of the writing, the author's unique use of language, the interpretive choices of the actors, the dramatic content of the material, and so on. As a rule of thumb, comedy is played faster than drama, but there are factors that make "fast" or "slow" an oversimplification. A more sophisticated way to establish the right tempo has to do with rhythmic changes to ensure that a scene isn't played at the same pace throughout. *Rhythm* is a recurrent beat in a musical sense, and a variety of changing rhythms alter the tempo of an actor's performance. I suggest my students work on rhythmic changes in Beats & Blocking so they are built in when the form comes together in run-throughs.

As the Beats are developed, I ask them to look for engaging rhythms, unpredictable rhythms, emphatic rhythms that will provide an interesting design for the scene. The tempo should accommodate these rhythms which give a dynamic to a performance that cannot be achieved any other way. After years of acting in the theater, I can tell you that one of the best ways to keep an audience alert is to vary the dynamic and change the rhythms, avoiding a monotonous tempo that lulls them, inevitably, into inattention.

In this last phase of rehearsal, the more run-throughs the better. Small changes, additions or subtractions to the behavioral choices of the actors can be made, but the commitment to an agreed-on form is a must before a cast can relax and play the material spontaneously. Don't tinker with the form once it's set. Repetition of the form during run-throughs is what allows a Zen artist to let go of conscious control. Form becomes organic during the repetition, having been completely absorbed by the performer's Bodymind; then, and only then, does it become a guidance system for the flow of living energy that vitalizes an actor's performance, moment to moment.

Answers to the seven questions that preceded rehearsal—Who am I? Where am I? What do I want? Why do I want it? Who do I want it from? What's in the way of my getting it? How do I get it?—should emerge during run-throughs. If all has gone well, these answers have been woven together into one rich tapestry of internal and external behavior. Seamlessly, a story will unfold that is well-executed, exciting, and original in every detail. At last, the actors are ready to leave rehearsal behind and play their roles. If they have rehearsed properly, from first to last, they can relax and have a good time. Performance will take care of itself.

Performance

"To act well, and to act well repeatedly, has to become an obsession." This is the opinion of Michael Redgrave, one of the most respected British actors of the 20th century. [His daughter, Vanessa, is, in my opinion, one of the two or three great actresses of this generation.] I quote Sir Michael from *The Actor's Ways and Means*, an exquisite little book I read years ago and revisited as I was finishing this chapter. Basically I agree with him, except in my experience "obsessed" is too mild a word to pin on the actors, writers, and directors I've known who will settle for nothing less than perfection in their art. I refer to this volume here because it focuses almost entirely on the rules for acting in *Performance*.

Redgrave's book reminds me of how rewarding it is to spend a few hours in the company of a cultivated, literate actor who loves the drama and has so thoughtfully studied the history of his profession. His book, based on four lectures he delivered to the drama department at Bristol University, is also a reminder that too few of my countrymen can offer anywhere near the informed chronicle that he does of the craft of acting in the Western theater. Michael Redgrave was a scholarly thespian who viewed his considerable accomplishments with a wry sense of humor and an admirable humility. His knowledge was impressive, but he wasn't impressed with his knowledge, displaying an envious willingness to admit how much he didn't know about the art form for which he was famous.

For instance, when he discusses Stanislavsky, he says: "I must confess that for some years now I have felt almost bored at the sound of his name and decidedly self conscious even in uttering it. However, I am ashamed to admit this, and in trying to make some plan for these talks, I quickly became aware that I could not bypass this landmark of the theatre with no more than a salute. For the work of Stanislavski [sic] is the only successful attempt which has ever been made to come to terms with the fundamentals of the actor's art."

Redgrave goes on to recall the problems he and so many of his fellow actors had when they first read *An Actor Prepares*. He reflects honestly on his instinctive tendency to reject any attempt to codify what seems to him the often mysterious nature of performance art. But he resolves his misgivings with these words: "The misunderstanding we may have about Stanislavski [sic] could probably be cleared up in a few minutes' conversation if one were to converse with him. And at this moment, after re-reading many of his words, and thinking what I would say to you about him, I can think of no one with whom I would more wish to have a talk."

Not that Redgrave denigrates teachers or theorists who preach a system or a methodology; he is simply unashamed to be performance-oriented. Being a pragmatist, he is more interested in *what* works in performance than *why* or *how* it works. From his viewpoint: "the great moments or evenings in the theatre, those which leave the strongest impression on the spectator, often arise from the unconscious of the player and are not susceptible to analysis either by him or by the beholder. As it has been put, in yet another way, these are the times ... when we can say that the performance has 'flight,' or 'leaves the ground.'"

Even from these few quotes, it's obvious that Redgrave is not only performance-oriented, but theater-oriented as well. He was part of a cadre of celebrated British actors, most notably Sir John Gielgud, Sir Laurence Olivier, Sir Ralph Richardson, and Noel Coward, who, like him, initially made their reputations on the stage, later reaching a broader audience in the cinema, then promptly returning to the theater to challenge themselves with the great roles in theatrical literature.

On the other hand, in this country during the last seventy-five years, actors who found success on the Broadway stage immediately went to Hollywood and rarely returned to their roots. As a consequence, on this side of the Atlantic the development of the actor's art and a reverential view of acting as a valued profession has suffered a setback over several generations. Lest we forget, theater is the actor's natural habitat, while film is a director's medium. Actors thrive in front of live audiences, where they can flex their artistic muscles and take command of the performance from beginning to end. In Britain, performance artists of the highest rank—Redgrave, Olivier, Gielgud, and the others who often directed themselves and each other on the stage—were uncomfortable giving up that managerial role when they acted in films. They were accustomed to being in charge and taking total responsibility for their performances.

Parenthetically, in *The Actor's Ways and Means* Redgrave refers to the Stanislavsky "method" on numerous occasions, but he never once mentions Lee Strasberg's name. He discusses the paramount importance of the actor's voice and body, the power of "the magic If," the "circle exercise" (expanded awareness) and other Stanislavskian principles and techniques as if they comprised the only "method" available to a British actor in mid-century. It's as though he had never heard of the *affective memory* exercise or The Actors Studio, whose alumni had overrun the American cinema. From Sir Michael's standpoint, Method actors who were so popular in this country might as well have been in a different profession.

In a way, they were. Brando, Dean, and directors like Kazan all got their start in theater and promptly went to Hollywood. The trend had begun during the '30's when players Franchot Tone and John Garfield left the Group Theatre behind, emigrated West, and became movie stars. Strasberg, by nature an authoritarian, always stressed the dominant role a director plays in the dramatic arts; he saw the actor in a submissive, secondary role. His students, first at the Group Theatre and later at The Actors Studio, were willing cogs in an art form dominated by directors. Because of their training they were a perfect fit in the Hollywood hierarchy, in what would become the commercially-dominant film industry.

Stanislavsky, on the other hand, was an actor first, a teacher second, and a director by default. He was a man of the theater; acting was his passion, and he saw the actor's performance as the decisive aspect of dramatic art. He had no interest in any medium that didn't put actors as artists on a pedestal and keep them there. Is it any wonder that his aesthetic never took hold in the mid-century American drama club, whose members paid lip service to the art of acting but, in truth, worshipped only the star on the dressing room door? Revisiting Michael Redgrave's inspirational treatise on acting put my own life in perspective and made me realize how vain my search had been for the principles Stanislavsky represented when I migrated to New York more than forty years ago.

Unless one has worked extensively in the theater, it would be impossible to appreciate the importance of a few spectators who randomly come together as an audience in the creation of performance art. My dictionary defines *performance* as "a presentation, especially a theatrical one, before an audience." Having grown up in the movies, I knew that on a film set the director is the audience. An actor, therefore, must trust the man or woman behind the camera for an objective, immediate response. In addition, in the movies a performance is recorded on bits and pieces of film that will be assembled in post production by the director and an editor. Hopefully, a movie actor has had enough experience in the theater, heard the laughter, sensed the tears, and felt the collective response of an audience to deliver those fragments of his or her performance to the editing room as a comprehensive whole.

The audience in the broadest sense is composed of ticket holders, critics, stagehands, playwrights, investors, grips, producers, theater owners, drama students, Academy members, network programmers, the youthful popcorn set, the informed, the uninformed, you and me. Everyone who goes to the movies, watches television, or attends a stage production is a member of the audience. Not one of us has to take a test for expertise in evaluating a dramatic presentation, and just by buying a ticket or changing channels, each of us has the right to make a judgment and form our own opinions of performance art.

Since audiences are made up of many individuals, they are veritable stews of subjective reactions, difficult to analyze, qualify, or verify. Nonetheless, after my years in the living theater, I know that every new audience has its own recognizable identity. As old-timers will confirm, you never get exactly the same reaction twice. Some kind of mysterious alchemy molds a group of strangers into an identifiable psychic field, which reacts to your performance for the first time, every time. The folks out there in the dark have not been rehearsed; they react the way they react. They can't help themselves.

A journalist once asked Laurence Olivier, "What's the actor's biggest problem?" His reply was short and sweet, "To keep the audience from going to sleep." Since most audiences are aligned in rows of seats that face one direction, toward the stage or screen, some actors take it for granted that they will automatically pay attention. Though spectators are sandwiched between other spectators, physically trapped until the lights come up, they're free to mentally roam the cosmos or fall into a deep slumber should the performance fail to hold their interest. In truth, the obligation is on the dramatic artist (actor, writer, and director) to create drama so mesmerizing that members of the audience are afraid to let their minds wander for fear they might miss something.

They should be riveted on the stage or screen from the moment the lights dim in the theater.

What means do you have at your disposal to "keep the audience from going to sleep" if you're an unconscious actor? First, tell them a good story. An audience—indeed, any group of listeners—is a sucker for an interesting yarn that will keep them interested. Gifted raconteurs pique the listeners' interest when they first open their mouths; in the same way, the actor as storyteller must command the audience's attention the first time he or she enters or the performance will not, to paraphrase Redgrave, get off the ground.

You are ready to do this if you have come up with provocative, original answers to the seven basic questions and are able to dramatize the character's point of view instantaneously. I remember reading that Anthony Hopkins had such a definite idea about how Hannibal Lecter should be discovered by the camera when he first came on screen in *Silence of the Lambs* that he told the director, Jonathan Demme, just how the scene should be shot. If you've seen the movie, Sir Anthony's entrance is a prime example of what I'm talking about.

The point is, start telling your story instantly and get the audience on your side. Before you can do this, however, you have to clue them in as to who you are, what your problem is, and why they should care about your solving it. Emotionally they have to be rooting for you, but if they don't understand you or are confused about the motivation behind your behavior, they can neither be for you nor against you, depending on your role in the piece. The audience should root for you to find the grail if you're the good guy, or get your comeuppance if you're the bad guy. Hero or heavy, it makes no difference; they have to have strong feelings about what happens to you, or you're not telling your story very well.

As I've said, never play an obvious heavy as the heavy; what you'll end up with is a bad guy with no saving graces, a cardboard character devoid of humanity. It won't matter to the audience whether you live or die if there's nobody to root for, one way or the other. Once again, in *Silence of the Lambs*, Anthony Hopkins transformed Hannibal the Cannibal, the most reprehensible of characters, into an offbeat hero; he later admitted that Hannibal Lecter, though a tortured madman, was hopelessly in love with the young Jody Foster. I advise all Zen artists to find light in the most despicable of characters and plumb the dark side of every thinly-written protagonist in a white hat.

As the story of your performance unfolds, reinforce the built-in urgency, milk the surprises large and small for all their worth and, in the interest of mounting suspense, hold off the moment of resolution until the very last minute. If the spine of your role is solid and during performance you supply the emotional thrust necessary to fuel the rising arc of intensity, all will go as planned, and you can ride a wave of increasing tension to the end. Reducing the fuel will slacken the tension, and the audience will feel a letdown and lose interest in your story.

The dictionary tells us that *per*—the Latin preposition "through"—combined with *formare*—"to form thoroughly"—turns out to be literally, *through form*. In the methodology I teach, all of the actor's life force flows through the Bodymind as well as the rehearsed structure which is the form of the role. A skilled unconscious actor's performance is forever old and new, predetermined and improvised, pre-set and discovered moment to moment, all at the same time. This balanced integration of spontaneous intuitive flow through meticulously designed form is what makes my Process unique.

More than anything else, unconscious actors live their roles in the present tense. Every emotional impulse they feel is a reaction to the spontaneous energy generated by them and their fellow actors in union with the audience. Every moment is new, unpredictable, utterly truthful, and inevitable, in the now moment of performance. In every scene, the audience is the other character, part of an improvisation that fills the theater and creates a brand new theatrical event at every performance. The same thing happens take after take on a film set; the only missing element is the group dynamic that only an audience can provide in the living theater. Never forget, the audience is a not-to-be-ignored collaborator in your performance when you're acting on the stage.

And don't be surprised that the minute the good guy wins and the bad guy loses, the paying customers are ready to go home. Once the perceived hero finds his or her "promised land," there's nothing more for them to root for. They can be content that once more, good has triumphed over evil—in the drama at least—and a similar outcome can take place in their lives. Such are the marvelously positive reinforcements of a good dramatic story well told. Many audiences have been inspired and encouraged to hang on for a better day.

Of course, once an unconscious actor encounters the public, it's too late to question decisions made in rehearsal. I tell even the most inexperienced student, never second-guess yourself. Commit. You have no greater power as a performing artist than an unwavering, deeply-felt commitment to your point of view. Give up being right or wrong; others may criticize or disagree with your choices, but you have to stand by your decisions. If your performance works for audience after audience, you have clearly done something right.

Being right or wrong matters little to unconscious actors anyway, because that would suggest their egos are in the way. They must bring selflessness to the art, making contact with audiences on a whole other level. I believe an actor's willingness to bring his or her unprotected humanity to each role is what affects audiences more than anything else. Skill is an empty façade. Reveal your innermost truth when you're playing a character, and audiences can't help responding; try to manipulate them with clever ideas, and you'll leave them cold.

A passionate heart reigns supreme in the drama business. Zen artists go beyond simply communicating with a group of spectators. They seek oneness with all humanity. They dig down into the depths of their consciousness, mining all the love, the humor, the sexuality, and yes, the fear, the anger, and the heartache in their instruments to earn a sympathetic rapport with their fellow beings. Uninhibited living energy is the link which holds us all in communion. As Duse demonstrated more than a hundred years ago, in modern acting there's no better way to become one with audiences than to share your living essence with them. Stanislavsky agreed: "The actor creates the life of the human spirit of the role from his own living soul, and incarnates it in his own living body. There is no other material for the creation of a role."

Quoting from *Stanislavsky in focus*, he goes on to say: "you never lose yourself on stage. You always act in your own persona as artist. There's no walking away from yourself." Stanislavsky is obviously referring to the greater Self, not the precious ego that some actors attempt to glorify in their acting. Showing off is hardly performance art; turning oneself into a mere entertainer to buy popularity is not what he had in mind. "Love the art in yourself, not yourself in the art," is one of his most repeated quotations.

While commercial success is not the best criterion for artistic achievement, neither is worldwide fame a sign that actors have been seduced by or given themselves away to the marketplace. The famous actors I've worked with over the years well deserved their celebrity and were more dedicated to doing their best work than the lesser mortals who disparaged them. For a true Zen artist, a successful career is never inconsistent with transcendent art. As I see it, the more excellence in your performing, the better chance you have of reaching a wide, appreciative, and loyal audience.

We're nearing the end of the story: one man's journey toward mastering performance art in acting and in life. In the beginning, The Unconscious Actor was a conception, a prototype, a creature of the imagination. But over the years it has come alive as real human beings have learned to practice unconscious acting. In a generic sense, he or she is any performing artist who thrills audiences worldwide, exhibiting the principles described in this book in the discipline of their choice. To name a few of my heroes: Tiger Woods, who has set a standard of pre-eminent artistry on a golf course; Oprah Winfrey, whose empathetic openness is on display five days a week for millions of fans in her television audience; Mikhail Baryshnikov, a Zen artist of the highest magnitude, a prophet who's combining dance, music, and stylized language into an art form that could nudge contemporary theater toward a new kind of dramatic expression.

In my own field, I sense that I'm watching an approximation of ultimate artistry when a performer seems to be totally present, telling me a deeply personal story, and discovering the life of the character for the first time every time he or she plays the part. Over the years I've seen Zen artists on the stage, in film, and on television, and I've talked about these performances in the workshop, using them as examples of unconscious acting. I know little of other ancient theatrical traditions—the Barong, Kabuki, or Noh, for instance—so the expertise I have is limited to dramatic art in Western theater. Like Stanislavsky, I've spent a lifetime observing and learning from the performances of actors in that arena. I've scoured newspapers, books, magazines, and watched numerous talk shows for quotable words of those I've admired so I can bring them into class as teaching aids.

Performers who stand above the crowd are sometimes able to talk about what they do, but sometimes they are unable—or unwilling—to analyze their methods and reveal their inner workings. Some actors perform brilliantly, but the last thing they want to talk about is how they do it. I only quote those incomparable artists who are doers rather than theorists, who have generously shared their thoughts about acting based on their own professional experience.

Invariably they share a common background; in the absence of an updated, well-publicized, comprehensive methodology, they have been forced to follow their instincts and develop a technique of their own. This will take them a decade or two of experimentation. When they are finally accomplished actors, they often worry that too much analysis might jeopardize the instinctual purity of their art. But some are still willing to be forthcoming with an interviewer.

In a *New York Times* interview Jeanne Moreau, longtime queen of French cinema, said, "There's no thinking, no reflection—as if some force went through me and says . . . no, it must be this way, not that."

I'm reminded of a passage in *Zen in the Art of Archery* when Eugen Herrigel was accused of having too much conscious control as he trained to become an archer. Herrigel asked Master Awa, "How can the shot be loosed if 'I' do not do it?"

"'It' shoots."

"And who or what is this 'it'?"

"Once you have understood that you will have no further need of me."

Ms. Moreau apparently didn't need to question the force moving through her Bodymind. Like other Zen artists, "There's no thinking, no reflection" when she is in performance, as she allows her intuitive impulses to flow through the role with her thinking mind out of the way.

Recently a member of the workshop told me she was reading a book by David S. Reiss, *M*A*S*H: the exclusive inside story of TV's most popular show,* and she came across these words of Alan Alda who starred in the long-running series on CBS. "Like any artist, the actor has to be open to inspiration, and the unconscious. When you know what you're looking for, that's all you get—what's previously known. But when you're open to what's possible, you get something new, and that's creativity." I couldn't have capsualized the message in the book you're reading any better myself.

I'm grateful to Mr. Alda for his words of wisdom. I'm also indebted to one of the most admired actors in the world, Daniel Day-Lewis who was quoted in *Entertainment Weekly* as saying: "Essentially, the process of working towards the presentation of a life that isn't yours is a process of working towards unconsciousness. So if you've done the work properly, you're absolutely unconscious to what extent that life has become you or you have become that life." Like Alan Alda, Oscar winner Day-Lewis was defining himself as an unconscious actor, and the phrase has a certain ring to it.

I share these quotes with every new student; this unconsciousness is what you're going to learn here, I tell them. I'm not talking about acting while you're asleep or in a coma. You're going to be awake and fully functional whether you're in front of a camera or interacting with an audience.

Another obvious proponent of unconscious acting is Sir Anthony Hopkins. In *Los Angeles' Arts and Entertainment—*

VENICE, Hopkins said: "I simplified the 'Method' for myself. I gradually went back to the understanding that I devise a method of my own but I still use a lot of it." He went on to say: "And my wisdom, what little wisdom I may have, is that I don't know anything anymore. I don't know anything about acting anymore. All I know is that it's a process of letting go."

In this day and age, not knowing is a hallmark of greatness in performance art. I hope that the most successful Zen actors in the dramatic arts will talk about their methods, as Meryl Streep did on James Lipton's popular show, *Inside The Actors Studio*, on the Bravo channel. Ms. Streep, arguably one of our better actors, discussed her approach to acting with uncommon candor: "I come to each job with an open heart and trying to do my best . . . and with some connection to a character that I don't completely understand, although I know she lives in me. I don't question it. I don't really understand the zone or the state I go into when I do these things. I don't *know* how I'm going to approach it. It would be good to have one sort of way."

Lipton questioned her: "When you have to prepare for a role as thoroughly as you did Sophie [*Sophie's Choice*], do you leave room for spontaneity? For accidents? For those wonderful moments?"

Ms. Streep's emphatic reply: "Oh, God, I hope so. Yes, I do. That's the only thing that's worth looking at . . . is what nobody expected to happen in a scene. It's all the things that if you've been in a play, when somebody drops something or forgets a line, suddenly it all becomes alive and electric, and it all feels real. So, yes, the unexplained, the tangent energy, the spontaneous is what you dream of and wish for and hope appears."

Tom Hanks and Harrison Ford were also interviewed by Mr. Lipton. Hanks reminisced about telling his dad that, when he was talking to his movie father [Jackie Gleason] in *Nothing in Common,* he was really communicating with him: "which is the spiritual thing that actors can go through sometimes no matter what the project is. It's not unlike going to church. It's not unlike both the inspiration that you can get from the spiritual moment, but also the sense of relief, of confession, of self-examination. It can come out because of the role that you portray."

Ford, known in the industry as a dedicated craftsman, compared acting to what he had learned as a young man making a living as a carpenter: "The way of thinking about things I learned from carpentry. I began to understand what served me in acting as well, to work from the ground up, one thing on top of another thing, on top of another thing."

And then came Ford's description of what happens for him when he leaves the building blocks behind, when he transcends the craft: "I expect to grant my audience complete and total access. You have to be willing to live in front of people, let them see the good, the bad, the ugly, the weak, the strong, the conflicted, the terrible. It's not about you, again it's about the continuity between you and the rest of your race. It's about being human. And it's about sharing that humanity. It's amongst some of the most important moments of my life, the being able to do that. The question of the *willingness* to do it? I mean, it's to give yourself to that moment."

One night, I happened to turn on the *Charlie Rose* show in time to hear Nicholas Cage respond to Rose's question, "What do you bring to a film?"

Without hesitation, Cage said, "My soul." My ears picked up. Cage went on: "I want to be in control while being out of control. I don't want to know what I'm going to do."

When Rose posed the questions about his life as an actor— "What's the best for you? What could make it better?"— Cage answered, "If I can find a way to totally just bare my soul, to be totally naked on film, so that there was no delineation between my life and my persona on film—maybe that would be pure."

Cage grinned and glanced off camera. "My team is back there, and I'm talking about spirit. And they told me you don't want to talk about spirit on the *Charlie Rose* show, [but] I'm open-minded. Is there something out there, and if there is, come on in, because I want you to help me act."

Charlie Rose became uncharacteristically enthusiastic. "You are great! That's why directors like you. Here's a guy who's willing to go out on the edge and give you the best he has without knowing *himself* where it's going to end."

Yes, quite unexpectedly, on national television, Nicholas Cage and Charlie Rose were discussing the Process I was writing about. As were the other noted artists I've been quoting. It seems that this route to performance art has deeper roots in the collective unconscious than I had previously realized. Somehow, Stanislavsky's sublime ideas about artistry in the drama and his seminal training methodologies for actors in the Western theater, both European and American, have survived for over a hundred years. He is alive and in robust health in the 21st century.

The same can be said for Eleonora Duse. Toward the end of the biographical appreciation of Duse quoted earlier, Helen Sheehy writes about Eva Le Gallienne's close relationship with the legendary star who treated the younger actress "as a colleague, encouraged her, and allowed her a glimpse into her private world." As a result, Le Gallienne was in a position to repeatedly study her idol in performance. "From her front row seat," Sheehy tells us, "she observed there 'was no hiatus between the thoughts and feelings of the characters Duse played, and herself as their interpreter. It was *one* process.' Le Gallienne believed that Duse's art was a combination of 'perfectly concealed technical virtuosity' coupled with creative imagination, 'the power of an astute and virile mind,' and a body 'which had been molded into a flawless instrument.'" I can think of no better way to succinctly describe a blueprint for the dramatic artistry I have been discussing throughout this book.

I believe the trend is definitely in the right direction, and Zen artistry is in the genes of a small but growing army of actors in the drama business. I wrote this book not so much to reach them, the recognized practitioners we all admire, but for every performer in the Western theater who dreams of making a significant contribution to the art of acting. I say to you, wherever you are, be proud of yourself and "follow your bliss." Know who you are, know where you came from, know that the profession you are part of dates back thousands of years and that your ancestors are smiling down on you with appreciation and support.

I have deliberately stressed the historical aspects of acting in this book because I've found that too many of my coworkers know too little about their family tree. But don't be misled. The story of The Unconscious Actor is less about the lessons of the past or the fine work being done in the dramatic arts today, than it is a call to arms for the actor of the future. If you're a newcomer, I suggest you learn as much as you can about your genealogy, honor the intrinsic nobility of the acting profession you are entering, and see yourself as a superb artist, nothing less. The road to success is paved with artistic integrity and an unquenchable thirst for excellence.

Should the reader aspire to fulfillment in another field, I urge you to explore the mechanics of creativity in your workaday lives. You may call me a terminal idealist, but I can't help envisioning a day when legions of unconscious warriors, Zen artists of every persuasion in the arts, in business, in sports, and yes, even in politics, will bring an enlightened approach to the creation of a better world worthy of a brand-new millennium. If any part of you shares that vision, the sooner you get moving, the better. As Goethe reminds us: "Whatever you can do or dream you can, begin it. Boldness has genius, power and magic in it. Begin it now."

Recommended Reading List

(In Alphabetical Order by Author)

ADLER, Stella—*The Technique of Acting*. New York: Bantam Books, 1988.

ALLEN, David—*Stanislavski For Beginners*. New York: Writers and Readers Publishing, Inc., 1999.

ARTAUD, Antonin—*The Theatre and Its Double* (Mary Caroline Richards, translator). New York: Grove, 1958.

BENEDETTI, Jean—*Stanislavski: An Introduction*. London: MEUTHEN Ltd., 1982.

BOLESLAVSKY, Richard—*Acting: The First Six Lessons*. New York: Theatre Arts Books, 1933.

BRESTOFF, Richard—*The Great Acting Teachers and Their Methods*. Lyme, NH: Smith and Kraus, Inc., 1995.

BROOK, Peter—*The Empty Space*. New York: Touchstone, 1996.

CALLOW, Simon—*Being an Actor*. New York: St. Martin's Griffin, 1995.

CAMERON, Julia—*The Artist's Way*. New York: Penguin/Putnam, 2002.

CARNICKE, Sharon M.—*Stanislavsky in focus*. Amsterdam: OPA (Overseas Publishers Association), 1998.

CHAIKIN, Joseph—*The Presence of the Actor*. New York: Atheneum, 1987.

CHEKHOV, Michael—*To the Actor*. New York: Perennial Library, 1985.

CHOPRA, Deepak—*The Seven Spiritual Laws of Success*. San Rafael, CA: Amber-Allen Publishing/New World Library, 1994.

CLURMAN, Harold—*The Fervent Years*. New York: Da Capo Press, Inc., 1983.

CROALL, Jonathan—*Gielgud: A Theatrical Life 1904–2000*. New York: Continuum, 2001.

DAW, Kurt—*Acting: Thought into Action*. Portsmouth, NH: Heinemann, 1997.

DIDEROT, Denis—*The Paradox of Acting* (Walter Herries Pollack, translator). New York: Hill and Wang, 1957.

EDWARDS, Betty—*Drawing on the Right Side of the Brain*. New York: Jeremy P. Tarcher/Putnam, 1989.

FELDENKRAIS, Moshe—*Awareness Through Movement*. New York: Harper & Row, 1972.

FERGUSSON, Francis—*The Idea of a Theater*. Garden City: Doubleday and Co., 1949.

GALLWEY, W. Timothy—*The Inner Game of Tennis*. New York: Bantam Books, 1979.

GASSNER, John—*A Treasury of the Theatre: Volume One*. New York: Simon and Schuster, 1951; *A Treasury of the Theatre: Volume Two*. New York: Simon and Schuster, 1951; *A Treasury of the Theatre: Volume Three*. New York: Simon and Schuster, 1951.

GELB, Barbara and Arthur—*O'Neill*. New York: A Delta Book, 1964.

GRANT, Neil—*History of Theatre*. London: Hamlyn, 2002.

GROTOWSKI, Jerzy—*Towards a Poor Theatre*. New York: Simon and Schuster, 1969.

HAGEN, Uta—*Respect for Acting*. New York: Hungry Minds, Inc., 1973.

HARTNOLL, Phyllis—*A Concise History of the Theatre*. Great Britain: Thames and Hudson, 1968.

HERRIGEL, Eugen—*Zen in the Art of Archery* (R. F. C. Hull, translator). New York: Pantheon Books, 1960.

HETHMON, Robert H.—*Strasberg at The Actors Studio.* New York: Theater Communications Group, 1965.

HORNBY, Richard—*The End of Acting.* New York: Applause Books, 1992.

HUNT, Gordon—*How to Audition.* New York: HarperCollins, 1995.

KNEPLER, Henry—*The Gilded Stage: The Years of the Great International Actresses.* New York: William Morrow & Company, Inc., 1968.

KRISHNAMURTI, J.—*The First and Last Freedom.* Wheaton, IL: Quest, 1967.

LEWIS, Robert—*Method—or Madness?* New York: Samuel French, Inc., 1958.

LE GALLIENNE, Eva—*The Mystic in the Theatre: Eleonora Duse.* Arcturus Books, 1973.

MASON, Marsha—*Journey.* New York: Simon & Schuster, 2000.

MEISNER, Sanford and Dennis Longwell—*Sanford Meisner on Acting.* New York: Vintage Books, 1987.

MORRIS, Eric—*Acting from the Ultimate Consciousness.* Los Angeles: Ermor Enterprises, 2000; *No Acting Please.* Los Angeles: Ermor Enterprises, 2004.

OSBON, Diane K.—*Reflections on the Art of Living: A Joseph Campbell Companion.* New York: HarperCollins, 1991.

REDGRAVE, Michael—*The Actor's Ways and Means.* London: Nick Hern Books Limited, 1995.

ROBERTS, Jane—*The Nature of Personal Reality.* San Rafael, CA: Amber-Allen Publishing/New World Library, 1994

RODEGAST, Pat and Judith Stanton—*Emmanuel's Book.* Weston, CT: Friend's Press, 1985; *Emmanuel's Book II.* New York: Bantam Books, 1989; *Emmanuel's Book III.* New York: Bantam Books, 1994.

SHEEHY, Helen—*Eva Le Gallienne: A Biography.* New York: Alfred

A. Knopf, 1996; *Eleonora Duse: A Biography*. New York: Alfred A. Knopf, 2003.

SHURTLEFF, Michael—*Audition*. New York: Bantam Books, 1980.

SMITH, Wendy—*Real Life Drama: The Group Theatre and America 1931–1940*. New York: Grove Weidenfeld, 1990.

SONNENBERG, Janet—*Actor Speaks*. New York: Crown Trade Paperbacks, 1996.

STANISLAVSKY, Constantin—*My Life in Art* (J. J. Robbins, translator). New York: Meridian Books, 1956; *An Actor Prepares* (Elizabeth Reynolds Hapgood, translator). New York: Routledge/ Theatre Arts Books, 1989; *Building a Character* (Elizabeth Reynolds Hapgood, translator). New York: Routledge/Theatre Arts Books, 1994.

STRASBERG, Lee—*A Dream of Passion*. New York: Penguin, 1987.

STUBBS, Jean—*Eleonora Duse*. New York: Ballantine Books, 1970.

TEMKINE, Raymonde—*Grotowski* (Alex Szogyi, translator). New York: Avon, 1972.

TOLLE, Eckhart—*The Power of Now*. New World Library, 1999.

WEAVER, William—*Duse: A Biography*. New York: Harcourt Brace Jovanovich, 1985.

WILBUR, Ken—*The Spectrum of Consciousness*. Wheaton, IL: Quest, 1993.

Index

A

ABC, 162
Abel, Walter, 51
Academy Award, 9
action, 35, 77, 88, 95,
    98, 107, 109, 133,
    156, 176, 184,
    190–191, 237, 243
action, 237, 239–241,
    249, 251
activities, 252
activities, 230, 232–233,
    236, 241, 243
Actors Studio, The, 61,
    64, 97–98, 102–105,
    112–113, 260;
    Director's Unit, 102;
    Playwright's Unit, 102
Actor's Ways and Means,
    The (Redgrave), 257,
    259
Adams, Maude, 38
Adler, Luther, 53
Adler, Stella, 53, 100,
    104, 106–107, 133
Aeschylus, 27–29
affective memory
    exercise, 13, 102,
    106–107, 133, 260

Ah, Wilderness (O'Neill),
    50
Albee, Edward, 95
Albert, Eddie, 51
Alda, Alan, 270
Alfred Hitchcock Presents
    (television show), 80
Alice (television show),
    161
All in the Family
    (television show),
    158–159
Allen, David, 191
Aloysius of Gonzaga,
    St., 18
American Academy,
    New York City, 121
American Mime
    Theater, 121–122, 192
An Actor Prepares
    (Stanislavsky), 59–60,
    84, 113, 129, 258
analysis, 14, 18, 137,
    141, 186, 216, 226,
    228, 231, 258, 269
analytical mentality, 14
analytical mind, 180
analytical prowess, 55
analytical skills, 25

analytical thought, 137,
    173, 186, 218, 227
Anderson, Maxwell, 50,
    52
Anderson, Robert, 68–69
Andreini, Isabella, 38
antagonist, 245
Anthony, Joseph "Jo,"
    228
anti-realistic expression,
    42
anti-realistic plays, 42
Antoine, André, 40
Apple Tree, The
    (musical), 157
Aristophanes, 27, 30
Aristotelian unities, 35
Arkin, Alan, 207
Arliss, George, 46
art of performance, 91
Artaud, Antonin, 95
Arthur, Bea, 158
Arthur, Jean, 51
Assignment in Brittany
    (film), 10
Astaire, Fred, 48, 66
Athenian acting, 29
Athenian dramatists, 28
Athens, 27

audition song, 2
auditioning, 4, 158
Aumont, Jean-Pierre, 10
avant-garde, 94, 96, 104
Awa, Kenzo, 143–146
Awake and Sing (Odets),
    53
awareness, 26, 175–176,
    178, 182, 184–185,
    193–195, 197–199,
    260

B
Bakshy, Alexander, 39
Baldwin, James, 101
Ball, Lucille, 194
Bard of Avon. *See*
    Shakespeare, William
Barefoot in the Park
    (Simon), 157, 194,
    225
Barker, Margaret, 53
Barong, theatrical
    tradition, 268
Barry, Philip, 50
Barrymore, Drew, 38
Barrymore, Ethel, 38
Barrymore, John, 38
Barrymore, Lionel, 38
Baryshnikov, Mikhail,
    268
Batjac Productions, 55
beats, 12–13, 230,
    242–244, 247, 249,
    252, 254–255
Beats & Blocking, 22,
    241–242, 244,
    246–247, 249,
    251–253, 255
Beautiful Mind, A (film),
    245

Beckett, Samuel, 95, 97,
    126
Beery, Wallace, 10
Béjart, Armande, 38
Belasco, David, 44
Benton, Robert, 225
Bergman, Ingrid, 118
Berhman, S. N., 50
Berlin, Irving, 65
Bernhardt, Sarah, 41–42
Berra, Yogi, 90–91
Beyond the Horizon
    (O'Neill), 49
Big (film), 118
Birth of a Nation, The
    (film), 47
Blake, William, 126
Blitzstein, Marc, 84
blocking, 242–244, 247,
    250, 252, 254
Bloy, Leon, 16
body language, 41
body of the actor, 12,
    25, 27, 29, 33, 94, 100,
    103, 109–110, 121,
    129–131, 134–135,
    190–193, 198–199,
    201–204, 209, 213,
    215–216, 243–244,
    260, 267, 274
Bodymind, 129–130,
    184, 197, 202, 204,
    222, 256, 265, 269
Bogart, Humphrey, 48
Bohnen, Roman, 53
Bohr, Neils, 141
Boleslavsky, Richard, 99,
    106
Bolger, Ray, 51
book musical, 48–49, 51
Booth, Edwin, 43

Boys Town (film), 6, 9
Brahm, Otto, 40
Brand, Phoebe, 53
Brando, Marlon, 61,
    63–65, 67, 105, 260
breathing, 86, 131, 144,
    193, 197, 222
breathing exercise, 131
Brecht, Berthold, 42
Brice, Fanny, 45
Brigadoon (musical), 84
Broadway, 46–47, 50,
    52–54, 70, 81, 83–84,
    86–87, 89, 91–95, 97,
    105, 110, 116, 122,
    153, 211, 259
Broadway musical, 86
Bromberg, J. Edward,
    53
Brook, Peter, 95
Brooks, Mel, 155–156
Brown, Clarence, 10–12
Buddha, 126, 173
Building a Character
    (Stanislavsky), 60, 84,
    113, 129, 158
Burbage, Cuthbert, 34
Burbage, Richard,
    34–35
burlesque, 31, 45
Burns, Lillian, 10
Burrows, Abe, 87, 117,
    153–154
Bus Stop (film), 68
Butterflies Are Free
    (Gershe), 124
Byington, Spring, 51

C
Cage, Nicholas, 273
Cagney, Jimmy, 48

Calhern, Louis, 51
Campbell, Joseph,
  127–128
Carlin, Gloria, 137
Carnegie Hall, 166
Carnicke, Sharon M.,
  105–107, 109–110
Carnovsky, Morris, 53
Casale, Madame Lucia,
  140
Cassavettes, John, 72–75
Cathedral High School,
  Los Angeles, 16
CBS, 72, 122–123,
  150–151, 160–162,
  164
Chaiken, Joe, 95
character: character
  acting, 12; character
  actors, 12, 153, 231;
  physicalizing the
  character, 7
character, portraying,
  6–7, 11–12, 65–66, 79,
  121, 132, 139,
  245–246, 249, 251,
  253, 263–264, 266,
  268, 271
characterization, 12, 65,
  78
Charles II, King, 38
Charlie Rose (television
  show), 273
Chart of the Stanislavski
  System (Lewis), 83–84
Chayefsky, Paddy, 77
Chekhov, Anton, 39, 46,
  97–98, 103, 230; on
  Duse, Eleonora, 139
Chekhov, Michael, 10,
  99–100, 132, 192, 202;
  To the Actor, 100, 192

Chesterton, Gilbert
  Keith, 159
Child, Julia, 18
Chip Off Olympus, A
  (Tasca), 151
Christian, 15–16, 31,
  120
Christian Brothers, 16
Chuang Tzu, 173
circle exercise, 260
Citizen Kane (film), 56
Civic Repertory
  Theater, 46
Clark, Bobby, 45
classic play, 98
classic themes, 52
classical, 62
classical actor, 29, 32, 43
classical comedy, 31, 36
classical style, 65
classical theater, 84
classicalism, 32, 35, 44
classicism, 65, 108
classics, 32, 46, 65
Clift, Montgomery, 61
Climax! (television
  show), 76
Clive, Kitty, 38
Close, Glenn, 175, 194
Clurman, Harold,
  52–53, 106, 108, 112;
  Fervent Years, The,
  108, 112
Cobb, Lee J., 53
Cohan, George M.,
  44–45, 50
Coleridge, Samuel
  Taylor, 6
collective unconscious,
  273
Colman, Ronald, 2

Columbus, Christopher,
  174
Comédie-Française,
  36–38
comedy, 28, 30–32,
  35–36, 45, 50, 65–66,
  84, 117, 149–151, 153,
  155–160, 164, 207,
  225, 255
comedy of manners,
  30, 35, 50, 84
comedy of manners, 35
commedia dell'arte,
  32–35, 38, 74
Commentaries I
  (Krishnamurti), 119
Commentaries II
  (Krishnamurti), 119
Commentaries III
  (Krishnamurti), 119
communicate, 126,
  174–175, 211–213,
  226, 232, 251
communication, 8, 20,
  137, 168, 175, 202,
  211–213, 229, 266,
  272
communication
  exercises, 229
Conditions exercise, 122,
  134–135
Congregation of the
  Passion, 20
conscious breathing,
  197
conscious thought, 175,
  216
Converse, Tony, 149
Cooper, Jackie, 9
Conquering Hero, The
  (musical), 86
Corbin, John, 141

Corneille, 35
Cornell, Katherine, 46
costume, 7, 25, 28–29,
    62, 64
cothurni, 28
Cotton Club, New York
    City, 85
counter-realism, 42
Covan, Willie, 85
Coward, Noel, 50, 65,
    159, 225, 259
CPR (Character/
    Place/Relationship),
    229, 234, 236, 246
Crabtree, Lotta, 38
craft of acting, 7, 10, 14,
    19, 36–37, 55, 60, 76,
    83, 91, 99–100, 106,
    108, 118, 121, 131,
    135, 140, 146, 148,
    166, 170, 185, 189,
    220–221, 231, 253,
    257, 271
craftsman, 79, 158, 190,
    271
craftsmanship, 13, 60,
    94, 147, 188, 242
Crawford, Cheryl, 13,
    61
create, 120, 128, 135,
    139, 170, 174–175,
    177, 179, 182, 201,
    219, 221–223,
    236–237, 244, 246,
    253
creative imagination, 27,
    100, 274
creative impulse,
    185–186, 218
creative process, 171,
    178, 205
creativity, 16, 18, 26, 32,

74, 96, 109–110,
    144–145, 171,
    173–177, 179–184,
    188, 190, 192, 198,
    218, 270, 275;
    mechanics of,
    171–189
Crosby, Bing, 2–3, 5–6,
    23, 56, 85
Crosby, Everett, 3
Crowe, Russell, 245
Cukor, George, 11–13,
    71, 117
Curtis, Paul, 121–122,
    134

D

Da Vinci, Leonardo, 126
d'Annunzio, Gabriele,
    140
Dante, 126
Darwell, Jane, 5–6
Davis, Bette, 48
Day-Lewis, Daniel, 270
De Mille, Agnes, 151,
    167
De Niro, Robert, 213
De Vega, Lope, 35
Dean, James, 61, 64, 67,
    260
Death of a Salesman
    (Miller), 62
Del Rey Players, The,
    23
Demme, Jonathan, 263
Depanis, Guiseppe, 139
Desire Under the Elms
    (O'Neill), 52
Destination Gobi (film),
    55–56
Dillman, Bradford, 50
Director's Unit, 102

Douglas, Melvyn, 80
Downey's, 105
D.R. Studio, 165, 167
drama, history of,
    26–54
dramatists, 27–28, 32,
    39, 43, 96, 213–214,
    224, 236, 245, 252
Dream of Passion, A
    (Strasberg), 111, 178
Drew, John, 46
Drew, Mrs. John. *See*
    Lane, Louisa (Mrs.
    John Drew)
Duncan, Isadora, 141
Dunnock, Mildred, 61,
    73, 80
DuPont Show of the Week
    (television show), 72
Duse, Eleonora, 41–42,
    138–142, 191, 266,
    274
Duse (Weaver), 139

E

Eastern mysticism, 110
Edward, Brother, 16
Eighty Yard Run, The
    (Shaw), 79
Eighty Yard Run, The
    (television broadcast),
    79
Einstein, Albert, 126
Eldridge, Florence, 50
*Eleonora Duse: A
    Biography* (Sheehy),
    140
Elizabethan actors, 38
Elizabethan England,
    34, 37
Emerson, Ralph Waldo,
    141, 182

emotion, 13, 84,
107–109, 111, 126,
133, 181, 183,
185–186, 198–199,
204–208
emotional impulse, 204,
265
emotional-memory
exercise, 178
emotional-memory
exercise, 178
emotional spontaneity,
181
ensemble, 57, 70, 73,
116, 118, 169, 195. *See
also* Civic Repertory
Theater; *commedia
dell'arte;* Group
Theatre; Moscow Art
Theatre, The
Entertainer, The
(Osborne), 118
Entertainment Weekly
(magazine), 270
epic-realism, 42
Erickson, Leif, 53, 68
Euripides, 27, 29, 54
European drama and
theater, 27, 31–34, 38,
41–43, 46, 48, 51, 54,
65, 94–95, 273
Evans, Cora, 17–19, 59,
120
Evans, Mack, 17–18
event, 186, 237, 239, 241
Exercise(s), 102,
134–135, 137, 146,
148, 168; *affective
memory* exercise, 13,
102, 106, 133, 260;
breathing exercise,

131; circle exercise,
260; communication
exercises, 229;
Conditions exercise,
122, 134–135;
emotional-memory
exercise, 178;
emotional-memory
exercise, 178; Flow,
190–215; imaging
exercises, 222;
improv exercises,
102; *Name and Bow,*
209–210; physical
exercises, 121, 130;
private moment
exercise, 102–103;
psychological gesture
exercise, 100, 202;
repetition exercise, 100;
sense memory exercise,
102; solo exercise,
147
Expressionism, 42

F
Faculty, The, 164
Fairbanks, Douglas, 46,
48
farce, 30, 35, 50, 66
farceur, 45
Farmer's Daughter, The
(film), 3
Fervent Years, The
(Clurman), 108, 112
Feuer, Cy, 87, 154
Fields, W. C., 45
Finney, Albert, 130
*First and Last Freedom,
The* (Krishnamurti),
118–119

Fitzgerald, F. Scott, 72,
75
Fletcher, Louise, 239
Flight of the Eagle, The
(Krishnamurti), 119
Flow, 110, 137, 139, 177,
181, 186, 190–218,
222, 236, 256, 265,
270
Flower Drum Song
(musical), 86
Fonda, Henry, 5–6, 23,
48, 56, 117–118
Fontanne, Lynn, 46
Foote, Horton, 77
Ford, Harrison, 272
Ford, John, 4–5, 8
Form, 216–219
formal thought, 218
Formalism, 42
Forrest, Edwin, 43
Fosse, Bob, 86–87, 153
Foster, Jody, 264
Fox. *See* Twentieth
Century Fox
Foy, Eddie, 45
Frankenheimer, John,
72–75
"Franklin D. Roosevelt
Jones" (song), 2
Free Theater, 40
Freedom From the Known
(Krishnamurti), 119
Freeman, Y. Frank, 2
Front Page, The
(MacArthur and
Hecht), 50

G
Gable, Clark, 48, 56
Garfield, John, 53, 260

Garrick, David, 37–38
Gary (student), 147–148
Gaslight (film), 118
GE Theater, 80
Gelosi, 38
Genet, Jean, 94, 103
George M! (musical), 92
Gershwin, George, 48–49
Gershwin, Ira, 48
Ghandi, Mahatma, 141
Ghosts (Ibsen), 40, 42
Giant (film), 67
Gielgud, John, 65, 259
Gilroy, Frank D., 101
Girl Crazy (musical), 48
Gish, Dorothy, 48
Gish, Lillian, 48
Glass Menagerie, The (Williams), 118
Gleason, Jackie, 272
Globe Theatre, 34
Goethe, Johann Wolfgang von, 36, 275
Golden Boy (Odets), 53
Grady, Billy, 67–68
Graham, Martha, 122, 126
Grant, Bud, 124
Grant, Cary, 48
Grapes of Wrath, The (film), 3–6, 118
greater Self, 17, 110, 144–145, 172, 176–177, 182, 214, 267
Greek theater, ancient, 27–30, 37
Green, Paul, 53
Greene, Graham, 16, 23

Greim, Jacob T., 40
Griffith, D. W., 47
Grotowski, Jerzy, 95
Group Theatre, the, 48, 52–53, 61, 70, 99–100, 106–108, 112–113, 260
Gunsmoke (television show), 80
Guys and Dolls (musical), 49
Gwenn, Edmund, 153
Gwynne, Nell, 38

H
Hagen, Uta, 101, 200
Hamlet (Shakespeare), 130
Hammerstein, Oscar, II, 48
Hanks, Tom, 118, 169, 211, 272
Happy Time, The (Taylor), 84
Harris, Julie, 61
Hart, Lorenz, 48
Hart, Moss, 50, 65, 132
Hatha Yoga, 110
Hayes, Helen, 46
HB Studio, 101
heart and acting, 14, 54, 65, 126, 180–181, 183, 185–186, 190, 192, 204–205, 216–218, 266, 271
Hecht, Ben, 50
Heflin, Van, 53
Heisenberg, Werner, 141
Hemingway, Ernest, 23, 97

Hepburn, Katharine, 10, 51, 56, 117
Herrigel, Eugen, 142–145, 269
Hickman, Darryl: army life, 57–58, 68; auditions, 3–4, 69, 81, 83, 86–87, 124; body work, 121, 129–131, 134; child actor, 1–16; New York and Broadway, 81–114; teaching, xv, 115–275; television work, 72–78, 80; and wife Lincoln, Pamela, 121; writing in college, 23–24
history of acting, 24–54
history (type of play), 35
Hoffman, Dustin, 148, 201
Hollywood, 3, 15–17, 20, 48, 61, 69, 73, 75, 78, 83, 124, 259–260
Homecoming, The (Pinter), 96
Hope, Bob, 48
Hopkins, Anthony, 227, 263–264, 270–271
Horowitz, Vladimir, 166
House of Connelly, The (Green), 53
How to Succeed in Business Without Really Trying (musical), 87, 92, 153–154, 157

Human Comedy, The
(film), 10–11
Hurt, William, 183

I
I Love Lucy (television
show), 194
Ibsen, Henrik, 39–42,
46, 54, 103
Iceman Cometh, The
(O'Neill), 50
idea, 115, 179, 182, 186,
188, 200–202, 209,
217–218, 228, 231,
242, 246
If I Were King (film), 2
image(s), 12, 74, 115,
126, 179, 182,
185–186, 191, 199,
201–204, 209,
217–218, 228, 237, 244
imagination, 12, 14, 27,
33, 55, 100, 107,
128–129, 179–180,
182, 185–186, 191,
199, 201–202, 204,
222, 227–228, 267, 274
imaging exercises, 222
improv, 74, 102, 192,
217
improv exercises, 102
improvisation, 32–33,
36, 74–75, 213, 236,
265
*Improvisation for the
Theatre* (Spolin), 192
improvise, 73–74, 125,
155
impulse(s), 25–26, 75,
122, 134, 137, 148,
181–182, 185–186,

192, 204, 209, 216,
218, 227, 265, 270
Independent Theater,
40–41
Inge, William, 68, 103
Inside the Actors Studio
(television show), 271
instinct, 26, 55, 63, 145,
155–156, 170, 190,
269
intellect, 36, 55, 126,
128–129, 144, 218
*Introduction to Acting: A
Handbook on the
Stanislavsky Method*
(Strasberg), 113
intuition, 115, 137, 144,
181–183, 185–186,
191, 199, 209, 227
intuitive energy, 186
intuitive flow, 137, 192,
209, 216, 218, 265
intuitive impulse, 209,
216, 227, 270
intuitive response, 230
intuitive urges, 182
Ionesco, Eugene, 95,
103
Irving, Henry, 37–38
Isidore, Father, 19
Island in the Sky (film),
55

J
Jackass Mail (film), 10
Jackson, Glenda, 95, 145
Jefferson, Joseph, 43
Jesus, 173
Joe Allen's, 105
John of the Cross, St.,
126

Jonson, Ben, 35
Jolson, Al, 48, 85
*Joseph Campbell
Companion, A*
(Osbon), 127–128
Judeo-Christian culture,
27
Julius Caesar (film), 65
Justinian, Emperor, 38

K
Kabuki, theatrical
tradition, 43, 268
Katselas, Milton,
124–125
Kaufman, George S.,
50, 65, 132
Kaye, Danny, 48
Kazan, Elia, 53, 61, 63,
70–71, 105, 236, 260
Kean, Edmund, 37
Keeper of the Flame
(film), 10, 12
Kelly, Gene, 48
Kemble, John Philip,
37–38
Kern, Jerome, 48
Kerr, Deborah, 68,
70–71
Kerr, John, 68
Kerr, Walter, 95–96
King, Martin Luther, Jr.,
141
Kingsley, Sidney, 52
Krishnamurti, J.,
119–120, 126, 133

L
La Dame aux Camélias
(Dumas, fils), 139

La Scala, Beverly Hills, 79
Laboratory Theatre, 106
Lahr, Bert, 51
Lane, Louisa (Mrs. John Drew), 38
Lao Tzu, 126
Lawrence, Gertrude, 48
Lawson, John Howard, 52
Le Gallienne, Eva, 46, 274; *Mystic in the Theatre, The*, 137–138, 140
Lear, Norman, 150, 153, 157, 159–161, 195–196
Leaves of Grass (Whitman), 127
Lekain, Henri-Louis, 37
Lennon, John, 141
Levene, Sam, 51
Lewis, Robert "Bobby," 60–61, 81, 83–85, 98, 100–101, 104–105, 107, 113, 132
Life Ahead (Krishnamurti), 119
life force, 188, 198–199, 201, 205, 207, 209–210, 215, 217, 265
Lightning Strikes Twice (film), 55
Liliom (Molnar), 42
Lillie, Beatrice, 48
Lincoln, Pamela, 121, 150
linear thought, 143

Lion in Winter, The (Goldman), 118
Lipton, James, 271–272
literary actor, 37, 43, 54, 217
literary theater, 97
live television, 72–73, 75–80
living theater, 51, 77, 81, 91, 262, 265
Loesser, Frank, 87, 117, 153
Long Day's Journey Into Night (O'Neill), 50
Looker (film), 130
Louis XIV, 34
Love, Phyllis, 73
Love of Life (television show), 122–123, 149
Loy, Myrna, 80
Loyola University, Playa Del Rey, California, 23–24, 57
Lucas, George, 127
Lunt, Alfred, 46

M
MacArthur, Charlie, 50
MacGowran, Jack, 95
Mack Sennett Bathing Beauty, 2
MacMurray, Fred, 51
Maids, The (Genet), 94–95
Malden, Karl, 61
Man Who Came to Dinner, The (Kaufman and Hart), 50–51
manifesto, 59
Mansfield, Richard, 43
Marat/Sade (Weiss), 95

Marceau, Marcel, 96
March, Frederick, 50
Marlowe, Christopher, 35
Marlowe, Julia, 38
Martin, Ernie, 86–87
Martin Beck (theater), 116
Marx, Karl, 51
Marx Brothers, 45
*M*A*S*H*: the exclusive inside story of TV's most popular show* (Reiss), 270
masks, 29
Mason, James, 65
Mason, Marsha, 134, 148, 151
Matinee Theater (television show), 76
Maude, 158
Mauriac, François, 16
McCambridge, Mercedes, 55
McLeod, Norman Z., 10–11
McQueen, Steve, 80
mechanics, 44, 156, 176, 184, 188, 192, 197, 254; of creativity, 171–172, 176, 184, 188, 192, 218, 275
Meet Me in St. Louis (film), 68
Meisner, Sanford "Sandy," 53, 79, 100–101, 105, 232
Meisner technique, 167–168
Men of Boys Town (film), 6–10

Menander, 30
Merman, Ethel, 48
Merton, Thomas, 17, 120
metaphysical, 62, 110, 136, 183
Method, the, 61, 63–64, 67, 74, 99, 101, 113, 132, 220
Method actors, 62, 66, 105, 129, 159
Method and "Poetic" Theater, The (Lewis), 84, 98–99
Method director, 70
Method of physical actions, 107
Method—or Madness? (Lewis), 60, 81, 83
Metro-Goldwyn-Mayer, 6–7, 9–11, 67, 69–70
MGM. *See* Metro-Goldwyn-Mayer
Michelangelo, 126
Midnight Cowboy (film), 201
Milland, Ray, 3
Miller, Arthur, 54, 62, 103, 225
Miller, J. P., 77
miniseries, 162, 164
Minnelli, Vincente, 11, 67–72
Miracle on 34th Street (film), 153
Molière, 34–36, 38, 54
Molnar, Ferenc, 42
moment to moment, 75, 134, 148, 194, 202, 208, 211, 218, 236, 241, 256, 265

monk, 19–20, 22, 28, 59, 125, 142
Montana, Joe, 165–166
Moore, Victor, 45
Moreau, Jeanne, 269–270
Moreland, Don, 142
Moriarity, Michael, 116, 118
Morrison, Patricia, 3
Morse, Robert, 87
Moscow Art Theatre, The, 10, 41, 97–100, 108, 110, 114, 128, 230
Motion Picture Home, Woodland Hills, California, 153
motion picture industry, 3
motion pictures, 28, 46–47, 50, 69, 76–77
Mourning Becomes Electra (O'Neill), 52
movie star, 1, 15, 59
movies, 1, 3–4, 8, 10, 14, 20, 24, 47, 55, 57–58, 61–62, 67–69, 76–77, 80, 91, 100, 118, 153, 156, 195, 223, 227–228, 261, 263
musical comedy, 65–66, 84–85, 87, 91–92, 117, 164
My Heart's in the Highlands (Saroyan), 84
My Life in Art (Stanislavsky), 58–60, 93, 109, 111, 115, 135
My View of the World (Schrödinger), 126–127

mystic bridges, 175
Mystic in the Theatre, The (Le Gallienne), 137–138, 172
mystical artists, 126, 138, 174–175
mystical discipline, 143, 172, 182
mystical path, 141
mystical perception, 19
mystical process, 128
mystical religious experience, 17
mystical world of superconscious, 192
mysticism, 110, 120, 127–129, 133, 141, 173
mysticism in the Process, 133, 138
mystics, 17, 126, 128, 141, 172–173, 177

N
Name and Bow (exercise), 209–210
National Velvet (film), 14
naturalistic acting, 66, 104, 132, 136
naturalistic drama, 43
naturalistic stagecraft, 40
naturalistic theater, 62, 125
Nazimova, Alla, 46
NBC, 162
Nelson, Ruth, 53
Nemirovich-Danchenko, Vladimir, 41
Neo-Classicism, 42
New York actors, 48, 50, 67, 70, 73, 75, 78
New York City, 72, 79,

81–82, 85–88, 91, 93,
    95–96, 99, 103, 105,
    114, 124, 138, 142,
    147, 149–150, 159,
    162–163, 201, 261
Newman, Paul, 78–80
Nicholson, Jack,
    238–239, 254
Nijinsky, Vaslav, 126
no thought, 176, 226
Nobel Prize, 49, 95–96
Noh, theatrical
    tradition, 268
Nolan, Lloyd, 53
non-realistic plays, 42
Nothing in Common
    (film), 272

O
O'Brien, Margaret, 10
O'Connor, Carroll, 158
Odets, Clifford, 52–53
Of Thee I Sing (musical),
    48
O'Keefe, Georgia, 126
Oklahoma! (musical), 49
Oliver, Sandy, 86
Olivier, Laurence, 118,
    259, 262
Olivier, Laurence,
    Stone-Age, 25, 27
On the Waterfront (film),
    67
Once in a Lifetime
    (Kaufman and Hart),
    50
*One Flew Over the
    Cuckoo's Nest* (film),
    238–239
One Life to Live
    (television show), 150

O'Neill, Eugene, 48–51,
    54
O'Neill, James, 49
onkos, 28
Open Theater, 95
Osbon, Diane K., 127
Oscar (Academy
    Award), 5, 55, 151,
    170
Out of Control, In Full
    Command, 152–275

P
Paley, William, 123–124
Paramount, 161
Passionist monastery, 19
Passionist monks,
    19–20, 22
pastoral, 35
Pearce, Joseph Chilton,
    197
performance art, 25, 45,
    88–89, 94, 99, 101,
    107, 125, 129, 136,
    143, 146, 148, 150,
    156, 169, 178,
    182–185, 188, 192,
    208, 216, 258,
    261–262, 267, 271, 273
performance artist, 6,
    26, 94, 144, 166, 178,
    181, 185, 209, 214,
    241, 259
performers, 27, 29, 45,
    78, 85, 88–91, 125,
    169, 188, 194–195,
    206–207, 213–214,
    217, 223, 244, 248,
    256, 268, 274
Perry Mason (television
    show), 80

Persoff, Nehemiah, 80
Philco Playhouse
    (television show), 72
physical actions, 107,
    109, 243, 251
physical exercises, 121,
    130
physical imagery, 192
physique of the actor,
    121
Pinter, Harold, 96–97
Pirandello, Luigi, 42,
    138–139
Place, 229, 232–233, 241,
    246
Place for Polly, A
    (Coleman), 122
Plautus, 30–31
Playhouse 90 (television
    show), 72, 76, 78, 80
playwrights, 28–30,
    32–34, 36, 39–40, 43,
    46, 51–52, 54, 62, 74,
    104, 114, 118, 188,
    214, 261
Playwright's Unit,
    102–103
Poetic theater,
    theatrical style, 85,
    92, 95, 98–99, 103,
    132
Police Tapes
    (documentary), 162
Polish Laboratory
    Theater, 95
Porter, Cole, 48
Powell, Jane, 10
Power and the Glory, The
    (Greene), 16
Prep, the, 193, 195–196,
    198, 201, 204, 209

Preston, Robert, 118
Principle(s), 173–183,
    193
prior event, 237, 241, 249
Private Life of the Master
    Race, The (Brecht), 42
private moment exercise,
    102–103
Process, the, xv, 19,
    133–134, 136, 138,
    143, 145–146, 148,
    151–152, 167,
    169–183, 189–192,
    200, 202, 213,
    216–219, 221, 241,
    265, 273
protagonist, 245, 264
psychological gesture
    exercise, 100, 202
Public Theater, The, 95
Pulitzer Prize, 48–50, 92
Punch and Judy show,
    98

Q
Quintero, Jose, 50

R
Racine, 35
Raja Yoga, 110
rational thought, 128
Ratoff, Gregory, 10–11
Raye, Martha, 3, 51
realism, 39, 42, 44, 93,
    129, 136
realistic acting, 41, 95
Rebel Without a Cause
    (film), 64
Redgrave, Michael,
    257–259, 261
Redgrave, Vanessa, 257

Regina (opera)
    (Blitzstein), 84
rehearsal, 2, 25, 57, 72,
    74, 76–77, 79, 87,
    155–156, 165–166,
    168, 221–256
rehearse, 73, 77, 116,
    167, 203, 219, 221,
    223–224, 228–229,
    234, 253, 256, 265
Reilly, Charles Nelson,
    101, 117, 164
Reiss, David S., 270
Relationship, 229, 233,
    241, 246
repetition exercise, 100
Respect for Acting
    (Hagen), 101
Reynolds, Debbie,
    164–165
rhythm of the scene,
    158, 255
rhythms, 25, 49–50, 95
Ribot, Théodule
    Armand, 111
Rice, Elmer, 49–50
Rice, Jerry, 165–166
Richardson, Ralph, 259
rising arc of intensity,
    236, 245, 251, 264
Robards, Jason, Jr.,
    49–50
Robbins, Jerome, 61
Roberta (musical), 87
Robinson, Bill, 85
Robinson, Todd, xvi
Rodgers, Richard, 48
Rogers, Ginger, 66
Roman Church, 17, 31,
    120

Roman Church
    mysticism, 120
Roman dramatists, 32
Roman theater, ancient,
    30–32
romance, 35
Rooney, Mickey, 6–10
Rose, Charlie, 273
Rose, Reginald, 77
Royal Shakespeare
    Company, 65, 130
Rumi, 126
Russell, Lillian, 45
Russian Tea Room,
    New York City, 101

S
Sacramento Music
    Circus (theater), 86
Samuel French
    (bookstore), Los
    Angeles, 105
Sardi's, New York City,
    101, 105, 118
Saroyan, William,
    10–11, 52, 84
Saturday Night Live
    (television show), 235
Saxe-Meiningen, Duke
    of, 40
scene study, 61, 124,
    134, 148, 191, 200,
    213–214, 216–219,
    221–222, 225
Schaffner, Franklin,
    78–79
Schrödinger, Erwin, 126
Screen Actors Guild,
    245
screenplay, 77, 224
script, 8, 11, 13, 54, 56,

73–75, 78, 80, 89, 124, 157, 161, 188, 200, 213, 216, 218, 223–225, 227–228, 231, 237, 239, 242, 252–253

Seagull, The (Chekhov), 39, 230, 232

Seaton, George, 153

Secrets, 229, 236–241, 246, 254

Seeds of Contemplation (Merton), 17

Seinfeld, Jerry, 155

Self, 17, 66, 110, 127, 143–145, 172, 176–177, 182, 190, 195, 197, 214, 267

sense memory exercise, 102

series, television, 80, 162, 164, 270

Serling, Rod, 77

Seven Story Mountain, The (Merton), 17

Shakespeare, William, 35–36, 70, 103, 130, 132, 225

Shaw, George Bernard, 39, 41, 103

Shaw, Irwin, 52, 79

Sheehy, Helen, 140–141, 274

Sherwood, Robert, 50

Showboat (musical), 48–49

Siddons, Sarah, 38

Side By Side (television pilot), 149

silence, 96, 139, 156, 251

Silence of the Lambs (film), 263–264

Simon, Neil, 92, 117, 159, 194, 225

singing, 45, 65, 85–86, 91, 95

sitcoms, 157–159, 161, 168

situation comedy, 149–150, 153, 159, 161

Six Characters in Search of an Author (Pirandello), 42

Sixth Infantry Division, Fort Ord, California, 57, 68

Skinner, Otis, 46

Skippy (film), 9

Smith, Art, 53

social criticism, 35

Socrates, 30

solo exercise, 147

Sondheim, Stephen, 49, 132

Song of Russia (film), 10, 99

Sophie's Choice (film), 223, 271

Sophocles, 27–29, 54, 132, 235

soul, 14, 18, 44, 47, 54, 109–111, 123, 139, 141, 161, 184–185, 190–192, 201, 218, 231, 267, 273

soulful, 218, 231

souls, 31, 230

spirit, 19, 26, 34, 44, 49, 59, 109, 111–112, 129,

141, 188, 219, 233, 243, 267, 273

spiritual, 129, 132

spiritual aspirations, 16, 92

spiritual contents of role, 191

spiritual core, 173

spiritual dimensions, 111

spiritual discipline, 173

spiritual energy, 184

spiritual forces, 140

spiritual fulfillment, 19

spiritual identity, 110

spiritual implications, 125

spiritual impulse, 192

spiritual moment, 272

spiritual "mother," 19

spiritual seeker, 15

spiritual Self, 197

spiritual transcendence, 59

spirituality, 59, 110, 119, 137, 174

Spolin, Viola, 192

spontaneity, 36, 101, 118, 137, 179, 181, 217, 236, 271

spontaneous, 25, 179, 272

spontaneous character, 199

spontaneous creativity, 179

spontaneous energy, 134, 265

spontaneous expression, 177

spontaneous feelings, 208
spontaneous ideas, story lines, 179
spontaneous images, 202–203
spontaneous impulse, 148, 216
spontaneous interaction, 90
spontaneous intuitive flow, 265
spontaneous language, 213
spontaneous reactions, 240
stagecraft, 40, 117
Stanislavski for Beginners (Allen), 191, 230
Stanislavsky, Constantin, xv, 13–14, 41–42, 58–59, 76, 84, 93, 98–100, 105–112, 114, 128–130, 133–138, 141–142, 158, 168, 173–174, 178, 190–192, 220, 230–232, 237, 243, 258, 260, 266–268, 273–274; *An Actor Prepares*, 59–60, 84, 113, 129, 258; *Building a Character*, 60, 84, 113, 129, 158; on Duse, Eleonora, 138; *My Life in Art*, 58–60, 93, 109, 111, 115, 135
Stanislavsky in focus (Carnicke), 105–106, 267

Stanley, Kim, 97
Stapleton, Jean, 158
Stapleton, Maureen, 61, 101
Star Maker, The (film), 2, 6, 85
Star Wars (film), 127
Stern, Jack, 85
Stevenson, Robert Lewis, 44
Stewart, Jimmy, 8
Strasberg, Lee, 13, 52–53, 62, 64, 74, 79, 97, 99–100, 102–104, 106–110, 112–113, 129–130, 220, 259–260; and The Actors Studio, 61; *Dream of Passion, A*, 111, 178; on Duse, Eleonora, 138, 141; *Introduction to Acting: A Handbook on the Stanislavsky Method*, 113
Streep, Meryl, 169, 223, 271–272
Street Scene (Rice), 49
Streetcar Named Desire, A (Williams), 63
Strindberg, August, 39, 54, 103
Studio, The. *See* Actors Studio, The
Studio One (television show), 76, 80
styles of drama, acting, 35, 39–40, 42–43, 49, 61, 65, 88, 96, 98, 103–104, 112, 131–132, 255

stylistic demands, 159
stylistic elements, 132
stylistic extension, 136
stylistic point of view, 97
subtext, 13, 229, 236–242, 244, 246, 248, 251–253
subtextual beats, 12
subtextual choices, 237, 239–240
subtextual design, 239
subtextual logic, 242
subtextual motivation, 243
subtextual reality, 236
subtextual track, 242
subtextual truth, 76
subtextual work, 12–13, 254
Sullavan, Margaret, 51
Sullivan, Dr. Frank, 54
superconscious, 110, 112, 136, 141, 173, 178, 192
supra-textual drama, 125
Surrealism, 42
Sweeny, Joe, 73
Symbolism, 42
System, the, 13, 60, 76, 83–84, 98–100, 106–107, 111, 113–114, 130, 132–133, 137, 192, 220, 230

T
Tandem/T.A.T., 157–158, 161
Tartuffe (Molière), 109
Tasca, Jules, 151

Index 293

Taurog, Norman, 7, 9, 13
Taylor, Elizabeth, 10, 14–15
Taylor, Laurette, 118
Taylor, Robert, 10
Tea and Sympathy (Anderson), 68, 70
Tea and Sympathy (film), 68, 70–72, 76
teachers, 10, 12, 24, 41, 52–53, 59–60, 74, 79, 84–85, 99–101, 105–106, 111–113, 117, 121–122, 124, 132–133, 146, 164, 167–170, 173, 183, 191, 193, 202, 207, 217, 220–221, 237, 258, 260
Teahouse of the August Moon, The (Patrick), 84
teleplays, 77
television, 72–73, 75–80, 83, 92, 122, 149, 151, 161–162, 164, 223–224, 234, 261, 268, 273
Television City, Los Angeles, 72, 74
television series, 80, 162, 164, 270
Temple, Shirley, 1, 14
tempo, 158, 254–255
Terence, 30–31
Terry, Ellen, 38
text, 25, 41, 54, 74, 97, 103, 121, 134–135, 137, 169, 208, 213–214, 216–217,

221–223, 225–227, 230, 233, 236, 239, 241, 243–244, 246–248, 253
textual drama, 36
46th Street Theater, New York City, 154
The Music Man (musical), 118
theater, history of, 27–54
Theater Guild, 52
Theater of Cruelty (theatrical style), 95
Theater of the Absurd (theatrical style), 42, 95
Theodora, Empress, 37–38
Thespis, 29
Think on These Things (Krishnamurti), 119
Thoreau, Henry David, 141
Thorpe, Richard, 10–11
thought, 18, 84, 128, 137, 143, 145, 173–177, 186, 196, 216, 218, 227
thought box, 179
thought form, 186
thought-less, 90–91
Three Sisters, The (Chekhov), 97–98, 110
Tiger on a Chain (television broadcast), 149
To the Actor (Chekhov, M.), 100, 192
Tolstoy, Leo, 141

Tone, Franchot, 53, 260
Tootsie (film), 201
Town Hall, New York City, 120
Towne, Robert, 225
Tracy, Spencer, 6–8, 10, 13, 23, 48, 56
tragedy, 28, 30, 32, 35, 160, 207
transitions(s), 12–13, 242–243, 249–251
Triangle Theater, New York City, 125, 151
Tucker, Sophie, 45
Twentieth Century Fox, 5, 14, 55

U
unconscious, 13, 26, 110, 174, 177, 179, 186, 191, 201–202, 218, 228, 237, 244, 258, 270
unconscious, collective, 273
unconscious acting, 19, 41, 137, 146, 167, 171–172, 175–176, 180, 182–183, 200, 208–209, 214, 227, 231, 235, 268
unconscious actor, 2, 7, 55, 148, 172, 175–176, 183, 190, 200, 203, 216, 218–219, 221, 240, 242–243, 263, 265–266, 270
Unconscious Actor, The, xv, 14, 138, 146, 164, 171, 177, 182, 209, 215, 267, 275

unconscious forces, 6
unconscious mind, 222
unconscious
  performance, 178
unconscious self, 205
unconscious warriors,
  275
unconscious writer, 18
unconsciousness, 185,
  190, 216, 270
University Club, The,
  New York City, 122
Untamed (film), 3
U.S. Steel Hour
  (television show), 76

V

Van Gogh, Vincent, 141
Van Zeller, Hubert, 120
Vance, Vivian, 194
Vidor, King, 55
voice, 12, 26–27, 29, 33,
  45, 51, 54, 84, 98, 103,
  110, 129–131, 134,
  181–183, 191–192,
  198–199, 201, 204,
  209, 213, 215–216,
  251, 260
Voltaire, 37

W

Wagner, Richard, 126
Waiting for Godot
  (Beckett), 95
Waiting for Lefty
  (Odets), 53
Wallach, Eli, 61
Walsh, Bill, 166

Wanted, Dead or Alive
  (television show), 80
Warner Bros., 55
warriors, unconscious,
  275
Wayne, John, 55–56
Weaver, William, 139
Webb, Clifton, 51
Webber, Andrew Lloyd,
  49
Wellman, William,
  55–56
West, Mae, 48
Where the Heart Is
  (television show), 123
Where's Charley?
  (musical), 92, 157
Whiteside, Sheridan, 50
Whitman, Walt, 127
Widmark, Richard, 55
Widower's House (Shaw),
  41
Wild One, The (film), 64
Wilde, Oscar, 65, 132,
  225
Wilder, Thornton, 50
Williams, Tennessee,
  54, 62–63, 235
Winfrey, Oprah, 268
Winter Dreams
  (television broadcast),
  72, 75, 78
Winters, Jonathan, 155
Wise, Robert, 55–56
Wolfe, Thomas, 23
Wolfington, Peg, 38
Woods, Tiger, 268
Woodward, Joanne,
  78–79

Woolley, Monty, 50
Wright, Frank Lloyd,
  141
Wynn, Ed, 45
Wynter, Dana, 73

Y

Yoga, 110–111
York, Dick, 68, 70
You Are There (television
  show), 72
*You Can't Take It With
  You* (Kaufman and
  Hart), 50
Young People (film),
  14

Z

Zen, 111
Zen, and art of acting,
  115–151
Zen acting, 143
Zen actors, 146, 271
Zen artistry, 183, 192,
  202, 274
Zen artists, 145, 170,
  172, 176–177, 184,
  188, 190, 214,
  230–231, 255, 264,
  266–269, 275
Zen Buddhism, 143
Zen in the Art of Archery
  (Herrigel), 142–143,
  172, 269
Zen Master, 143–144,
  173
Ziegfeld, Florenz, 45
Zoo Story, The (Albee),
  95

The Unconscious Actor Lives!

Darryl Hickman is eager to share with you the ground-breaking Process he has developed for teaching *the mechanics of creativity*® to help you attain the highest level of performance in the arts, in business, or in your everyday lives.

For his fellow actors and other colleagues in the drama business he provides:

- an ongoing, weekly workshop in Los Angeles for actors, writers, and directors;
- master classes at prestigious colleges and universities;
- lecture-demonstrations at established repertory companies and regional theaters;
- CDs and audio cassettes of this book; and
- DVDs and videocassettes demonstrating the Process.

For other readers interested in mastering the art of performance, Mr. Hickman wishes to make seminars and training programs available to:

- corporate America;
- professional conventions;
- sales conferences; and
- groups interested in helping its individual members maximize creativity, achieve desired goals, and acquire skills that will lead to superior performance in his or her chosen field.

www.darrylhickman.net